FEEDBACK FOR FAST FUTURE!

In his book Fast Future! John Doehring clearly defines the large-scale trends impacting our world, and then sharply illuminates the important implications that each of these will likely have on our business. John's insights are compelling and relevant, and he provides leaders with pragmatic and useful advice on the actions that are necessary. John's view that controlling and improving our own organization is central to future success squares perfectly with our beliefs. Fast Future! is a must read for all leaders who want to achieve business growth and success, both today and tomorrow!

Stephen Hickox, CEO *CDM Smith*

"John Doehring is an insightful business leader who identifies and explains the top trends that will most impact business in the years to come. John paints a compelling picture of a future where the pace of change continues to accelerate, and he combines his foresight with practical advice for business leaders who look to not to be a victim of the change ahead, but to embrace and profit from it. John's insistence that through under-standing both your company and the larger trends ahead your business can survive, and even thrive, in such a future is a great lesson for any leader."

William C. (Bill) Siegel, PE, President and CEO, *Kleinfelder*

In Fast Future! John Doehring provides us with insights into the future of business that will be risky to ignore. As a business leader, I appreciate that John's book isn't simply thought-provoking for the sake of being provocative. He is also instructive, offering ideas, approaches, and actions - and pointing us in the directions that will help to make our organizations successful in the Fast Future!

Michael P. Sanderson, PE, President/CEO, *Sanderson Stewart*, 2014 U.S. Chamber of Commerce Dream Big Small Business of the Year

"Compelling and engaging. John Doehring's easy style and straightforward approach belie his razor sharp observations about the current and approaching forces of change acting on organizations. He neatly dissects the most transformational upheavals facing society, and then applies his observations directly to organizational practice. If you and your team are not addressing these uber-trends, ___ *for what is ahead.*

John's practical, tactical discussion questions o ___ *map for those who intend to flourish in the eve* ___ *n us. As he has for years, John Doehring again d* ___ *y, in this new and thought-provoking call to Fas*

Michael C. Spoor, CEO, *Bravo Energy* ___ *ca*

"In his new book Fast Future! John Doehring has hit it out of the park! John reviews each of the ten major, "uber-trends" impacting our world, and then draws our attention to why these developments will matter to the organization. As he looks into the future, John's extensive business experience positions him well to address what is most relevant in the workplace today. Consider Fast Future! your own, personal guided tour of the journey ahead - one you'll find enormously helpful."

Gerri King, Ph.D., Organizational Consultant and Author of *The Duh! Book of Management & Supervision: Dispelling Common Leadership Myths*

"What an exciting and frightening time we live in. Everything seems to be changing, and as leaders we must strive to find answers, alternatives, and proactive solutions to the challenges coming our way each day. Fast Future! is a thought provoking look at this future, and what we can do to prepare for the new world of business. As John Doehring suggests, we all must become better futurists, to make sense of the magnitude of information, problems, and opportunities that creep each day into our lives and careers. This book is a must read for all in the game of business!"

Ronald D. Worth, CAE, FSMPS, CPSM, Assoc AIA, CEO, *Society for Marketing Professional Services*

"Fast Future! provides a compelling and visionary insight into the challenges and opportunities of running a business in the 21st century. Our world is changing in deep and fundamental ways, and the outcomes cannot be fully anticipated. The only path to long-term success is to develop a culture of institutional flexibility that enables the company to accept and adapt to change as a fundamental part of doing business. Ditching the management jargon, John Doehring speaks in a straightforward and concise voice, and communicates these critical concepts readily, while providing a useful foundation for business success in a transformative future where the only certainty is change. This book will be a must-read for all of our staff as we look to take advantage of the opportunities of the coming Fast Future!"

Lee Jordan, Operations Manager, *GATE, Inc.*

"Fast Future! is a must read for savvy business owners who desire to control their own destiny. In it John Doehring presents thoughtful insights and perspectives, substantiated with real data, that demonstrate the revolutionary and accelerating changes in today's business climate that will challenge the way successful organizations operate, grow, and prosper. John makes a compelling case for the importance of business leaders to pick their heads up, look forward, and to define and strive for their long term goals - through mastery of their mission, vision, and business strategy."

David E. Pinsky, P.E., President and CEO, *Tighe & Bond*

FAST
FUTURE!

FAST
FUTURE!

Ten Uber-Trends Changing Everything in Business and Our World

...and What the Coming Transformation Means for Your Business Today

JOHN D. DOEHRING

Published by Advantage, Charleston, South Carolina.
Member of Advantage Media Group.

ADVANTAGE is a registered trademark and the Advantage colophon is a trademark of Advantage Media Group, Inc.

Printed in the United States of America.

ISBN: 978-1-59932-526-2
LCCN: 2014956741

This publication is designed to provide accurate and authoritative information in regard to the subject matter covered. It is sold with the understanding that the publisher is not engaged in rendering legal, accounting, or other professional services. If legal advice or other expert assistance is required, the services of a competent professional person should be sought.

Advantage Media Group is proud to be a part of the Tree Neutral® program. Tree Neutral offsets the number of trees consumed in the production and printing of this book by taking proactive steps such as planting trees in direct proportion to the number of trees used to print books. To learn more about Tree Neutral, please visit www.treeneutral.com. To learn more about Advantage's commitment to being a responsible steward of the environment, please visit www.advantagefamily.com/green

Advantage Media Group is a publisher of business, self-improvement, and professional development books and online learning. We help entrepreneurs, business leaders, and professionals share their Stories, Passion, and Knowledge to help others Learn & Grow. Do you have a manuscript or book idea that you would like us to consider for publishing? Please visit advantagefamily.com or call 1.866.775.1696.

For Megan.

Faith, hope, and love.
But the greatest of these is love.

ACKNOWLEDGEMENTS

When authors complete a book, they often claim that the project was a large collaboration, and that without the help of many others it would not have been possible. This is certainly true of Fast Future! This book is the summation of a long journey through the years and careers that involves many, many people. Without each and every one of you, this work would have been substantively different, and surely diminished.

I want to start by thanking our clients. Throughout the years, you have provided thought-provoking ideas, challenging assignments, and an energizing path to success for our business. You have trusted me to step behind the curtains, and to help you improve and grow your firm. Quite often, you have invested considerable resources and great personal effort—with little guarantee of success. Instead, we were motivated by a shared belief that extraordinary results were not only possible, but truly achievable through the power of good ideas, clarity of purpose and objectives, clear and direct communication, and lots and lots of hard work.

Next, I'd like to thank an important group of business associates, colleagues, bosses, and mentors who have supported me, taught me about management and leadership, and instilled in me a lifelong passion for recognizing and exploiting change, continuous organization improvement, choosing the maverick and contrarian path, and pursuing inspirational leadership. Thank you Les White, Mike Robinson and Pete Davidson from my early days at Exxon, Dan Stevens and Jim Hastings from my later Exxon career, business partner and co-founder Mike Spoor from Windward Petroleum, Don Pomeroy and Kevin Pottmeyer of Geologic Services Corporation, and Mark Zweig, founder of ZweigWhite. And thank you to all of the others along the way who have educated and guided me, served as role models, and helped me to shape my own beliefs, worldview, mission, and vision.

Other professional colleagues contributed as well, some through direct and personal relationships, others as a speaker, trainer, or expert, and still others simply through the power of their own printed words. Many of these I met through the National Speaker's Association, Institute of Management Consultants, and World Future Society. Likewise, I'm indebted to the tremendously talented educators during my graduate education at New York University's Stern School of Business, and in my undergraduate years at the University of Texas at Austin.

I'm also sending a heartfelt thanks (and many kudos) to the folks at Advantage Media Group. Adam Witty, Denis Boyles, Ann Hanson, Lauren Caster, Alison Morse, Scott Neville, George Stevens, Megan Elger, Claire Watson, Jenn Ash, and Patti Boysen guided me expertly through the mysterious process of book publishing and marketing, kept me on track and on schedule, and ultimately delivered a finished product that is light years ahead of what I could have done without them. The obvious lesson here is this: when in doubt, hire the best.

It's also clear now that little would have happened without the constant support of a loving family. Early on, my parents John and Jane Doehring convinced me (somehow) that I was special, that could do anything I wanted, and that I was destined for eventual greatness. Surprisingly, I never questioned this somewhat irrational faith, and simply believed it to be true. Alas, I didn't become a doctor, but I've been blessed still to overflowing with five beautiful children and a wife who has supported me far beyond what I have expected or deserved. I'm truly blessed.

And speaking of blessings, I must finally acknowledge the importance of faith. It's not always a popular (or even welcome) subject—especially in the business world—but my belief in God and Jesus Christ has sustained me many a day through the creation of this book, and through the inevitable ups and downs of business and life. Without a savior, it's difficult to ascribe much meaning to anything. With him, it's obvious from where the blessings come, and ultimately who deserves the real credit for everything.

John Doehring
December 2014

TABLE OF CONTENTS

PART I
INTRODUCTION

THE FAST FUTURE

Our future isn't just coming—it's here. Change is hot, it's in, and it's everywhere. Over the next 25 years, grand-scale, highly disruptive, and often astonishing changes will radically reshape virtually everything around us—in business and our world. This transformation will soon usher forth a new global society, virtually unrecognizable from the present. It's going to be a wild ride.

Today, the velocity of change is already impressive. And the pace of change is accelerating—so tomorrow promises an even faster transformation. And, most importantly, the speed of change continues to accelerate faster than our expectations. As a result, we're constantly surprised, always chasing the new, falling further and further behind the curve.

This then is our story—it's a future that's already arriving now, accelerating still faster all the time, and each day further outpacing our expectations—and very soon perhaps, even our ability to comprehend.

This is the Fast Future.

1

Introduction

"A journey of a thousand miles
begins with a single step."
—Lao-tzu

I'm not a futurist.

Well, at least not in the classic sense of a formally trained, academically focused *foresight* specialist. My gig is *business*—and specifically helping companies, professionals, and leaders to improve their businesses, and to capture greater success in work and life.

Some people study the future because that's what they're trained to do. Others pay attention because the future is interesting, fascinating, compelling. Still others watch because that's where the money is—where they can discover emerging opportunities and make a buck.

Like many firm owners, I spend most of my time working *in* my business—satisfying clients, hustling new projects, and fitting in the other stuff of a successful enterprise. But beyond that, I've spent a great deal of time over the last several years focusing specifically on the *future*, and comprehending what I can of the road ahead.

I'm fascinated by this picture—the changes that are occurring in our world even today—and in particular the large-scale, *uber-trends* that are transforming (or will) virtually everything in our economies, industries, markets, and business—as well as in our global society, communities, and lives. As I work to comprehend this future, my main focus has been to understand the *meaning* and *implications* for business success. Ultimately, I'm after an action agenda: what organizations, companies, professionals, and leaders can and must do today to capture sustainable growth, profit, and success tomorrow.

You see, I'm a futurist.

I've enjoyed an interesting and diverse career. I've experienced a lot, from a variety of different vantage points. I spent 16 years at a large multinational oil company, one of the biggest business organizations in the world. I've worked since then in much smaller firms—mid-market companies, entrepreneurial startups, and as an independent professional. I've learned in an incredible array of roles—scientist, project manager, front-line supervisor, business group manager, senior executive, management consultant, organization trainer, professional speaker, business owner, and entrepreneur. I've contributed on the technical side, in sales management, and as a general and executive manager—in industries including petroleum, environmental consulting, product sales and marketing, industrial products distribution, design and construction, and today as a management consultant focused on business strategy, growth and operational improvement, and organization development.

Through all of my experiences, organizations, and roles, I've made a couple of observations that I believe are critically important, and foundational, to understanding business today. The first is this:

Very few business organizations or leaders are today preparing adequately for the Fast Future that is coming— and in some cases, is already here.

In truth, so many companies and leaders are doing nothing (or next to nothing) that we can confidently conclude that real trouble lies ahead. In fact, thousands, tens of thousands, and perhaps millions of these organizations, all around the world, are likely to falter substantially (either completely or in part) in the next decade. Given the magnitude, intensity, and pace of global change—juxtaposed against this enormous *organizational lethargy*—this failure seems inevitable, and even unchangeable.

As this book will describe, the Fast Future ahead will be messy— unpredictable, inconsistent, and unfair. Opportunities and threats will tax organizations in many different ways, and will lead to both big winners and big losers in the business game. We'll all be affected, and at times feel displaced, disengaged, and dispirited.

But among this dizzying disruption, we'll also see much good in the future ahead. No guarantees, but I find great hope here, born of a second observation:

Successful organizations and individuals are those not who best guess the future ahead, but those who know most clearly who they are, what they want, and how to get there.

For success-oriented firms and leaders, goals are achieved not through controlling the uncontrollable, but instead through mastery of their own selves—through mission, vision, enterprise strategy, executing action plans, great teams, and leadership.

Savvy readers will recognize here a list of the basics of business—and not much new. Ironically then, success in a turbulent, topsy-turvy, ever-changing Fast Future comes primarily through a disciplined focus on matters that don't themselves change much—like clarity of purpose, compelling objectives, a focus on execution, and the importance of quality people. These core concepts remain foundational to a firm's success.

The strategic importance of these business basics is not at issue. Few leaders will argue their value. Instead, the main problem in most companies today is *priority*. Managers in firms both large and small focus most of their effort on short-term things: current projects and inventory, quarterly sales forecasts, next week's payroll. It's the classic struggle between important and urgent, and urgent always wins. Important items are deferred until next week, next month, or next year—until tomorrow. Of course, in all too many instances, this tomorrow never comes.

Now, add to this familiar story the Fast Future piece—the disruptive, rule-changing, and ever-accelerating change monster—and the important but not urgent problem is profoundly exacerbated. Now not only do we put off important tasks until tomorrow, but we also risk badly misjudging just what tomorrow is. In a stable environment, the result is that we delay in perpetuity. In the Fast Future world, we delay for a tomorrow that actually arrives today, uninvited, and before any of us are ready for it.

So, what is the progressive business leader to do?

Our investigation of the future, and in particular these *uber-trends*, doesn't always provide clarity. In fact, more often than not, our study leads not to answers, but to more questions. Still, this investigation is crucial because it's here—in the search for understanding, in wrestling with the implications, possibilities, and scenarios—that the successful leader finds true meaning. Sometimes our assessment is spot on, and the actions we choose immediately successful. Other times, we miss the boat spectacularly, and charge out in a direction that is completely wrong. Leaders learn that not only action, but also *agility* matters a great deal—their ability to be nimble, flexible, and adaptable to shifting conditions and outcomes. So here's a toast to swift starts, fast failures, and a healthy skepticism of status quo success.

In the chapters that follow, I've organized my discovery of the Fast Future into 10 categories—10 major *uber-trends* that I believe will have transformational importance in businesses, in our world, and in our lives. Some will argue with this taxonomy, and that's okay. Whether or not there really are 10 trends (perhaps it's 11—or is it nine?) isn't important. It's a lumping and splitting exercise. What matters most is understanding—the type that leads to strategic thinking—in looking at the changes ahead, the acceleration of the change, and the likely outcomes of the uber-trends. Implications are very important, and taking action is crucial.

I've likewise wrestled with the relationships and interconnections between the uber-trends. Some—such as technology and information—appear to be foundational, at the center of the Fast Future storm. Others—including globalization, marketplace, and the evolution of community—are more likely derivative, driven themselves by the forces of technology and other trends. These relationships are complex, but again, it's the *implications* of the changes in our businesses and lives that are most important.

And so what I offer here is a picture, a glimpse (however imperfect) of what's probably ahead. This picture is at times more general, and at times more specific, but it's always designed to *motivate action*.

Keep in mind that this amazing, transformational future is only a part of the story. The current lack of attention and action, and the short-term, status-quo focused, change-averse nature of so much of business today is the other part. Two incongruent paradigms, headed most certainly for a spectacular collision.

Let me be blunt. What I expect in the years ahead is disease, death, and even disaster. I see a business battlefield of carnage and chaos, and, in some cases, near-catastrophe. This will be especially true in industry segments that today are relatively stable, with long-term historical success, predictable markets, and (so far) little outside threat. This recipe has lulled many a company and its leaders into a sense of quiet comfort, entitlement, and even arrogance. For these, the Fast Future is going to be a bumpy ride. And in the big picture, as many as half of these firms simply won't make it, failing quickly (collapse and bankruptcy) or slowly (declining revenues, squeezed profits, poor transitions). I expect this in half of existing businesses.

Some will disagree with my assessment, believing that I'm unnecessarily dramatic, and too pessimistic. Maybe, though I don't think so.

And frankly, I'm not pessimistic at all. On the contrary, I see the Fast Future as profoundly positive, filled with extraordinary 21st-century opportunity. I believe that our world will become considerably more open and transparent. Global business will likely focus much more on merit and results (so will our society in general—today we're witnessing the very messy beginnings of this revolution). Those who've previously been locked out of the global opportunity will find the keys to new avenues for success. Gazillions of new businesses and business owners will step up and try their luck. On the other hand, legacy industries, markets, companies, and countries that were built on the control, constraint, and deceit of information and power will be increasingly assailed by the rising meritocracy. For many, this battle will be very difficult, and the endgame ugly.

As you read *Fast Future*, I hope that you, too, will become more fascinated by the future, these 10 uber-trend developments, and the extraordinary journey we're all about to take. But I also want to remind you to keep an eye toward the importance of these changes on your business. Remember to think "so what?"—that is, the meaning, implications, and actions needed for success. Answers may come slowly, but the questions themselves will be rich in value, and will help to steer you and your firm on the right path forward.

Now, shall we journey forward together, on a brief tour of the Fast Future?

2

The Economy, Forecasting, and the Road Ahead

*"Economics is extremely useful, as a form
of employment for economists."*
—John Kenneth Gailbraith

E conomy … Shmeconomy

Does the health of the current economy really matter to your business?

Your answer is yes. Of course it does. Economic health means consumer confidence and business investment, and that translates to demand for products and services. Without demand, growth is difficult, competition increases, and profits slip away.

Still, when we look at the longer term, and at the uber-trends transforming our world, what's going on in today's economy (up or down) is really less important than you might think. Compared with the Fast Future ahead, much of what we're concerned with day to day is, I think, frankly irrelevant.

Yes, audiences are skeptical. Time and time again I've found that we must pause and acknowledge the economy at hand—the boom, downturn, and recovery, the short-term trend—what's currently happening in business and markets today. Without this acknowledgment (and some empathy for those struggling to succeed), many will turn off the Fast Future message.

Leaders will say (occasionally out loud), "This guy doesn't understand our business," or, "That won't work in our industry," or, "That's a no-can-do in this market." I suppose that we're all like this, to a point. Left unchallenged, we simply focus too much on the short-term, on uncontrollable elements, and on external forces pushing us around. We create excuses and justify our helplessness—and view ourselves as victims—because that is easier than focusing on *action*. We dismiss the opportunities in front of us (if we see them at all) as not applicable to our situation, industry, firm, or self. Sound familiar?

To confess, I've long been biased strongly (perhaps irrationally so) the other way. I've never been very comfortable blaming my own results (or lack of success) on the current economy. It feels like a cop-out. To be sure, the economy has been strong and growing for most of my career. Downturns have been short, recoveries quick. I've been fortunate.

However, business leaders must distinguish between *macroeconomics* (the big economy and trends) and *microeconomics*—the forces of supply and demand, and the relationship between one buyer and one seller. In virtually every situation I've seen (either as manager or consultant, in products and in services, and in organizations large and small), what's necessary for success is often *just a little, not a lot.* A couple of additional clients, a few more projects, a slightly better pipeline or conversion rate. *Just a little, not a lot.* At any given time, it's this handful of new business opportunities that separates success from failure. In fact, most businesses can't handle very much growth in the short term without other constraints (limited production capacity, staffing shortfalls, financial resources) slowing or stopping progress. On the other hand, more fully utilizing the organization's *current* capacity usually delivers a big difference in short-term results. (Sustained, longer-term growth requires additional resources and investment.) The point is that if short-term success requires just a little incremental growth, then why should it matter (much) what's going on with the greater economy? Why care about the market as a whole when all you need is one additional customer? Indeed, tough times may call for a different strategy or tactics, or require additional effort.

But unless the company already dominates a market, then it's not the economy that is limiting, but something else—namely the organization's own self-imposed constraints, its beliefs, abilities, and actions.

What is it that you and your firm *really* need for success? Ten new clients, or two? A couple of additional projects? One new service line or an office location? What would 10 percent or 15 percent improvement in your firm look like—in terms of new customers, projects, services, or markets? And what's *really* standing in the way of you achieving this?

ECONOMY ON THE US HOME FRONT

The economy of the United States, generating $16.7 trillion in annual GDP (2013), is the world's largest. It is big, strong, and robust.[1] (Figure 2-1 compares the 2013 GDP output of the world's top 10 economies, valued on a purchasing power parity basis.) The U.S. economy has been up and down for much of the last century—though mostly up. Downturns have been regular, but by comparison, brief. This cyclical trend will likely continue—mostly up, but sometimes down, at least over the next few decades. (It's the nature of business, both at home and abroad, to be cyclical and dynamic.) However, it's also likely that we'll see some big changes along the way, as Fast Future uber-trends shift and modify these cycles through underlying structural change.

FIGURE 2-1. TOTAL ANNUAL GDP OUTPUT, TOP TEN NATIONS

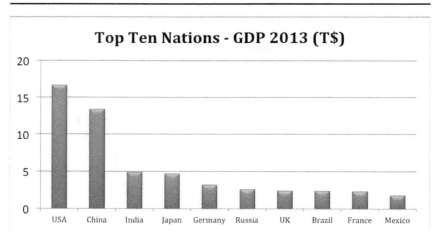

Source: CIA World fact Book, https://www.cia.gov/library/publications/the-world-factbook/rankorder/2001rank.html.

The collapse of late 2008 rocked the US (and global) economy like nothing any of us has seen. (Even a 20-year-old greenhorn in 1929 would today be a centenarian.) Almost immediately (it seemed), everything stopped. The fall was fast and deep. This collapse was widely compared to 1929, which, of course, resulted in a swift, long-lasting, and devastating global depression. This time around, governments across the world jumped in fast, with extreme measures, to prevent a similar catastrophe.

Figure 2-2 represents domestic GDP growth, and highlights the severity of the late 2008 crash.[2] As shown, the US economy actually cooled off substantially by early 2008, and by the fourth quarter was in free fall. (I'm sure you'll remember this time, and exactly what it felt like. I certainly do. I can see the faces in the audiences I spoke to back then. The shell-shocked surprise, anxiety, and fear. Blank stares.) Few saw this coming. And even those who were wary of a bursting bubble were surprised by the speed and intensity of the fall. (So this is what an oncoming economic depression feels like!)

FIGURE 2-2. QUARTERLY GROWTH (REAL GDP) OF THE US ECONOMY

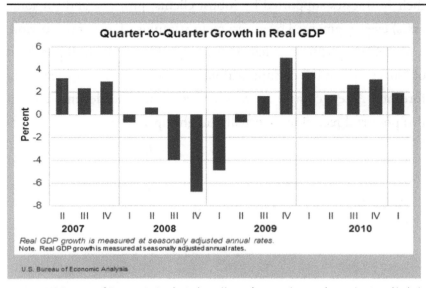

Source: US Bureau of Economic Analysis, http://www.bea.gov/newsreleases/national/gdp/gdp_glance.htm

Figure 2-2 also indicates that the US economy rebounded quickly, re-entering positive territory by mid-2009. You might not remember this part so clearly—the recovery was, for many, not so obvious. In fact, how an organization experienced the downturn and recovery was highly correlated with the particulars of that business— individual clients and customer types served, services and products offered, local and regional geographies covered. Within the professional services sector (where much business is either local, or focused in specific market segments), experiences varied widely. For instance, some architecture firms (commonly on the leading edge of new design and construction work) saw a near-instantaneous evaporation of their business, as clients in sector after sector pulled back on plans. Some of these firms were forced to cut staff sharply in 2008—often by 30 percent, 50 percent, or more. Many were bankrupt by early 2009. By contrast, many engineering firms (especially those in strong geographies and/or with particular market focus) roared right through, their businesses supported by robust clients, projects, and (in some cases) even augmented by government stimulus. (During this period, a few of our clients insisted on a low profile, either feeling a kind of "survivor's guilt," or superstitiously avoiding a jinx of their good fortune.) A few companies experienced almost no decline, though this powerful recession eventually caught up with most.

FIGURE 2-3. QUARTERLY GROWTH (REAL GDP) OF THE US ECONOMY

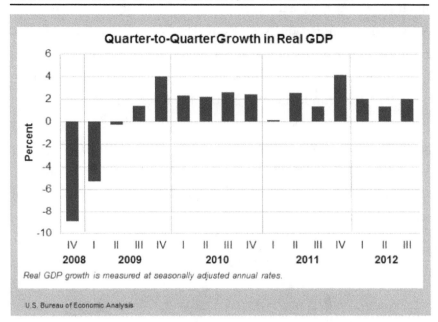

Source: US Bureau of Economic Analysis, http://www.bea.gov/newsreleases/national/gdp/ gdp_glance.htm

Figure 2-3 data shows that the economic story post-collapse has been one of moderate growth (generally 2 percent or less, punctuated by quarters of even slower progress).[3] During this time, the early recovery was uneven and fragile, a few steps forward and a few back. Continued uncertainty at home (repeated debt and funding crises and a general lack of movement in the federal government) and abroad (debt crises in the European Union, and political instability in the Middle East, North Africa, and elsewhere) conspired to impede an otherwise stronger rebound. Future uncertainty—especially in the jobs market—has prevented many from enjoying the fruits of the recovery.

Domestic unemployment, as highlighted in Figure 2-4, offers another view into the US economy. The chart shows the overall unemployment rate, starting with 2001.[4] The trend from mid-2008 forward is strikingly different from what came before. In fact, for most of the first three-quarters of the decade, domestic markets enjoyed unemployment in the 4–5 percent range—what economists consider "full employment." With the recession, unemployment shot up to about 10 percent by January 2010. It has fallen gradually since then, to below 7 percent at present. This is much better, but still high by recent standards. And, of course, no improvement is of much comfort to those who remain out of work, underemployed, or without a sense of long-term job stability.

FIGURE 2-4. US MONTHLY UNEMPLOYMENT RATE

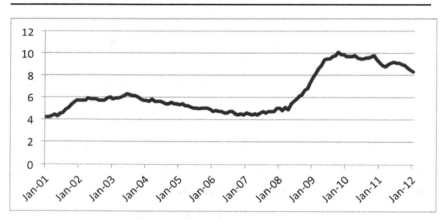

Source: US Bureau of Labor Statistics, http://www.bls.gov/news.release/empsit.nr0.htm

Here's another way to understand the recession of 2008. Figure 2-5 offers a snapshot of unemployment by individual US county, with average unemployment between May 2012 and April 2013.[5] (Darker colors denote a higher state unemployment rate.) As the map suggests, this recession was largely a tale of the two coasts, with deeper unemployment impact experienced on both the West Coast (especially in California) and the East Coast (especially in Florida), and with lesser pain in the US heartland. In fact, this recession is best understood as a bursting bubble—hitting hardest those areas that had been growing the fastest. Particularly overheated markets in Southern California, southern Florida, Las Vegas, and Phoenix experienced the steepest declines, highest unemployment, and most pronounced economic reversal. In contrast, regions that had been growing more modestly (off the beaten path, so to speak) weathered the storm much better. As one client CEO puts it, "It always hurts less to fall out of a basement window."

FIGURE 2-5. US MONTHLY UNEMPLOYMENT RATE BY STATE AND COUNTY

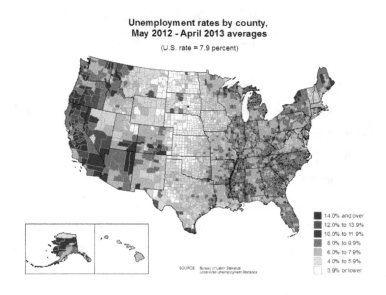

Source: US Bureau of Labor Statistics- http://www.bls.gov/web/laus/mstrtcr1.gif

Where are we headed? That's the big-money question, and the short answer is that nobody really knows. Don't let anyone (including me) tell you they know what's going to happen. Instead, pay attention, and figure it out yourself. Listen to the experts and the pundits, but always keep a careful eye and a healthy skepticism.

Economists are generally a conservative lot, reluctant to predict anything but the very near future. And most practitioners of the "dismal science" are not particularly good at it (neither are they, frankly, very good at describing the past—as evidenced by the often-large adjustments made to previously published economic data). Pay attention, listen, and learn—but keep your own eyes open.

ECONOMIC FORECASTING AND OTHER TALES OF MAGIC

The highly respected and noted economist John Kenneth Galbraith once said, "Economics is extremely useful, [particularly] as a form of employment for economists."

Of course, economics is helpful in providing understanding of how the complex and interconnected systems of our domestic and global economy are related to and affect one another. But forecasting the future, either the long or short term, is quite another matter. We must take stock of the trends and predictive indicators around us, but always with a healthy sense of skepticism and humility.

Take, for example, the economic forecast shown in Figure 2-6, which for a while was published monthly by *USA Today* and the advisory firm *IHS Global Insight*.[6] This system predicted US GDP growth, based on 11 leading indicators, as outlined in Figure 2-7.

FIGURE 2-6. US ECONOMIC FORECAST- USA TODAY AND IHS GLOBAL INSIGHT

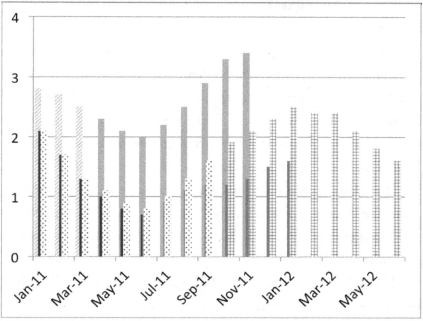

Source: USA Today and IHS-Global Insight, 2011–2012

FIGURE 2-7. LEADING INDICATORS OF THE USA TODAY AND IHS-GLOBAL INSIGHT

FORECAST

11 LEADING INDICATORS
Real federal funds rate
Interest rate yield curve
Corporate bond spread
Hours worked
Building permits
Non-defense capital goods orders
Money supply
Stock prices
ISM export orders index
Crude oil prices
Light vehicle sales

Source: USA Today and IHS-Global Insight, 2011–2012

You might think that a careful analysis of these obviously important parameters of economic activity would result in an accurate forecast, but it's not so. I followed the trail of this forecast for about a year (updates were suddenly discontinued in mid-2012). The forecast was often imprecise and sometimes way off—requiring considerable revision (of both future and past data). Overall, the picture was an up-and-down rollercoaster ride, and not particularly helpful for planning and action.

Let's look at the data from three separate periods to better understand the challenge of forecasting. The first estimate is from March 2011 (represented by gray slashed bars for actual data, solid gray bars for forecast data). The second forecast is from June 2011, shown with solid black bars for actual, and solid dark gray for forecast. The third estimate is from November 2011, and is depicted by gray dot bars for historical results and gray ladder bars for future estimates.

What do these forecasts tell us? Note first that the graph was itself modified (sometimes substantially) in each of the three periods. For instance, the prediction for GDP growth for November 2011 began at 3.3 percent, was revised downward to 1.3 percent, and then revised again upward to 2.1 percent. (The difference between a GDP growth of 3.3 percent [pretty strong] and 1.3 percent [pretty weak] is significant.) Close examination also reveals that "actual" historical GDP has also been updated, again sometimes significantly. My point here is not to critique this particular forecast or team, but to draw attention to the general difficulty of forecasting itself. As I've said, economists are not only imprecise in predicting the future, but they sometimes also struggle with predicting the past. Throughout its run, this *USA Today-IHS Global Insight* forecast offered a rollercoaster view of the road ahead, with a trend (either up or down) for a few months, and then a reversal over the next several months.

Overall, there wasn't a strong direction either way, and so uncertainty remained high.

In conclusion, we should recognize that the "dismal science" is just that: at best only part science, in which behavior is accurately described by scientific means. Economic behavior is also affected greatly by *human behavior*—in individuals and large populations—acting both rationally and irrationally.

All predictions, therefore, will be suspect, because they're about estimating human thinking and activity—a product of both logic and emotion.

WHERE GOETH THE PEOPLE?

What's ahead in the short term is often unclear, but over the longer haul, some trends (like population growth and movement) are more evident. There's no question that the population of the United States will continue to grow overall—at a relatively fast clip. In fact, the US Census Bureau expects that between the years 2000 and 2030 (we're halfway through this period), the nation's population will expand by nearly 30 percent. But this growth will occur at a much different pace in different regions of the country, and will result in a continued disparity in both growth rate and population density across the states.

With respect to population (total, density, and growth) the US states are already quite diverse. Figure 2-8 highlights the population distribution among states.[7] Of the slightly more than 308 million US citizens today, about one-third of these (100 million) live in just four states: California, Texas, New York, and Florida. Beyond these four mega-states, an additional 66 million people reside in the next six largest states: Illinois, Pennsylvania, Ohio, Michigan, Georgia, and North Carolina. Thus, more than half of the country calls one of these ten states home. In total, the average state size has a population of about 6 million. Without the four largest, the remaining average is about 4.5 million, and without the 10 largest, it's closer to 3.5 million. In reality, there really isn't much of an "average" state in terms of size. Isn't it striking how well this disparity in state size is represented by the US government model, constructed more than 230 years ago? Understanding this eventuality, our founders established a Senate where all states are equal, and a House with representation based on population. All states, of course, elect two senators, but several states (and territories) seat today just one representative, while the California delegation totals 53.

FIGURE 2-8. POPULATION DISTRIBUTION IN US STATES

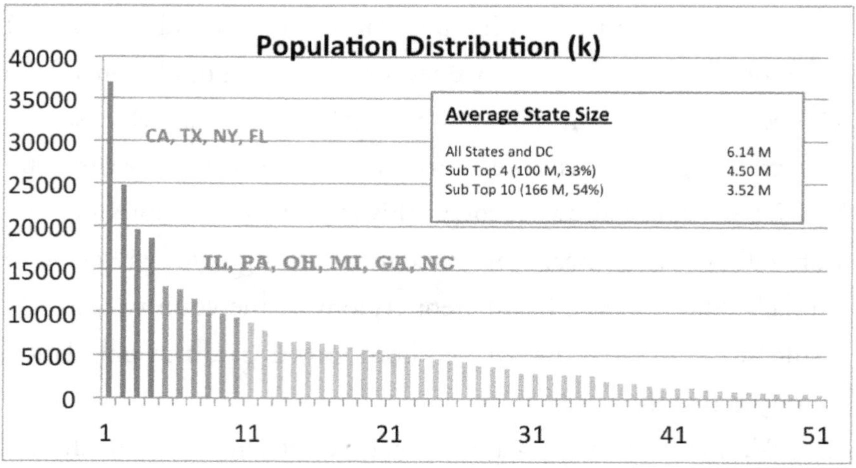

Source: US Census Bureau, http://www.census.gov/compendia/statab/cats/population.html

From this current population disparity, individual states will continue to grow at widely different rates. During the period from 2000–2030, Florida is expected to expand by nearly 80 percent, Texas by 60 percent, and North Carolina by more than 50 percent (Figure 2-9). In contrast, populations in most Northeastern states will increase much more slowly. For instance, Massachusetts, New Jersey, and New York are predicted to grow by just 10.4 percent, 6.5 percent, and 2.6 percent, respectively.[8]

FIGURE 2-9. GROWTH RATES OF US STATES–2000-2030

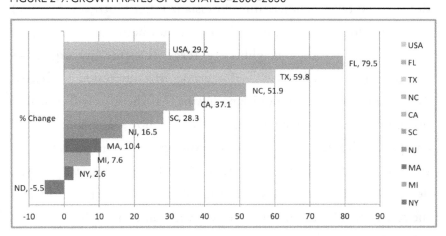

Source: US Census Bureau, Population Division, Interim State Population Projections, 2005.

Are these differences in size and growth rates really important? I think so, because so much of the success of business is tied directly to the local population served.

This "serve local" strategy is the most common approach seen, particularly with services firms. Even professional firms (consultants, engineers, architects, accountants, and lawyers) with global reach largely serve their customers locally, from nearby offices. Thus (larger, Fast Future uber-trends notwithstanding), growth in local markets, fueled by growth in the local population, will remain a primary correlation to business growth and success.

Here's an example. One of our clients is an engineering firm located in Louisiana. This company's principals want to grow, but they'd prefer to keep their business focused locally in Louisiana. The firm has had limited success through the years in branching out to nearby Mississippi and Alabama. But there are important implications (costs) of this choice, since Louisiana (after Hurricane Katrina) is expected to grow more slowly than other southern states, and a great deal more slowly than neighboring Texas. (Despite my urging—I am after all a Texan myself—this group isn't interested in Texas.) Their choice of focus in Louisiana means that the firm will probably not grow as fast as it could elsewhere. I'm not suggesting that all companies should chase the fastest-growing markets (that would be stupid), but instead that all must look at the *implications* of their decisions, and own up to the realities of the markets they target. In the case of this Louisiana firm, growth will come through battle with competitors, so the operational focus must include a more aggressive, "take it away from the other guys" strategy.

Additionally, even within specific states, the populations of towns and cities are growing and developing at different rates. In the future, some of these urban areas will begin to overlap and coalesce with one another to form even larger supra-urban, regional population clusters. As the authors of the *America 2050* study (www. america2050.org) suggest, by mid-century, growth in the United States will be defined in large part by 10 of these "mega-regions" (Figure 2-10).[9] Today, three of these regions are particularly recognizable: the Northeast Corridor stretching between Washington,

DC, and Boston; Southern California (joining greater Los Angeles and San Diego and surrounding areas); and Northern California (including San Francisco, Oakland, the East Bay, San Jose, and other communities of the Silicon Valley). Several of the other mega-regions are rapidly developing as well.

FIGURE 2-10. THE EMERGING MEGA-REGIONS

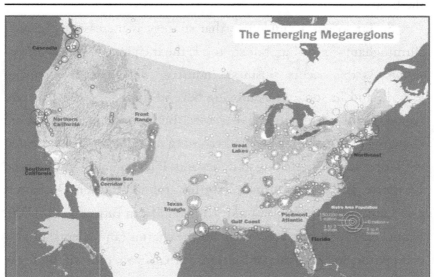

Source: www.america2050.org

Again, our main question is "so what?" Why are these potential mega-regions important to business?

Since much of business is often local, leaders can become myopically over-focused on the local area, and not watch what's developing nearby (but not right in) their sandbox. Many of us are too provincial in our outlook—overestimating the importance of the current area and business, and overstating the differences and barriers between areas. In the future, this provincialism will lead to missed opportunities and threats.

Consider this example. Suppose you're the principal owner of a small firm in Birmingham, Alabama. (Birmingham is a unique southern city with an industrial character.) Your company has prospered, basically, by following a simple formula of taking care of the local clientele.

So far so good, but today that strategy is increasingly at risk. Birmingham is growing, but so, too is the incipient *Piedmont Mega-region*. As this occurs, business, industry, and clients are evolving as well, and in some cases moving beyond local suppliers to larger regional and even national partners. Because client markets are changing too, many clients are becoming more regional themselves, with operations stretching out beyond Birmingham—to Atlanta, Charlotte, or Raleigh-Durham, North Carolina. (Raleigh-Durham is also a unique southern city, but it's different from Birmingham.) Will your clients stick with you, or fall for the charms (and talents) of new competitors from Atlanta or Raleigh? Perhaps you, too, will find new business opportunities in the mega-region—*if you look*. This is the path ahead for the progressive leader, navigating familiar opportunities today while discovering more about the change and opportunity of tomorrow.

Globalization isn't limited to outsourcing production to India, or cheap products from China. Increasingly, it will also mean looking at Raleigh-Durham—all the way from Birmingham.

PART II
UBER-TRENDS

3

The Astounding Acceleration of Technology

RAPID TECHNOLOGICAL DEVELOPMENT WILL TRANSFORM EVERYTHING—AND THE PACE OF THE CHANGE IS ACCELERATING.

"Any sufficiently advanced technology is indistinguishable from magic."
—Arthur C. Clarke

W e're living today in exponential times, amid a technological revolution of astonishing scale. Though it might not be clear for another century, this transformation will be at least as important as previous disruptions—the Industrial Revolution of the 19th/20th centuries, the scientific and cultural revolutions of the Renaissance before that, and the Agricultural Revolution thousands of years earlier. Each of these periods was defined by a step-change in human endeavor and progress, and profound impact on the human condition. And each of these disruptions has come more frequently, as the pace of technological developments accelerates through history.

Technology *is the most important trend*. It's the core driver of the Fast Future ahead.

In appreciating the technology revolution, our challenge is not that we don't see it, but that we *do*. The impact of technology is pervasive. We're all in it—not only as observers, but also as participants. Still, familiarity with the obvious is a problem. If we knew nothing about the change, we might be inclined to learn; since we know (or think we know), investigation seems less critical. But unless you're paying very close attention, it's easy to miss the latest developments, and to misjudge the implications of change. And it's nearly impossible today to keep up with everything, and to fully grasp the scale, velocity, and meaning of it all. We're like lobsters in a pot— the water still cool but warming. Everything feels fine, though big trouble lurks ahead.

At times, we're enthralled by technology (lining up at Apple stores to purchase new versions of gizmos we already have). At other times, we're paralyzed by change (should I purchase a Blu-Ray player, or are these passé?). Some are irrationally infatuated (the iPad will fix all of our communications issues), while others are irrationally skeptical (Internet access kills all productivity in our organization).

Everywhere, technology is exploding exponentially. Fast-growing segments include computers (hardware and software), information (we'll look at this in the next chapter), biotechnology, and nanotechnology. And while each of the sub-fields is exploding, there is also increasing convergence of segments into dynamic new fields, with this convergence further accelerating the development and impact of technology in our world.

The technology endgame (if there is one) is unclear— but lack of clarity is a poor excuse for not paying attention, asking good questions, and preparing for the transformative change ahead.

None of us can escape the reach of the technology and the Fast Future.

COMPUTERS: THE HEART OF THE REVOLUTION

At the core of the revolution is the computer. Computers have pumped the life-blood of technological change at an ever-increasing pace, particularly in the last 50 years or so. But computers and computing power are older than you might think, with roots dating back thousands of years. The abacus, perhaps the first computational device, was created in Babylonia about 5,000 years ago. Later, the Antikythera Device, a mechanical, lunar-month calculator, was developed around 80 A.D. William Oughtred invented the slide rule in 1622, and the following year Wilhelm Schickard created the first mechanical calculator. Binary mathematics was developed in 1679.

Other notable and related inventions included the typewriter (1829), telegraph (1831), magnetic recording (1899), vacuum tubes (1906), flip-flop circuit (1919), electric typewriter (1935), and Turing's foundational computer principles (1936). Then, from the late 1930s to 1950s, a steady stream of increasingly more powerful mainframe computers arrived, with names like the Mark 1, Z1, Z3,

ENIAC, EDVAC, EDSAC, BINAC, ACE, and UNIVAC. Most of these were built for academic research and/or business solutions.

After World War II, development accelerated further, and computers ushered in a modern technology era. The mid-1950s saw the creation of silicone-based transistors, first-generation hard drives, transistorized computers, and Fortran programming. By 1959, a second generation of powerful computers (with transistors rather than tubes) began to make the scene. Two companies, Fairchild Semiconductors and Texas Instruments, each independently developed integrated circuits. IBM became the dominant manufacturer of commercial computers, while Xerox introduced the first commercial copy machines. The 1960s witnessed continued development: magnetic disk storage, BASIC programming, and the first video games. Control Data Corporation (CDC) released its first super-powerful Cray computer, while Digital Equipment Corporation (DEC) offered to the market the first *mini-computer* (at the then-absurdly low price of $18,500). This period also saw commercialization of the semiconductor, floppy disk storage, and the first mass-produced microprocessors from Intel.

By the 1970s and 1980s, the story of computers is more familiar: garage startups that became Microsoft and Apple, the first generation of personal computers, Wang's office automation system, VisiCalc software, cellular telephones, MS-DOS, the Apple II, the IBM PC AT and XT, and an explosion of various PC clones. This was followed by Apple's graphic user interface, the ascendancy of Windows software, computers by IBM, Compaq, Gateway, Dell, and HP, and most recently, the overwhelming success of products made by Apple—the Mac, iPod, iPhone, and iPad.

FASTER AND FASTER

It's clear that the pace of computer development is increasing. Various metrics demonstrate this acceleration—two examples include the processing speed of the world's fastest computers, and the overall processing speed-per-unit cost.

Since 1993, the *TOP 500 Supercomputer Sites* has analyzed processing speeds of the world's fastest supercomputers, and has provided a ranking of these results semiannually each year.[1] Figure 3-1 charts the trend for the fastest supercomputer (number 1) and the slowest (number 500), and the sum of all supercomputers in the top 500 (with trend-lines projected out to 2020). This data suggests a *geometric* acceleration of processing speeds (linear relationship on a logarithmic scale).

FIGURE 3-1. PROJECT PERFORMANCE OF THE WORLD'S FASTEST

SUPER-COMPUTERS

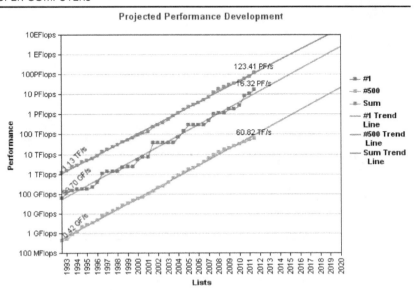

Source: Top 500 Supercomputer Sites, http://www.top500.org.

Futurist Ray Kurzweil has analyzed the evolution of computing power through time, and notes that "the exponential growth of computing is a marvelous quantitative example of the exponentially growing returns from an evolutionary process."[2] According to Kurzweil, it took 90 years for the computer industry to achieve its first MIPS (million instructions per second) per $1,000. Today, about 1.2 MIPS per $1,000 are added every hour. This exponential acceleration in *computing power per unit cost* is charted in Figure 3-2.

FIGURE 3-2. AVAILABLE COMPUTING POWER PER UNIT COST

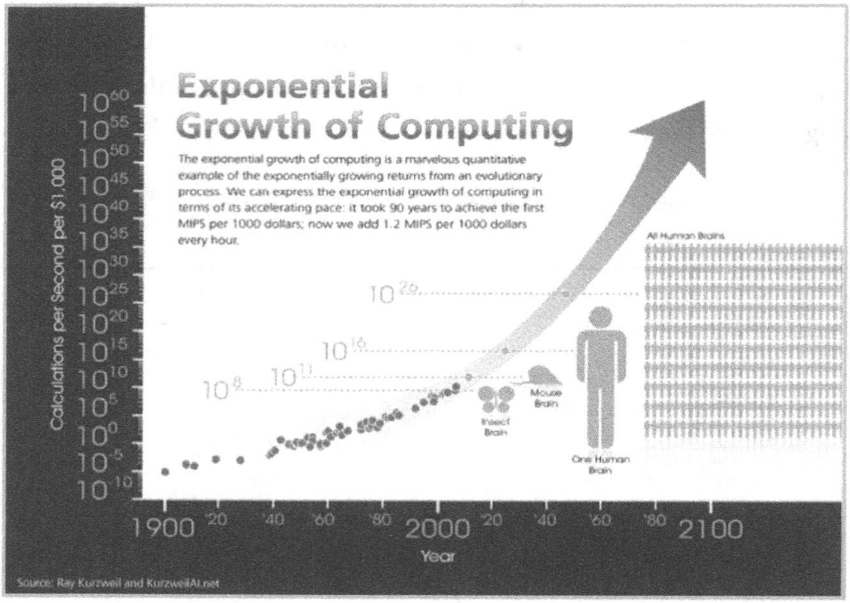

Source: Ray Kurzweil, and KurzweilAI.net.

Kurzweil says we're on the verge of creating a computer that will exceed the computational capacity of a human brain. Even more impressive, he predicts that continued progress will soon (50 years) lead to computing power that exceeds the *entire human species*.

If accurate, it's not just futuristic science fiction, but a rapid and profound disruption—today.

SMALLER AND SMALLER

In addition to speed, processors have also shrunk—a bunch—and the pace of development here has accelerated, as well. The first generation of integrated circuit semiconductors (late 1960s) were based on "gate length" size regions (inside the transistors) of 10 micrometers or more. By 2008, most products employed chips more than 100 times smaller than this—in the 65–90 nanometer range (about 1,000 times less than the width of a human hair). Today, chip features are even smaller at about 45 nm, with industry poised to introduce new silicone-based 3-D transistors using gate lengths as small as 22 nm.[3]

Many designers believe that industry has pushed silicone-based chip miniaturization near to its physical limit. Some are now working on new designs with new materials, including new alloy "nano-wires," with gate sizes around 10 nm.

Miniaturization is important for two reasons. First, smaller circuit features allow for further concentration of computing power, resulting in lowering computing power per dollar investment (see Kurzweil above). Second, miniaturization promotes the continued development of chip "on-boarding," allowing greater integration of computing power with ever-more-mobile applications. Though computer chips are already nearly ubiquitous (computers are in everything), there remains an unlimited array of additional possibilities—smaller, smarter, and faster tools for the human environment (including on-boarding inside the human body itself before long). This is "the Internet of everything."

MORE CONNECTED

Beyond speed and size, computers are becoming vastly more connected, forming an immense global array (a cloud) of connected power. This larger network includes both the world's most powerful mainframes, as well as millions and millions of individual PCs. Group grid sizes vary widely, from several units (in corporate or educational environments), to thousands and (before long) millions of personal units. Some grids are stable and relatively permanent; others completely ephemeral—briefly linking and then unlinking as projects are finished. While connected, grid computers draw on the computational capacity of multiple sources to achieve a common objective—a sort of "virtual super-computer."

The cloud is more effectively employed every day, in computationally intensive scientific, mathematical, and academic problems, as well as in various commercial applications (drug discovery, economic forecasting, seismic analysis, and back-office data processing). A primary advantage of distributed computing is that each network node (unit) is cheap; it's a basic computer, not a supercomputer. Linking into a grid provides supercomputing power, but at a considerably lower cost. A primary disadvantage of distributed computing is the relatively slow speed of its connections. As a result, cloud computing is best suited for applications that require multiple, parallel processing computations, without the need for intermediate communication.[4]

BIOTECHNOLOGY

In 1981, I was in college, completing a degree in biology. I don't remember much talk then about "biotechnology," and I certainly don't recall many job prospects in the field. (At that point, all Biology majors became doctors—either rich MDs, or poor PhDs.) Today, biotechnology is developing into a 21st-century business juggernaut. But in its most basic sense, the field of biotechnology—that is manipulating living organisms to suit a human purpose—has been with us for thousands of years, beginning with Neolithic agriculture.

The United Nations Convention on Biological Diversity defines biotechnology as *"any technological application that uses biological systems, living organisms, or derivatives thereof, to make or modify products or processes for specific use."*[5] For thousands of years, humans have worked to improve agricultural, in a quest for optimal crops (including methods of planting, fertilization, pest control, and cross-breeding genetic variants to increase yield and economic return). Other important biotechnology developments involved the brewing of beer and other alcohols, fermentation of foods (grapes, dairy, and breads), and pasteurization and other preservation techniques.

But biotechnology is more than just food. In 1917, Chaim Weizmann used a pure microbiological culture of *Clostridium acetobutylicum* to produce *acetone* (a component in the manufacture of explosives) in an industrial process. Biotechnology was also crucial to antibiotics: Alexander Fleming's 1928 discovery of the mold *Penicillium* led to commercial applications of *penicillin* by 1940.

Still, biotechnology is only now beginning to impact society beyond these several applications. In fact, the modern era of biotechnology began in 1980, not with a scientific breakthrough but in a court of law. Then, the US Supreme Court ruled (*Diamond v. Chakrabarty*—the case involved a bacteria capable of breaking down crude oil) that a genetically modified microorganism could be *patented*, opening the way for biotechnology *commercialization*.[6] Since this ruling, significant developments have occurred in many areas, and today the pace of biotech innovation is rapidly accelerating. Progress is occurring in four major areas, as detailed in Figure 3-3.

FIGURE 3-3. AREAS OF BIOTECHNOLOGY DEVELOPMENT

Category	Areas of Progress—Examples
Agriculture—food	organic food products (beer, milk), crop yield and crop resiliency, enhanced nutrition
Agriculture—non food	biodegradable plastics, vegetable oils, biofuels
Medical/health care	drug production, gene therapy, genetic testing, cloning
Environmental	bioleaching for mining, bioremediation

Rapid advancements are also occurring today in the field of *bio-informatics*, or *computational biology*. Efforts here involve greater use of computers in the study of large and complex biological information systems. One successful example is the Human Genome Project (HGP), a massive initiative of the US Department of Energy, designed originally to fully reference the entire human genome and all human genes. At the time of the project kickoff (1990), the HGP envisioned computational work of astounding proportions, with a planned study interval of fifteen years (2005). But because of large-scale, worldwide participation in the project, along with better-than-expected computer processing, the study was actually finished ahead of schedule in 2003. Since that time, researchers have used HGP results to pinpoint the specific genes associated with more than 30 human disorders.

NANOTECHNOLOGY

Nanotechnology? Though it sounds a bit futuristic, the idea of nanotechnology is rather simple: *manipulating matter on the atomic or molecular scale*. Nanotechnology is fundamentally about developing stuff—structures, devices, or materials—at a *very small size*, and then assembling these from the bottom up (one molecule at a time). The field of nanotechnology is today quite diverse, and includes dimensions of conventional physics, organic chemistry, molecular biology, semiconductor physics, and micro-fabrication and assembly.

The modern field of nanotechnology is new, with origins tracing back to the invention of the scanning tunneling microscope (1981) and the discovery of fullerene particles (1985). The term *nanotechnology* itself was coined originally by Norio Taniguchi in 1974, and later popularized by K. Eric Drexler in his 1986 book *Engines of Creation: The Coming Era of Nanotechnology*. It was Drexler who first proposed the idea of a "nano-scale assembler" that could build a copy of itself, and other items of complexity, through atomic level assembly.[7]

A nanometer (nm) is very small—one billionth (10^{-9}) of a meter. The field focuses on objects in the scale range of 1 to 100 nm. For comparison, the double helix of human DNA has a diameter of about 2 nm, and the smallest of cellular life forms (bacteria in the genus *Mycoplasma*) are around 200 nm in length. Here is another comparison: a nanometer is to a meter as a marble is to the size of the Earth. Or this: A nanometer is the approximate amount that an average man's beard grows in the time it takes him to raise a razor to his face!

The commercial promise of nanotechnology focuses on the "molecular assembler" in construction—producing materials by aggregation, one atom at a time. The premise is that molecular machine assembly is analogous to traditional industrial machine manufacturing. But there is a great deal of debate over the efficacy of the manufacturing possibilities. Molecular machines are still in their infancy. Research continues on many fronts, including the development of new nano-materials; molecular assembly through bottom-up and/or top-down approaches; bio-mimicry; and various other (and sometimes very speculative) directions.[8]

Today, the future of nanotechnology is also hotly debated—where the field is headed, and the important implications of further development. There are a wide range of potential applications—in medicine, energy, electronics, and bio-materials—each with considerable promise. But concerns are prevalent as well, from the potential impact on global economics, to environments and ecosystems, and even to various doomsday scenarios. These concerns warrant further analysis, discussion, and debate.

But nanotechnology already matters in our world. In fact, in August 2008, the *Project on Emerging Nanotechnologies* estimated that more than 800 nanotech-related products were already publicly available, with the list of new commercial applications growing by three to four new products per week.[9] Most of these are "first-order" (materials) applications, using nano-materials such as titanium dioxide (sunscreen, cosmetics, surface coatings); carbon allotropes (gecko tape); silver (food packaging, clothing, disinfectants, and household appliances); zinc oxide (various products); and cerium oxide (a fuel catalyst). These materials improve the various products they're used in: longer-lasting tennis balls, straighter-flying golf balls, and harder bowling balls. Clothing made with nanotech materials lasts longer, and keeps you cooler in the heat. Band-Aids infused with silver nano-particles help to heal cuts faster. Many other products—in automobiles, computers, video games, and medicine—promise to become cheaper, lighter, faster, or smarter through the use of nanotechnology.

COMING TOGETHER

Technological development is exploding everywhere, change is ubiquitous, and the pace of progress is increasing. Computer technology, information technology, biotechnology, nanotechnology—it's all evolving at breakneck speed. The more you look, the more you see, and the more amazing the picture is. And that's the way it is going to be.

But still there's more, because in addition to the rapid evolution of technology, today we're also witnessing many new associations and connections between technology fields. The rapid acceleration of cheap computing power, availability and transparency of information, and *many* more participants in the global conversation—are together driving a new *convergence* in technology. In the future, there will not only be specialists—biotechnologists and nanotechnologists—walled away and self absorbed in protected, academic-like research settings, but also many more focused on the commercialization of these new technologies, quite often in the *spaces between specialized fields*. As a result, technology disruption will also be characterized by this *convergence*—a connection and blending of advancements in various (and previously disparate) fields.

One example is the new field of *bioinformatics*, melding basic biological investigation with rapid advancements in computer and computational technology. The result is significant progress in initiatives like the Human Genome Project (HGP) mentioned above, and in subsequent applications related to the study and prevention of human disease.

Important work is proceeding on many fronts today, and it's easy to postulate a continued advancement in the future. Imagine the new breakthroughs—harnessing the power of cloud-connected computing to design new products constructed through nanotech assembly, and then onboarded in biological applications (including humans) to improve productivity, health, and happiness! It's both exciting and energizing—and a little scary. There will, of course, be significant issues, and perhaps tremendous risks—but also likely astonishing improvement in the human condition.

THE IMMINENT SINGULARITY?

So, where does it all end?

In his 2005 book *The Singularity Is Near: When Humans Transcend Biology*, author Ray Kurzweil paints an astonishing view of what he see ahead, and not so far in the distance.[10] Kurzweil argues that by the midpoint of the 21st century, humanity will (largely through the power of computer and information technology) fundamentally transcend the constraints of human biology and evolve into an essentially new species. The crux of his theory is rooted in exponentially accelerating technological change. As computers and other machines become faster, cheaper, and more proficient, they will focus on, and attack, the ever-more-challenging issues of humanity. Innovative solutions to these problems will provide continued innovation, and will (by about 2050) result in a mind-crunching pace of development, beyond the capacity of human understanding. At that point, the rate of technological change will be asymptotic—a mathematical *singularity*—as though (from the human perspective) an entirely brand new and otherwise unrecognizable world is created each new day. Kurzweil doesn't suggest that the machines will take over (like a bad science fiction movie), but that humans will rely on machine power to fully understand and exploit the universe opening around them.

Kurzweil is a controversial futurist, so it's not surprising that his views are hotly debated. What's most amazing to me concerning this picture of the future is that it's only 30 to 50 years away! In fact, Kurzweil postulates that our generation (or perhaps the one that follows) will be the last without the ability (and freedom) to choose how long we will live. Functional immortality! Sound crazy?

Is it true? I don't know. But much of this argument is relatively straightforward, and even compelling. His predictions are at least possible. Moreover, Kurzweil's ideas, and the *Singularitarian* viewpoint, are gaining traction. In a *Time Magazine* cover story *"2045: The Year Man Becomes Immortal,"* Lev Grossman refers to believers as a "movement."[11] As Grossman notes, not all Singularitarians are Kurzweilian purists; there is a good deal of diversity and opinion about what will happen and what won't, and when. But together they are different—a unique and growing subculture, about which Grossman says:

> Singularitarians share a worldview. They think in terms of the time, they believe in the power of technology to shape history, they have little interest in the conventional wisdom about anything, and they cannot believe you're walking around living your life and watching TV as if the artificial intelligence revolution were not about to arrive and change absolutely everything. They have no fear of sounding ridiculous; your ordinary citizen's taste for apparently absurd ideas is just an example of an irrational bias, and Singularitarians have no truck with irrationality. When you enter

their mind space you pass through an extreme gradient in worldview, a
hard ontological shear separates Singularitarians from the common run of
humanity. Expect turbulence.

Probably most controversial about this Singularitarian view is the eventual transcendence of biological limitations—the current boundaries of human health as we understand it today. Singularitarians see these obstacles not as permanent and inevitable facts, but merely as extremely difficult (but solvable) problems. Grossman quotes popular futurist and English biologist Aubrey de Grey this way:

People have begun to realize that the view of aging being something
immutable ... is simply ridiculous. It's just childish. The human body is a
machine that has a bunch of functions, and it accumulates various types of
damage as a side effect of the normal function of the machine. Therefore,
in principle, that damage can be repaired periodically ... The whole of
medicine consists of messing about with what looks pretty inevitable until
you figure out how to make it not inevitable.

One possibility is that hyper-intelligent machines (armed with new tools from biotechnology and nanotechnology) will advance new solutions to overcome human aging. Or, alternatively, perhaps the new technology will allow transfer of the human brain/mind into a *sturdier vessel*—a manufactured, robot body. As a result, in either of these scenarios, post-Singularity humans would become essentially immortal.

Perhaps these Singularitarian predictions won't come true— constrained by obstacles as yet not fully known or understood. Or, alternatively, maybe we'll achieve these goals, but over a longer time frame. Still, it seems likely that some (and perhaps most) of this out-landish change will happen—maybe sooner rather than later.

The potential is enormous, and it's born in our basic Fast Future premise: Rapidly accelerating technological development and change will fundamentally transform everything in our world.

SO WHAT?

The picture we've painted of the road ahead is both certain and uncertain, clear and confused. Surely the continued development of technology will profoundly change our society and world—rendering it (before long) largely unrecognizable from today. On the other hand, the details of that future are most uncertain—the details nearly impossible to predict. So what are you and I, as business owners and leaders, supposed to do about this Fast Future, this rapid technological change?

Accelerating technological development will impact our businesses in at least three areas: (1) changes in our own industry, (2) changes in our clients' industries, and (3) changes in our society in general. And despite the lack of substantive clarity in the answers, it is incumbent that we continue to ask (and investigate) many critical questions concerning our future, such as:

▶ How will continued, accelerating technological change and development impact our industry—how we do the work, where we do it, who do we do it for, and who do we compete against?

▶ How will technological evolution change our clients' businesses in ways both large and small, incremental and transformational?

▶ How will technology continue to define and influence how we connect and collaborate with one another?

▶ How will technology alter our competitive landscape—changing who our competitors are, where they come from, and how we compete?

▶ How will technology—and the concurrent rise of information—affect our profession? Will we see (as with other professions) a change in the nature of customer knowledge, and even a growing amateur class of pseudo-professionals?

▶ How will biotechnology affect or influence our businesses, as it impacts the quality and longevity of human life?

▶ How will developments in nanotechnology affect our work, perhaps through the promise of far-less-expensive, or much-higher-performing, materials in our products?

▶ How would a step change in the price of energy (either up or down) impact our business, industry, and/or economy?

▶ How do we best manage our business operations within a context of constant uncertainty, volatility, and change—including these highly disruptive technological advancements?

▶ Which areas of technological development offer the greatest economic promise in our industry? Where are the leading areas of new opportunity?

▶ What technologies suggest the greatest threats to our business today? In five years? In 20 years?

Change and growth of technology is at the heart of today's Fast Future transformation. This will continue, and in an environment where the pace of the development is itself accelerating, the road ahead will only become more complex—and less clear. The progressive business leader must pay close attention, scanning the horizon for both opportunity and threat, and must nurture an increasing adaptability and agility inside the organization—to meet and exploit the Fast Future opportunity ahead.

MY OWN JOURNEY WITH THE REVOLUTION

When I graduated from college in 1982, all computers were mainframes. As a new technical professional, I learned that secretaries typed out forms (for approval of this or that) on our behalf. Mistakes were painted over with White-Out, and some forms still came in triplicate (carbon paper included—'CC' once stood for carbon copy!).

About this time, IBM released its Selectric typewriter. The innovative correction ribbon was a big hit, allowing one to type over a previous letter using white ink, and then to retype the correct letter in its place. Just three years later, I had an IBM XT personal computer on my desk. It used MS-DOS as its primary interface—no Microsoft Windows yet. I created and managed spreadsheets with Lotus 1-2-3 (before Excel), and printed these with a dot-matrix printer. (Success required using a special and unique string of characters to communicate between the computer and the printer.)

All important computational and data management stuff was still handled on the big mainframes, and, boy, were the folks in the IT department powerful! And yes, they lorded this power over everyone, and we cowered in the fear that they wouldn't help us. I remember vaguely a day when we were visited by two suits from IBM, who came like secret agents and locked themselves into the clean room, and there (supposedly) changed out a system chip at a reported cost of $500,000. That was 1985/86, so it was probably the equivalent of today's throwaway calculator.

We communicated inside the company then with an early form of instant messaging using the mainframe and dummy terminals. As the Internet became available in the early '90s, most large corporations at first refused to connect (security issues), and some even enacted policies against e-mail accounts, or against using company resources to connect to the outside.

By the early to mid-90s, we were beginning to employ laptop computers in our work, along with cellular "car phones" (each costing more than $1,000 per month). Internet use came along slowly. One of my NYU graduate marketing professors predicted in 1996 that no appreciable commerce would ever transact via the Internet! Oops, that was a miss!

I've ridden the wave with the millions, never an early adopter of technological gizmos, just a user of basic tools. And I've had my share: Palm Pilots, Blackberries, desktops and laptops, a dozen different kinds of phones. Mostly these were PC/Windows platforms, though I've moved in the last few years over to Apple products such as the iPod, iPhone, and iPad—nice stuff.

Indeed, how things have changed. Sometimes it's difficult to imagine how we'd get by without this technology. And it's even harder (and sometimes nearly impossible) to completely disengage from it, to successfully disconnect (even temporarily) from the grid. Like others, I've hauled my laptop to Third World countries; taken my work to the beach in New Jersey, Turks and Caicos, and Hawaii; and worked to stay connected in the backwoods (where the point is to get away from connection). Today, the challenge is not the technology per se, but how best to use it, and the ubiquitous information and connectivity that's available almost everywhere. Just imagine what the place will look like in another 20 years!

4

Information Ubiquity and the Rising Value of Knowledge

**THE AVAILABILITY AND TRANSPARENCY
OF INFORMATION WILL FUNDAMENTALLY
TRANSFORM ALL HUMAN ENDEAVORS, WITH
KNOW-HOW THE NEW COIN OF THE REALM.**

*"Information is the oxygen of the modern age.
It seeps through the walls topped by barbed
wire, it wafts across the electrified borders."*
—Ronald Reagan

CONNECTIVITY, SHARING, AND OVERLOAD

Today, we are all overwhelmed with information, but it's not news to anyone. An explosion in the availability and transparency of information has been underway for (at least) a couple of generations, though the pace of expansion is rapidly accelerating today. Now we're right in the middle of it, struggling each day to organize, process, and make sense of the overload. We suffer from (as author Sam Horn puts it) *infobesity*.[1] But, as with other uber-trends, our familiarity with and involvement in the change creates a blind spot.

Ultimately, an endgame seems evident—that information will radically transform all of human endeavor. And, very importantly, virtually all forms of power that are today predicated on the restriction (and control) of information will be greatly assailed (and most will fail).

These power structures will be replaced by more democratic, meritocratic systems and philosophies. I'm not arguing for a Pollyanna, feel-good version of world democracy. I fully expect the change will be imperfect, messy, and filled with tension (and even violence). Still, like water flowing downhill, the change will occur as a matter of course, propelled by the power of information itself.

The roots of the information revolution are grounded in the steady advances of communications technology and computing power. One might argue that this began in the 15th century, with commercialization of the offset printer by Johannes Gutenberg. Important later inventions included the telegraph, telephone, radio, and TV, which together propelled us into a new Information Age. Rapid acceleration of computing in the 20th century furthered the step change, and the rapid rise of personal computers, smartphones, and a globally connected Internet have ratcheted up the pace of change to an astonishing level today.

In his book *The World Is Flat*, author Tom Friedman argues that the technological infrastructure created in the second half of the 20th century (personal computer, Internet and browser, broadband fiber-optic cable network, and collaborative information-sharing standards and tools) together created a backbone on which this new level of information sharing (and ultimately a rapidly globalizing world) has occurred.[2]

As Friedman summarizes:

At this point, the platform for the flattening of the world [had] started to emerge. First, the falling of the walls, the opening of the Windows, and the rise of the PC all combined to empower more individuals than ever to become authors of their own content in digital form. Then the spread of the Internet and the coming to life of the web, thanks to the browser and fiber optics, enabled more people than ever to be connected and to share their digital content with more other people for less money than any time before. Finally, the emergence of standardized transmission pipes and protocols that connected everyone's machines and software applications, and also encouraged the development of standardized business processes for how certain kinds of commerce or work would be conducted, meant that more people were not just seamlessly connected but also were able to seamlessly work together on one another's digital content more than ever before. Put it all together and what you end up with is the creative foundation of a whole new global platform for collaboration. This was the genesis moment for the flattening of the world, and it came together in the mid-to-late 1990s.

So, what does the rapidly increasing availability and transparency of information look like today? One of the best summaries of the transformation in progress are those provided by *Scott McLeod and Karl Fisch, in their series of Did You Know videos* (2008, 2009, 2011), available at *http://shifthappens.wikispaces.com/. Though their revelations are increasingly outdated in an extraordinary fast evolving landscape, some of the highlights they've shared over the last few years are captured in* Figure 4-1:[3]

FIGURE 4-1. INFORMATION EXPLOSION–FACTS AND FIGURES FROM THE DID YOU KNOW VIDEO SERIES

- Some 130 million books in the world today, with the total growing by about 1 million new volumes each year (2010 Google estimate)
- Google today digitizing about 1,000 pages of existing books per hour
- Around 1 trillion web pages today; a 2007 survey estimated 109 million unique websites (up from about 70 million in 2005)
- About 2 billion information searches completed each day; in 2006 that number was 2.7 billion per month, and 31 billion per month in 2008
- The number of Internet connected devices: 1,000 in 1984, 1,000,000 by 1992, and 1 billion by 2008
- Approximately 2 billion people today with Internet connectivity
- Nearly 250 billion e-mails sent each day; 80 percent of these are spam (2009)
- Wikipedia launched in 2001; as of March 2012 reported 3.6 million English-language articles, 21 million

articles in total (in 280 languages); more than 26 billion pages; 400 million unique visitors per month, growing through the work of some 85,000 active contributors

- The Flickr photo-sharing site reports about 5 billion photos stored; Facebook around 50 billion photos
- Some 240 million televisions in the United States (for 300 million citizens); US users access 10,500 radio stations, and 5,500 magazines
- Three major US broadcasting networks (in business for a combined 200 years) report approximately 10,000 unique visitors per month; Facebook, MySpace, and YouTube (none of which existed before 2004) today see some 250 million combined visitors per month
- About 60 hours of new video are uploaded to YouTube every minute
- More videos uploaded every couple of months than could have played on the three major broadcast networks, all running 24/7, since 1948
- Around 5 billion cellphones in use worldwide; 25 percent of households in the United States use only cellular telephone service (no landline); Nokia manufactures 13 cellphones per second
- First text message was sent in 1992; in 2009, users sent 6 trillion text messages around the world; the average US kid texts more than 2,200 times each month
- In 2009, about 300 million mobile apps downloaded; in 2010, the number was about 5 billion
- The amount of digital information worldwide is expected to increase by 44 times between now and 2020

- In 2008, approximately 95 percent of songs downloaded were not paid for
- Several sources have estimated the number of words in the English language today at around 500,000, about 5 times the number of words in Shakespeare's time; a 2010 Harvard/Google study placed the current English word estimate at over 1 million, and growing at the rate of about 8,500 new English words each year
- It has been suggested that a week's worth of the New York Times offers more information than a typical person saw in a lifetime during the 18th century
- A 2008 study estimated about 4 Exabytes (4 x 1019) unique pieces of information were created that year; more information than was created in the previous 5,000 years in total
- Amount of global technical information is today doubling every two years

Source: "Did You Know" at http://shifthappens.wikispaces.com/.

Yes, information is exploding, and it's a function both of more information *creation*, and more information *creators*. Greater information creation is due in large part to the rapid growth of technology, science, and other endeavors. But the second point—the rapid rise in the number of those *creating* new information (content)—is itself driving an exponential acceleration of global information. Behind this are both the rapid expansion of Internet connectivity, and the ever-increasing variety of new social media communication platforms.

As Figure 4-2 shows, the number of worldwide Internet users has grown extraordinarily over the last 10 years.[4] As of 2012, Asia alone boasted more than 1 billion connected users (but only a quarter of the continent's population). Other regions have witnessed tremendous user growth as well, including Latin America and the Caribbean (1,200 percent), the Middle East (2,200 percent), and Africa (3,000 percent). Still, in terms of total population, overall Internet penetration remains low in many regions (less than 40 percent in Latin America and the Caribbean, about 35 percent in the Middle East, and just 13.5 percent in Africa). There is considerable room for continued growth in connectivity and use of the Internet and information.

FIGURE 4-2. WORLD INTERNET USAGE (2011)

WORLD INTERNET USAGE AND POPULATION STATISTICS (December 31, 2011)						
World Region	Population (2011 Est.)	Internet Users Dec. 31, 2000	Internet Users Latest Data	Penetration (% Population)	Growth 2000–2011	Users % of Table
Africa	1,037,524,058	4,514,400	139,875,242	13.5 %	2,988.4 %	6.2 %
Asia	3,879,740,877	114,304,000	1,016,799,076	26.2 %	789.6 %	44.8 %
Europe	816,426,346	105,096,093	500,723,686	61.3 %	376.4 %	22.1 %
Middle East	216,258,843	3,284,800	77,020,995	35.6 %	2,244.8 %	3.4 %
North America	347,394,870	108,096,800	273,067,546	78.6 %	152.6 %	12.0 %
Latin America / Carib.	597,283,165	18,068,919	235,819,740	39.5 %	1,205.1 %	10.4 %
Oceania / Australia	35,426,995	7,620,480	23,927,457	67.5 %	214.0 %	1.1 %
Total	6,930,055,154	360,985,492	2,267,233,742	32.7 %	528.1 %	100.0 %

Source: Internet World Stats, Usage and Population Statistics, at http://www.internetworld-stats.com/stats.htm.

The last decade has also seen a 150 percent increase in the number of North American Internet users, and a 375 percent increase in Europe. Internet penetration is much higher in the West (nearly 79 percent in North America and 61 percent in Europe). However, even the more technologically advanced nations have opportunity for growth and expansion of Internet leverage. Penetration rates for major geographic regions are compared in Figure 4-3.[5] Overall, the world's Internet penetration (2011) stands at 32.7 percent—about one-third of the world population.

FIGURE 4-3. INTERNET PENETRATION BY GEOGRAPHIC REGION

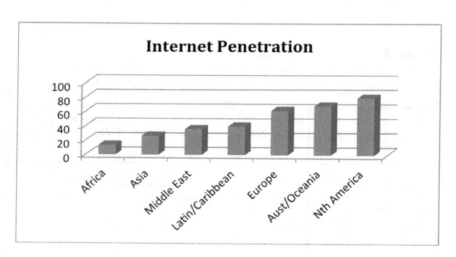

Source: Internet World Stats, Usage and Population Statistics, at http://www.internetworld-stats.com/stats.htm.

SOCIAL NETWORKS—A GAME CHANGER

To have claimed just a decade ago that social media would shake the very pillars of global media content creation and distribution seems unlikely. Few predicted that social media would completely revolutionize knowledge management (Wikipedia) or video production (YouTube). And even political experts missed how social connections (Facebook and Twitter) would drive social and political upheaval around the globe. And yet, of course, all of these things have occurred and, in many cases, in less than 10 years. The mind-numbing rise of social media has not only connected millions and millions of individuals in a global network that both allows and encourages information sharing, but this has also driven a rapid transformation in the nature of creativity and collaboration across our society. Social media encourages content *creation*, and it is radically reshaping the basic roles of creators and consumers. In the past, creators were credentialed experts in the "professional media." Consumers were amateurs, and a passive audience. New York University's Jay Rosen describes these folks as "those people formerly known as the audience," a poignant assessment of the new world order.[6] Today, we have millions of active, creative, and collaborative participants in the game.

Of course, the social media landscape is evolving at breakneck speed. There are many different platforms, including several large-scale sites, and many new, nascent startups. Some of these may become big winners, many won't catch on, and some will rise quickly and then fade, replaced by other more useful, relevant, or interesting ideas.

FACEBOOK

Since its 2004 creation by Harvard freshman Mark Zuckerburg, Facebook has grown into the largest, and arguably the most influential, social media networking service in the world. The company reported ending 2013 with 1.23 billion active monthly users—with more than 750 million of these users active daily (see Figure 4-4). The company reports that around a billion members use Facebook's *mobile* technology on cellular or smart phone devices. Approximately 80 percent of Facebook users reside outside of the United States or Canada. Facebook is today available in more than 70 languages; the operation is a fully global enterprise.[7]

Facebook's mission is to *"give people the power to share and make the world more open and connected."* By all accounts, the company has attained a high level of success with this, though there does remain additional opportunity for growth and development.

FIGURE 4-4. TOTAL FACEBOOK USERS

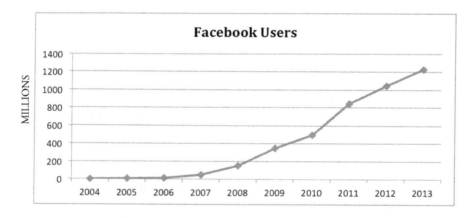

Source: Facebook.com

TWITTER

The micro-blogging service Twitter is only a little younger than Facebook, but it too is growing rapidly today around the globe. According to *MediaBistro* blogger Lauren Dugan (posted March 6, 2012), in 2011, Twitter grew 31.9 percent (number of users), that on the heels of 23.5 percent growth the prior year. At the close of 2011, US-based Twitter users were estimated at around 24 million.[8]

Twitter itself reports that in 2014, it has over 270 million active monthly users, and that 75 percent of these use mobile devices. About 500 million tweets are shared each day (twice as many as just a couple of years earlier). Some 77 percent of Twitter users reside outside of the United States, and the service is offered in more than 35 languages.[9] Twitter users are rapidly figuring out how to use the platform in new and valuable ways to communicate, share information, and (in some cases) change the world.

LINKEDIN

LinkedIn was founded in 2002, and within its first month of operation captured 4,500 members. In 2014, the service now boasts some 300 million members worldwide, in over 200 countries. The service is growing at more than two new members per second, and 66 percent of LinkedIn members are located outside of the United States. The platform is available today in 22 languages. Mobile users account for about 40 percent of total unique member visits to LinkedIn.[10]

LinkedIn's members conducted nearly 5.7 billion professionally oriented searches on the site in 2012. More than 3 million firms currently have LinkedIn Company Pages. There are 50,000+ developers using LinkedIn APIs to create new tools and services for professionals, and more than 300,000 unique domains actively using the LinkedIn Share button on their own sites (to send user content to LinkedIn). Finally, LinkedIn today includes some 2.1 million *LinkedIn Groups,* where members share insights and knowledge on subjects of unique interest.

YOUTUBE

YouTube is the world's largest video-sharing site, and today (2014) more than 100 hours of new video are uploaded every minute (almost two hours worth of video every second). More than 4 billion clips are viewed each day, and the site logs more than 1 billion users each month, about 40 percent of these on mobile devices. In aggregate, YouTube visitors watch more than 6 billion hours of material each month.[11]

Today, 80 percent of YouTube traffic comes from outside the United States, and the platform is localized in 61 countries and across 61 languages. In 2011, YouTube experienced more than 1 trillion total views. That represents almost 140 views for each human being on Earth!

More video is uploaded to the site each month than the three major US broadcast networks created over their first 60 years. Today, the YouTube player is embedded across tens of millions of websites worldwide. According to YouTube, there are more than 1 million content partners making money with their YouTube channels.

YouTube has also become considerably more integrated with other social media platforms. Each day, some 500 years of YouTube videos are watched on Facebook; over 700 YouTube videos are shared *each minute* on Twitter. Each week around 100 million people perform a social action on YouTube (e.g. likes, shares, comments, etc). Each Tweet results in approximately six new Youtube.com viewings, and Twitter now sees more than 500 tweets per minute which contain a YouTube link.

MYSPACE

MySpace offers a poignant and cautionary reminder of the fickle nature of the global Internet community, and our larger society as a whole. Though MySpace has repositioned itself as an entertainment-focused site, it's certainly taken a major step back from its once-preeminent position in social networking. In 2008, the company reported more than 200 million worldwide users, at the time the largest of the social networks. By mid-2011, the company's online fact sheet reported only 100 million total users. In 2014, the user community size is less certain (MySpace no longer provides either a fact sheet or historical timeline).[12]

There are, of course, many other relevant social media platforms operating today—Pinterest, Google+, Snapchat—and numerous others we've barely heard of. Some of these will become central to the global conversation, others not. Over time, these platforms themselves will become less important, less visible (think radio, TV, phones, cell phones, computers)—while the information—the content of the conversation—will continue to grow in relevance and importance.

INFORMATION—WHAT WILL IT MEAN?

It's obvious that something big is happening with information today. The convergence of advancing technology, information availability, and global connectivity is profoundly reshaping our world order. What it all means is unclear, but we're certainly destined for a future much different than today. A few of the implications:

COMMERCE

In the early 1990s, I was in graduate business school at New York University. The Internet (as we knew it) was still small, and primarily a vehicle for connecting very specific groups (online bulletin board services, group forums, and, of course, lots of pornography). The World Wide Web was an infant (Netscape went public in 1995, its *Navigator* Internet browser opening the web to the world). At that point, a marketing professor of mine made an emphatic prediction that no significant commerce would *ever* occur via the Internet! (I remember thinking even then that this prognostication seemed questionable.) Today, this comment is stunning—unfathomable by our current reality. In fact, it's much more plausible today to suggest the opposite—namely that virtually *all* commerce might soon be transacted (or at least enabled) via the Internet.

Global connectivity is changing commerce in other ways. The global market is becoming very fluid and frictionless, with products and services moving much more easily across geographic, economic, and cultural boundaries. Products and services markets are becoming increasingly disconnected from the place of manufacturing—it's less important where the work is being done (so long as it can be consumed satisfactorily somewhere else). Supply chains are quickly morphing and becoming much more fluid, even "atomized." And both mass marketing and mass production are less important, increasingly replaced with a new model of "mass customization," the specific product or service tailored directly to a market of one.

Because of the availability and transparency of information, markets, marketing, and all human commerce is evolving at exponential speed. These will never be the same again, and will continue to change at an ever-increasing pace.

POLITICS

Though few experts predicted it, there's no question that information power has profoundly affected political and governmental systems around the world. Enormous upheaval has occurred in an amazingly short time, most visible in the Arab Spring movements of the Middle East and North Africa. Here, social media platforms (Facebook, Twitter, YouTube) have played an important role in connecting individuals, informing markets, and galvanizing both opinion and action. Revolutions in Tunisia, Egypt, Libya, and Yemen resulted in the overthrow of autocratic governments. Other nations moved (either proactively or under pressure) to offer new reforms, freedoms, greater participation, or more transparency. Some countries remain in open conflict (Syria is today an unfortunate example), their outcomes unsettled. Dictatorial governments everywhere should take heed—the availability and transparency of information is changing everything. Governments can easily control one individual. But when citizens can connect, share, and collaborate in ideas and dreams, and can plan concerted action together, then unilateral power is greatly diminished. All power systems and structures based on the control and obfuscation of information are at risk today, and will increasingly be so in the future.

Upheaval in world politics and government is, of course, not limited solely to the Arab Middle East regions, or to autocratic governments. Indeed, information availability and use is reshaping the political landscape in nearly every nation. Powerful (but still developing) China must balance its desire for rapid economic progress with continued political stability and control—not an easy task. Other developing nations will be challenged to keep up with public opinion and expectation, as citizens begin to understand more clearly what's possible (and those expectations outrun the host country's ability to change and deliver). Developed Western nations in North America and Europe also face considerable challenge in the Information Age, including sustainability of the two-party political system in the United States, new legal challenges in free speech and personal security, and innovative approaches and methods for connecting politics with voters. In the 2008 US presidential election, a younger Barack Obama more effectively engaged a new generation of potential voters, and these younger and more connected citizens acted differently—contributing in February 2008 about $55 million over the Internet (5 times more than Obama's opponent John McCain). [13]

SOCIAL

In addition to the transformative changes in commerce and politics, information is radically reshaping the very fabric of global social structures. New technologies, tools, and tactics now provide a chance for millions of individuals to rethink community. In virtually all societies, a systematic movement toward online community is growing today through a "join, connect, collaborate, and create" progression of involvement. And this last stage—*creation*—is the most important development of all. Specifically, the information revolution is fundamentally less about information per se, and more about *creating* together (and for one another) after the connections have been made.

More joiners, larger communities, closer connections, additional creators—it's all coming, and all with a flatter, more democratic, more meritocratic global society. The Fast Future promises this transformative opportunity, and much of it for those who haven't participated before. Change will not, of course, be without challenge—ultimately creating both winners and losers. Nor will the change occur in a clean, linear progression (consider the state of change and "progress" in Iraq, Afghanistan, Libya, or Egypt). Still, over the long haul, the meritocracy will give millions an opportunity to better themselves, their families, and their communities through the power of technology and information.

KNOWLEDGE COUNTS MOST

In the Fast Future, knowledge and know-how will count for more than anything else.

Knowledge is important—this isn't new. The ability to know and do something has always been valuable. Those who could make and keep the fire, who knew where and how to hunt, or how to unlock the medicinal secrets of plants—these were the chiefs, the shamans, the wise of old. What is changing today is the context, and our rapidly expanding body of knowledge. In a fully global and connected world, barriers to acquiring this knowledge are falling rapidly. Knowledge is itself becoming more transparent, transient, and ephemeral. Knowledge is becoming commoditized.

Consider this: If there's just one specialist in the world in a particular subject, then he or she holds enormous value, power, and prestige. Today, that specialist likely lives in the West, and was probably educated in the United States. In contrast, consider that instead of just one, there are really 10 specialists worldwide who possess the same knowledge and know-how in equal parts. On second thought, let's make it 100 specialists—all the same in quality and expertise. These 100 specialists will be more dispersed geographically, and will increasingly live (if not be educated) in the *developing* world. And in an economy completely without boundaries (no, we're not there yet), each of these specialists will be less valuable (perhaps considerably less so) than the one. Prestige and power will be distributed. The world may be a much better place for all of this talent, but each specialist will face tougher competition.

And that's the Fast Future in a nutshell—an enormous amount of talent, skill, and expertise—all about to ascend the global stage in a truly connected world economy.

There have always been barriers to a fully open global market, including country, government, and political boundaries; race, gender, or religious constraints; language, secular beliefs, and other cultural roadblocks; and also time and geographic distance. Many of these barriers have worked to impede the sharing of information, knowledge, and know-how. Some were developed accidentally or through unintended consequence. Other constraints were imposed intentionally, on purpose, and with purpose. Some of it was ugly.

The power of knowledge helped the knowledgeable to control power. Today, this is changing rapidly (though not fast enough for some, and clearly not in all situations). Still, in most places, information does flow more freely, and citizens are gaining more of the knowledge and experience they'll need to succeed in the 21st century.

A TOWER OF BABEL

Language is the basic mechanism of communication; few human developments have been more important. Language is the foundation for human interaction (including commerce), and it remains a significant barrier today in global business. The inability to communicate with others impedes the flow of information, knowledge, and trade around the world.

Today, much of the globe's business is conducted in one of four primary languages: English, Hindi, Spanish, or (Mandarin) Chinese. As evidenced in Figure 4-5, English isn't the world's most common first language (Chinese is, by a wide margin), but it's the most global language, because so many learn English as a second language.[14] It is estimated that about one-fourth to one-third of all humans understand and speak some English.

FIGURE 4-5: THE PRIMARY LANGUAGES OF THE WORLD

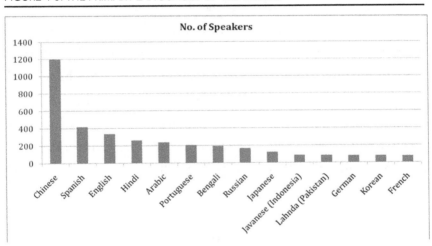

Source: Ethnologue: Languages of the World, Seventeenth Edition, 2014.

There are at present 5,000–6,000 languages spoken worldwide, though as many as a half of these are no longer known by children (and, thus, are at risk of extinction).[15] Many nations are pushing for standardization of their languages and dialects, and this is a major force in the rapid decline of languages. Another is the homogenization effect of globalization, a Fast Future trend that is accelerating.

While the number of languages is quickly declining, languages that remain are rapidly growing in size, continuing a trend that's been underway for more than 200 years. For example, modern English includes more than five times as many words as it did in Shakespeare's day, and these words are used in daily communications that vastly eclipse the scale of past experience. One estimate suggests that a week's worth of writing in the *New York Times* today represents a lifetime of reading in the 18th century. Language is becoming standardized on fewer platforms, but the survivors are rapidly growing in breadth.

As language becomes more standardized, global barriers are lowered, and expertise and experience flow more readily. This intensifies competitive pressure—more people in the know. Knowledge and know-how then combine with lower costs to create new value (think Chinese manufacturing, Indian IT support, or Colombian CAD work). It's easy to envision where this will head (in a hurry). Those formerly of more privileged position will face new competition; those previously outside of the game will find new opportunity. But in all cases, the conversation (and language) will be about *knowledge and know-how*—who knows what, and who can get it done.

A NEW GLOBAL CURRENCY?

Early economic trade began with simple barter—one product or service traded for another. This was useful because no one could do everything needed for survival. But simple barter (I'll trade you a mountain of fresh corn for your goat) presents a problem in its inflexibility and lumpiness. (I'm interested in your corn, but not so much in trading away my goat; how about a cow, I have two of those? And what to do if I only want a half a goat's worth of corn?) The solution was *money*—an enormously important early innovation in human development. With currency as an intermediary, trade was more flexible, fluid, and frictionless. The volume of trade, and size of markets, could grow much more quickly, and well beyond a handful of locals.

But money must be created, and its supply has long been controlled. For most of history, currencies were either made of scarce materials (such as gold or silver) or were backed by those materials. It's a relatively recent phenomenon to have paper money simply printed by a government, and backed only by that government's promise of redemption. Only a handful of nations have the credibility to deliver on the promise. Most currencies are heavily discounted to face value, and more than a few are essentially worthless.

Of course, money is scarce and has real value. It can only legally be obtained in trade—for products delivered, services provided, provision of labor, raw materials, or for money itself (lending or borrowing). But imagine a Fast Future scenario where labor is relatively less valuable—through transformational productivity—leading to greatly diminished labor demand. In this environment, what will people do to earn money? Many raw materials will remain scarce and valuable. But most goods and services might be provided at substantially lower cost, or not needed at all. Skills that are common won't be worth much in a fully connected global society, and much work will be of this sort. Truly distinctive talent—the knowledge and know-how to do extraordinary things—will be worth much more, and will remain in high demand. This suggests that only a part of products, services, and labor—that part which represents the distinction—will be worth anything. That's where the value (and money) will concentrate.

> So all organizations, systems and processes, and supply chains will have to adjust, and refocus their efforts on the value-concentrating part of their businesses.

The alternative, of course, will be to offer highly commoditized products, services, and labor at much lower prices—a viable strategy for those with scale and/or cost advantages. Either way, knowledge and know-how will become the most important (and true) currency of the realm.

And, in some cases, expertise may in fact become the *actual* currency of the realm—a return to the simple barter system of old. This will probably happen first at the lower end of the knowledge scale—those with one skill trading with those of another. This trade will work because the parties can agree on similar value (example: two hours of field labor equals one haircut). It's possible that higher-level knowledge workers can do the same, though it's more complicated when relative values are unclear (how many times does one have to mow a lawn to pay for orthodontic services?). These differences suggest a developing hierarchy in the know-how economy. At the lower-value end, service providers will be more commoditized. Examples might include landscaping, bookkeeping, or basic customer service. But higher-level services providers will also become more commoditized—software coders, marketing communications professionals, graphic designers. And one day (not too distant), virtually all services (brain surgeons, college educators, and company CEOs) will be commoditized to some degree, outsourced in whole or part to lower-cost (but still high-quality) alternatives. Like US-based CPAs who today send tax preparation work to India for completion, successful knowledge and know-how experts will focus on the highest-value-added components of their business.

EDUCATION AND THE FAST FUTURE

Commoditization means that the value of most products and services is constantly on the decline. Similarly, little knowledge and know-how will retain their value for long. Availability, transparency, and transportability of expertise will render much knowledge perishable, and what knowledge remains will rapidly decay in worth as it is distributed, shared, and copied. Because of this, true value will come not only through knowledge itself, but even more importantly, through the *ability to acquire* knowledge and know-how. In the Fast Future, continuous learning throughout life—for individuals, teams, organizations, and societies—will be a primary driver of economic value and sustainable competitive advantage.

In this light, isn't it ridiculous that we today cling to an antiquated education model developed in (and for) a much different time? In our current system, most formal education is loaded into the first quarter of life, with almost nothing else learned in the next 50-plus years. Increasing life expectancy (and healthier living) will exacerbate this imbalance. It's clear that the system must change, toward a more continuous life-long learning model. Many will have the capacity to do knowledge work for 50 to 70 (or more) adult years. More and more, that will require getting back to school—perhaps in several cycles—in a big way.

BACK TO SCHOOL—MY EXPERIENCE

After completing my undergraduate education (biology and geology), I went to work for Exxon Corporation—one of the world's largest multinational organizations. I'd originally planned to stay just a while, returning then to the university for a PhD. But my plan was sidetracked by a famil-

iar tale–marriage, kids, cars, homes, and such. Then a dozen years later, I enrolled in a graduate business program while continuing to work. Though Exxon paid for most of my education (a very generous program indeed), I'll never forget the skeptical pushback I received from most peers (and bosses). Few employees did this sort of thing, and the culture of this large but stodgy firm was strongly conformist. Much better (the thinking was) to simply devote the extra time and effort to the company itself–that was the best and shortest route to the top. And an MBA, rather than a technically focused path? For some, this was heresy. Even the idea of thinking beyond the firm–to what might lie outside of the comforts of the status quo–seemed risky to many of my friends and peers.

I'm not criticizing my former colleagues or my employer. Exxon was a top-notch firm and one of the better-run organizations in the world. (I suspect it still is today, though they've had to survive for 15 years now without me!) I've learned over the years to appreciate even more the company's values, systems, standards, and culture–all those things I griped about while there. This was a time of great transition in corporate America. The old model of the paternalistic company employer (one you invested all of your talent and emotion and trust in) was melting away around us–or so it seemed to me. A new paradigm–focused much more on self-management and on individual mission and vision–was sprouting, but made more sense to me. Many colleagues didn't buy fully into this notion of self-reliance, or the risks of taking unilateral action. Lots of these people stayed with the Company, safely inside the castle walls. Some have been very successful; others might regret not jumping themselves. For me, the move to earn that MBA, and the career choices that followed, has been most rewarding, and an important part of my adventure.

Over the past 40 years, we've witnessed a significant change in the organizations that employ workers. The notion of an individual career has evolved substantially. Historically, most people stuck with one occupation for life. During the 20th century, most stuck with one employer for life. Today, it's different—we've seen a *serialization of employment*—managing our careers by moving from one company or employer to the next. Some suggest that what's next will be a *serialization of careers*—changing not only who it is that writes the check, but also what we're doing—the occupation and roles of our work. Perhaps soon we'll change this several times during a career. Sometimes these shifts will come through carefully designed strategy and intention; other times it will result from need, or will develop haphazardly or serendipitously. But in all cases, a successful career will demand additional and ongoing education and development, and a great deal more flexibility and agility than required today.

A GLOBAL FREE AGENCY FOR PROJECT MANAGERS?

We may soon be headed into a world of 9 billion *freelancers*, each working in a jumble of jobs, projects, companies, and careers—each of us cobbling together both a living and a meaning from the global milieu. Many more of us will operate like the professional services providers of today—architects, engineers, accountants, lawyers, doctors, and consultants—the most successful of which concentrate their knowledge and know-how to create *value* for clients. We'll be professionals of many sorts: freelancers, contract workers, business consultants, artists, part-timers; some relatively obscure and some world-renowned.

This rapidly shifting new world order is likely to be structured increasingly around *projects*, as work itself becomes sliced, diced, and parsed into myriad short-term, temporary efforts in an ever more "atomized" supply chain. In this context, the basic knowledge and acumen of *project management* will itself become valuable. Many professionals already work in project-oriented environments, but many corporate workers and companies don't—instead they're still organized primarily in assembly lines, geographic teams, or functional silos. Project-based organizations are less permanent, more changeable, and are oriented more toward flexibility, agility, and shorter time horizons. In the Fast Future, we'll see more of this, as the work of more companies and industries become more project oriented.

Project management skills (including planning, scheduling, and budgeting) as well as general management and supervision, leadership, communications, relationship building, and change management, will be in much greater demand.

FAST FUTURE: SOME THOUGHTS ON WHERE WE'RE HEADED

As I've said, the Fast Future endgame isn't clear, but it will be big, and it will be different. The road ahead isn't just about change, but also about *opportunity*. In *Cognitive Surplus,* author Clay Shirky sketches out a view of the world that's developing, with new opportunities born of the technological acceleration, information availability, and a profound new sense of global interconnectedness.[16] Shirky offers several examples of the new "cognitive surplus" in action—people working together to create and deliver new value to society. These include PickupPal.com (carpooling), PatientsLikeMe.com (medical advice and care), Ushahidi.com (citizen reporting), and Pink Chaddi (political activism). Shirky claims that the extra, global cognitive surplus is already astoundingly large (he estimates that just 1 percent of the total is enough today to create 100 new full Wikipedia projects each year!). Moreover, he argues that the surplus will only grow as more of the world's citizens become connected and collaborative on the global platform.

Jeff Jarvis, author of *What Would Google Do?*, echoes a similar theme of big changes and opportunities ahead.[17] Jarvis argues that the current technology and information revolution will disrupt our world much more than we expect, just as has happened with previous disruptive revolutions. Jeff spoke not long ago at an NSA convention (professional speakers), and framed the disruptive revolution in poignant terms for the speaking profession—challenging the very notion of speaking, and the "speaker to audience" model. Jarvis sees that the future ahead will be characterized by a more collaborative context, with the speaker facilitating an interactive and living conversation that recognizes subject matter expertise, innovative ideas, and creative juices from all participants (beyond the platform leader). The paradigm will shift from that of speaker and audience, to facilitator (or conductor) and "the people formerly known as the audience." This paradigm will likely expand even further, well beyond the walls of the physical audience, to include the total "audience" of the world.

Another example of Fast Future change in our midst is Kickstarter.com, a 2009 crowdfunding site that connects creative entrepreneurs with prospective customers, clients, and adoring fans to *pre-fund* new projects. In 2012, indie rock singer-songwriter Amanda Palmer (former star of the punk band Dresden Dolls) raised nearly

$1.2 million in a then-record breaking campaign with *Kickstarter.*[18] Access to funding has always been a limiting factor for good ideas, and Kickstarter is one example of the new ideas that promise to radically reshape not only project funding, but also the fundamental relationship between creators and consumers, builders and buyers, performers and audience—indeed the very DNA of the marketplace. Again, a similar theme: the availability and transparency of information, linked with the transformative power of the web, to connect individuals in new, collaborative relationships.

In *World Wide Mind: The Coming Integration of Humanity, Machines, and the Internet* (Free Press 2011), author Michael Chorost postulates the evolution of an extraordinarily connected, learning, and evolving world that becomes increasingly "telempathic." Here, communities of linked individuals will share thoughts, emotions, and moods collectively, and through this act together in new ways as a group and as individuals.[19] Chorost argues that this system, with incipient signs of its development showing just now, could support a new system for brainstorming, "facilitated by the direct exchange of emotions and associations within the group (that) can happen at any time or place." *New Yorker* magazine contributor Jonah Lehrer has argued that team processes such as brainstorming don't work very well to facilitate creativity.[20] So, how about some real "brain-linking" instead, a whole new level of team collaboration?

It's a theme of many business analysts and futurists—as well as central to the point of this book—that the future will be much different, with bigger, more disruptive change than most of us think. Futurist Ray Kurzweil believes that this disconnect is tied to how humans think, and their natural bias for interpreting information in *linear* terms. Kurzweil argues that human brains are naturally wired this way, and that this makes sense, given the many human experiences that are linear in nature. But Kurzweil, others, and I expect something very different now—global change at an exponentially accelerating pace. In that case, we're all likely to under-appreciate the full magnitude of the transformation ahead.

Worldwide meritocracy is on the rise. In the Fast Future, those with knowledge and know-how will win and thrive, eventually irrespective of who they are, where they're located, or anything else. Knowledge, expertise, and experience—especially that which is truly unique—will matter most, and be valued by all. The marketplace will become more transparent, and knowledge will be most valuable currency around.

SO WHAT?

Again, while the road ahead is uncertain and the endgame unclear, many questions are important and worth asking in the firm today. Fast Future leaders are asking these questions, and taking action now. Some examples:

- ▶ How is the availability and transparency of information changing our business most?
- ▶ Where does our knowledge and/or control of information, help our business and value most? How should we protect that knowledge and information?
- ▶ Who has more knowledge and know-how concerning our industry and business today than they had in the past? What are they doing with this new knowledge?

▶ How is the new availability and transparency of knowledge and know-how fundamentally changing our customers, clients, supply-chain partners, and/or competitors? What will our industry and markets look like in 10 years? Twenty years?

▶ How will our work be accomplished in the Fast Future? What will change about team interaction and collaboration—as a result of technology and information flow?

▶ How is information and knowledge changing our clients' industries and markets, and how they do business?

▶ What are we doing today to provide our staff with more useful information, knowledge, and experience?

▶ What part of our business is (or could be) most easily commoditized if others knew more about it, or how to do it?

▶ What new ideas, innovations, or perspectives on education are we seeing and employing to help our staff and our organization prepare for the future ahead?

5

The Great Globalizing Globe

**OUR WORLD WILL EXPERIENCE RAPIDLY RISING GLOBAL
CONNECTIVITY ON VIRTUALLY EVERY DIMENSION POSSIBLE.**

*"It has been said that arguing against globalization is
like arguing against the laws of gravity."*
—Kofi Annan

WHAT GLOBALIZATION IS

G lobalization is an uber-trend we're all aware of, and
sometimes painfully familiar with. Still, as with other big
trends, our casual understanding is not enough to fully get it, or to
appreciate the magnitude, pace, and intensity of the change ahead—
and the implications in our world.

Globalization is a term that's frequently heard today. It can mean different things to different folks, so let's start with some definitions, the first two from Random House Dictionary, and the last three from World English Dictionary:

- ✓ *"The act of globalizing, or extending to other or all parts of the world"*
- ✓ *"Worldwide integration and development"*[1]
- ✓ *"The process enabling financial and investment markets to operate internationally, largely as a result of deregulation and improved communications"*
- ✓ *"The emergence of a single world market dominated by multinational companies, leading to a diminishing capacity for national governments to control their economies"*
- ✓ *"The process by which a company (or similar organization) expands to operate internationally"*[2]

I think of *globalization* in its more general context, as the overall connectivity of peoples around the world, and their economies, cultures, politics, societies, and governments.

The term is most commonly employed in the *economic* sense, concerning the production and distribution of goods and services, international trade, and the economic principles of specialization of labor and regional comparative advantage. Nevertheless, as economic globalization becomes pervasive, connectivity on other dimensions—political, social, and cultural—is also becoming central to the discussion.

The forces of globalization are not new (and the term itself has been around since at least the early 20th century). Still, globalization has become much more visible since World War II, particularly in the last 30 or 40 years. "Globalization" as a word entered into the mainstream US lexicon and culture in the 1980s.[3]

Here is what the *United Nations Economic and Social Commission for Western Asia* has said about globalization:

A widely used term that can be defined in a number of different ways. When used in an economic context, it refers to the reduction and removal of barriers between national borders in order to facilitate the flow of goods, capital, services, and labor ... although considerable barriers remain to the flow of labor ... globalization is not a new phenomenon. It began toward the end of the 19th century, but it slowed down during the period from the start of the First World War until the third quarter of the 20th century. The slowdown can be attributed to the inward looking policies pursued by a number of countries in order to protect their respective industries ... However, the pace of globalization picked up rapidly during the fourth quarter of the 20th century.[4]

In 2000, the *International Monetary Fund* identified four basic aspects of globalization, and said about each:[5]

Trade and Transactions

The amount and value of worldwide trade has increased substantially, though there remain significant variations between regions. (For example, many newly industrialized Asian economies have prospered greatly, while most countries in Africa have not.) Overall, developing countries have increased their share of world trade from about 19 percent in 1971, to 29 percent by 1999.

Capital and Investment Flow

Private capital investment in developing countries soared during the 1990s, and in many areas has replaced much of the developmental assistance and aid of foreign governments. Foreign direct investment has become the most important category of capital outlay.

Migration of People

During the period 1965–1990, the amount of internationally migrating labor forces doubled in size. Most of this movement of people has occurred between the least developed countries and more developed countries. Migration to the most developed countries is often constrained in some way, but it has occurred as well. Labor migration is cited as one mechanism for the convergence of global wage scales. Wage convergence then provides additional employment opportunities in the home country.

Dissemination of Knowledge and Technology

Exchange of information and technology is an integral component of globalization. Exchange of innovation and development has benefited both the least-developed and more-developing countries, as well as the most developed nations. Some developing countries have even skipped technological phases (for instance, with landline telephone infrastructure and service).

A BRIEF HISTORY

The origins of globalization are debated, but its roots date far back in human history. Since the beginning, humans have sought connection and trade with one another. As the tools and practices of agriculture developed, some peoples expanded beyond local subsistence farming, creating pockets of commercial specialization. By the third millennium BC, trade links developed between the Eastern Mediterranean area and the Indus Valley (Pakistan) region. By Hellenistic times, these interconnected cultures reached from Spain to India. Later, the Roman Empire joined with the Parthian Empire and Han Dynasty to form a *Silk Road* between China and Rome. Significant trade, and the mixing of global societies and cultures, continued here through the rising Islamic age, and later the Pax Mongolica of the 13th century. At this time, the first international postal service was initiated, and this era also witnessed the rapid spread of many disease epidemics, including the bubonic plague.[6]

In the 16th and 17th centuries, a new phase of globalization was defined by the serial rise of several European maritime empires (Portuguese, Spanish, Dutch, French, and British). In the 17th century, creation of the first forms of business corporations (such as the British East India Company [1600] and Dutch East India Company [1602]) intensified the focus of Western powers on colonization and exploitation. Burgeoning New World discoveries propelled many European nations into this race, leading to much international trade, economic development, and natural resource exploitation—as well as the exchange of peoples and cultures, plants and animals, and communicable diseases (the latter decimating a good deal of the indigenous population in the New World).

By the 19th century, the dawning industrial age yet again transformed global forces, creating a system more closely approaching our modern one. Industrialization led to higher production output, manufacturing economies of scale, and specialization of labor. These developments led to rapidly increasing populations, population concentration, and urbanization, and fast-growing demand for new products and services. Global opportunities for industrialization encouraged further economic and political exploitation and imperialism during this period. India, sub-Saharan Africa, and much of the Asia–Pacific region became integrated into the global economic system. Conquest in these areas provided enormously valuable natural resource inputs (fueling both continued industrialization output, and the coffers of the already-wealthy industrialists). Further international development was briefly interrupted by World War I and the large-scale Depression that followed. After World War II, global trade, economic development, and globalization resumed, along with the development of many new global institutions (the United Nations, World Bank, World Trade Organization, and International Monetary Fund).

THE VIEW TODAY

Large-scale globalization has touched the world's regions and populations quite differently—with both positive and negative effects. Some have prospered, while others suffered. But going backward now—that won't happen. Author Tom Friedman *(The World Is Flat)* has described the changes of globalization as "permanent."[7] He's right. More importantly, global transformation continues, and at an ever-increasing pace.

> The genie of globalization cannot be stuffed back into the bottle, and all peoples—whether for or against, beneficiaries or victims—simply must face this reality.

ECONOMICS

Opinions vary widely over the balance of positives and negatives of globalization. Economic and business interests sing the praises of increasing international trade and free marketplaces. But groups of disaffected workers, market sectors under assault, and politicians dealing with the fallout of change often focus on the downside of globalization, and lambast the global forces and policies involved.

Western economies have certainly benefited from a global marketplace, particularly in the extraction of natural resources (oil, minerals, forestry, and foods), and in the production of goods with cheaper foreign labor. And even as intensifying globalization eventually has "returned the favor" to formerly exploited areas in the East (examples: Japan, Taiwan, Korean, India, and China), most Westerners view global trade positively. Consumers benefit from lower-cost products across a large swath of the economy. Nevertheless, in the last decade or two, many more educated, trained, and experienced white-collar workers have become victims of the powerful forces of globalization. Transnational economic volatility, market bubbles and busts, and multiple recessions (with subsequent "jobless" recoveries) have indeed captured public attention. Displaced blue-collar auto and steel workers of the 1970s was one thing, but structurally obsolescent white-collar knowledge workers is quite another!

It's difficult to deny the significant increase of economic activity resulting from globalization. International trade in manufacturing goods has increased more than 100 fold over a 40-year period (from some $95 billion in 1955 to about $12 trillion in 2007).[8] In 2014, more than $1.5 trillion US is traded each day in the foreign exchange market in nationally denominated currencies, in support of this explosively expanding international investment. To be sure, the expansion has been geographically uneven, with some regions benefiting much more than others. For example, China's trade with the African continent has risen sevenfold in less than a decade (2000–2007).[9] International trade has usually reduced the cost of goods and services around the world as nations exploited their talents, focus, and advantages. For some, this comes primarily through inexpensive labor; in others, it's access to raw materials, a focus on technology and innovation, or particularly talented and skilled workers. Global competition has delivered both lower costs and an explosion of innovative new products and services.

Of course, there have been losers as well in the global game. Product innovation and step-change reduction in cost has rocked many an industry, region, and country. Non-competitiveness, obsolescence, and irrelevance have eliminated thousands of firms, and millions of jobs. Some countries (for instance, Haiti, Somalia, Burma, and North Korea) have largely been left out, often through their own economic protectionism and/or political isolationism. Other countries have witnessed a significant "brain drain" as talented workers leave for better opportunities abroad. And, unfortunately, despite the lifting of many boats around the world, extreme poverty remains a stark reality for millions and millions of people. This is the result of the (sometimes horrific) inequality in the sharing of wealth. A 1992 United Nations study found that the richest 20 percent of the global population controlled about 82.7 percent of the world's income, while the poorest 20 percent controlled only 0.2 percent.[10]

Global change is expected to continue. A 2007 Price Water-
house Coopers (PWC) report predicted that by 2050 the emerging
economies of the *E7* (China, India, Brazil, Russia, Mexico, Indonesia,
and Turkey) will altogether total some 50 percent *more* than those of
the current *G7* economies (United States, Japan, Germany, United
Kingdom, France, Italy, and Canada). This PWC study predicted
that China will overtake the United States, to become the world's
single-largest economy by around 2025, and that India will eclipse
China by 2050.[11] A similar 2010 report by Goldman Sachs estimates
that China could become the world's largest economy by 2020.[12]

The 2008 recession highlighted painfully just how profoundly
interconnected and interdependent the global economy has become.
The collapse of domestic US financial and real estate markets seriously
impacted economies across the globe. Similarly, financial weakness in
several European Union states (Greece, Portugal, Italy, and Spain)
slowed the U.S. economic recovery. Other world events—such as
the Japanese tsunami and nuclear crisis, persistent drought and other
weather events, and political instability in the oil rich regions of the
Middle East and North Africa—have reminded us all of the increasing inter-dependency of the economic fortunes of many nations
around the world.

POLITICS, CULTURE, AND SOCIETY

Globalization is concerned largely with economics, commerce,
and wealth creation, but these powerful forces affect much more than
the bank accounts of regions, nations, and people. Globalization has
greatly increased *transparency* in the world—through the availability of real-time information, news, and analysis. Many governments
built on the control of information and power are now under intense

scrutiny, assailed by new demands for openness and participation. Economic success on every continent (the Asian Tigers, South Africa, Brazil, and others)—provides new models for regional neighbors, and new pressures to join the global marketplace. However, openness to change (think *Perestroika* in the old Soviet Union) also comes with considerable risk to the establishment. China has embarked on a grand experiment, attempting to mix economic freedom with continued political control. (Ultimately this path forward in China is still uncertain, and success remains to be seen.)

The powers of globalization are also becoming increasingly *institutionalized*, as global organizations themselves ascend in importance. The United Nations, World Bank, World Trade Organization, International Criminal Court, and World Health Organization are examples of institutions growing in power and influence today. Even the European Union itself is an experiment in a new collectivism, and the institutionalization of globalization. These institutions (and others) will likely increase in influence as the world becomes a more interconnected, intertwined, and interdependent marketplace and society.

Globalization, international trade, and the (more or less) free flow of immigrant labor around the world are significantly homogenizing the traditions, languages, and cultures of the world. Information flows much more freely today, whether it's about American basketball, World Cup football, or consumer brands such as Coca-Cola, BMW, or Apple. This blending of world culture creates a sense of common dreams and goals, but also dilutes the diversity of backgrounds, perspectives, and beliefs of individual cultures.

With respect to language, there is clearly a blending today. Mandarin Chinese is the world's most commonly used language (850 million active speakers). Second is Spanish, with 350 million speakers; another 350 million or so speak English as their first language. Together, that's 1.5 billion of the world's citizens speaking one of these top three languages. English is reported (overwhelmingly) as the most popular *second* language of the world, and it's the primary language of economic opportunity and globalization. (Nearly half of the world's population has at least some acquaintance with English.) About 40 percent of the world's radio programs are broadcast in English, and at least one-third of the world's mail, faxes, and cables are delivered in English. English is the dominant language of the global Internet.[13]

Finally (and maybe most importantly), the coalescing trends of technology, information, and globalization have resulted in millions of peoples around the world grasping for a chance at *personal opportunity*. This idea (so deeply ingrained in the American psyche as the "American Dream") is now catching on everywhere around the world. This is new and extremely significant. The idea that one might aspire to become virtually anything has not been previously true (it's not entirely true in the United States, either, but more so here than in many places). In fact, for most of history, humans have made only small, incremental progress and change from generation to generation. There's been no particular basis for expecting that the next generation would do much better (or even pursue a different path at all). Most people simply follow their parents—in living habits, family structures, and vocational life. Globalization of economics, culture, and ideas is rapidly transforming the picture—and providing many with new hope, and a dream of real opportunity.

LOOKING AT THE CHANGE AHEAD

So, what's in store for the rapidly globalizing world of the Fast Future? Certainly, there will be much more change.

The globalization endgame will be an astounding transformation, with extreme global connectivity on almost every dimension of humanity possible. This will be both good and bad. In the long run, the benefits will largely outweigh the loss, with more winners than losers. Still, there's no denying that there will be many—countries, cultures, and millions of individuals—adversely impacted along the way.

Here are a few of the mini-trends of globalization that I believe will be critically important:

OUTSOURCING (OFFSHORING)

From a purely economic view, outsourcing—shifting business (manufacturing, production, administration, design) to other nations with comparative cost advantages, domain expertise, or skilled labor—just makes sense, and is beneficial to the global economy. Moreover, it's here to stay, and its use will accelerate. With economists, outsourcing is generally a positive. But with politicians, and in the general discourse, it's often a negative (and nearly a crime)—particularly in developed markets losing ground to other nations. The truth is somewhere in between. Completely free global trade is today still only a goal, not a reality. Barriers and unfair trading practices exist in many regions and it's not a level playing field.

Business decisions are made every day concerning outsourcing, often with imperfect data, and without full consideration of longer-range consequences. These decisions sometimes lead to structural changes in the competitiveness of regions, nations, or industry sectors, and often these can't be easily reversed.

Frankly, many politicians are disingenuous about outsourcing, promising their constituents they will reverse the trends, close the borders, and "bring back the jobs." By and large, these are promises that can't be kept. Jobs are moved to capture advantages. Without addressing these differences (usually labor cost), a reversal doesn't make much sense. To really win, governments must instead focus on long-term structural improvement, and primarily through more effective tax and trade policy, or through training/retraining of the domestic workforce. Focusing on what's already happened (the jobs already lost) is like directing water to flow back up the hill.

INSOURCING

Though the offshoring of jobs remains a powerful force in global economics, the reverse—insourcing (or onshoring) work into the country (moving business and trade from less developed to more developed nations)—is also occurring. This too will accelerate. This is the rest of the story, moving opportunities around to better match with specific resources (money, raw materials, and people). Labor may be consistently less expensive in a certain region, but labor is only one input in global production. Increasingly, producers will create supply chains customized for individual markets. In some of these, it will make sense to manufacturer *domestically*, in proximity to design or to customer service—for those markets that value personal attention, response time, or managerial control, more so than manufacturing cost.

SUPPLY CHAIN

Profound change is on the way for the world's supply chains—in every economic sector, industry, and geographic region. Supply chains are mutating in both structure (who participates and how they collaborate) and stability (how often participants shift their roles and relationships). As supply becomes more fluid, incredible new global opportunities will arise. As manufacturers, producers, distributors, and retailers become increasingly comfortable with new relationships, fluidity will accelerate still further. This experience has played out already in many industries, and it's coming to all. Even professional services firms (with a long history of supply chain control, local focus, and a high resistance to change) will see rapidly increasing globalization pressure, and exploding new opportunities to partner with others.

VERY SMALL FIRMS

Atomization—that is, the nearly complete dissolution of existing structures into their smallest component parts — of industry supply chains will provide significant new opportunities for companies of all sizes, but in particular for millions of very small (fewer than 10 employees) firms heretofore not as successful on the world stage. This small firm movement will gain steam in part through the rapid advancement of technology and information, but also through the rapid development of global markets. Mega-scale, multinational corporations with strong brands will continue in their global success, but simultaneously, hordes of very small firms will also capture significant growth, profit, and success in the Fast Future.

DISASSOCIATION

Looking even further out, globalization suggests perhaps an even more profound change. Connectivity and fluidity, outsourcing and insourcing, and the near-constant flux in all of business may eventually lead to a nearly atomic level *disassociation* of all work—task from project, project from process, producer from consumer, etc. *Where* the work is done will become far less important (and eventually perhaps irrelevant). The Fast Future will offer a nearly frictionless, virtual economy without boundaries, where opportunities flow (like water downhill) to the optimal producer, manufacturer, or supplier. Globally connected technology and communications systems will shrink the distance between producers and customers to insignificance. Many consumers will play the role of project manager or general contractor for their own projects, managing the various pieces themselves, or alternatively hiring a dedicated project manager for a particular project. *Who* does the work will remain critical; *where* the doers are physically located, likely much less so.

RISE OF THE GLOBAL INDEPENDENT

In a fully connected global network, the role and value of the corporation will change significantly. We may be headed toward a system of mostly (much) smaller organizations, teams, and independent professionals—who can adapt quickly to changes in product and project requirements, changes in skills and talents needed, and changes in customer objectives and expectations. The marketplace will likely be much different from that of the past—and the corporation-dominated paradigm of the Industrial Age. This could be viewed as a return to what came before: the independent practitioner, craftsman-oriented economy. In this world, the competitive landscape will be defined by millions and millions of independents—advisors, consultants, contractors, specialists, freelancers, etc., banding together to accomplish important work, and to achieve collaborative synergies where possible and valuable. This independent class will operate and succeed using the tools of the new Fast Future to connect instantly with clients and partners wherever they are.

Of course, developments toward this endgame won't always be pretty. Reward will rise for some and diminish for others. There will be blood and money—and lots of both.

And there's not much we can do to stop, or even slow, this powerful trend. It's where we're headed. The secret of globalization is no secret at all.

SO WHAT?

The implications and likely changes of globalization will affect individual markets, segments, and industries—along with the firms within them—in different ways, and on different timetables. Some industries (like mining, steel, or automotive) have been fighting the global onslaught for decades already. Others (like most professional services fields) have been considerably more protected—so far.

And even if the consequences of globalization (either in the short term, long haul, or both) aren't completely clear, leaders of organizations today must wrestle with the idea, asking important questions about the potential impacts and opportunities that lie ahead.

Here are some examples:

- ▶ How many in our firm can find Bogotá, Columbia; Islamabad, Pakistan; Ho Chi Minh City, Vietnam; or Jinan, China, on the global map?
- ▶ Which of our products or services are likely to be in greater demand in a global Fast Future marketplace? Which will be in less demand?
- ▶ What new products or services should we pursue now to exploit the globalizing marketplace?
- ▶ What areas of geographic expansion make the most sense for us? Should we pursue more aggressively further expansion domestically, or internationally, or perhaps both?
- ▶ What are we doing today in the firm that could be done better, faster, or cheaper by someone else?
- ▶ What are we not doing today in the firm that we might accomplish for another organization—doing it better, faster, or cheaper than they do it today?
- ▶ What game-changing innovations would threaten our current business most—and what are we doing about these now?
- ▶ What new competitor threats are developing? For whom is our current business their globalization opportunity?

6

The Morphing, Mutating, Shape-Shifting Marketplace

THE AGE OF RISING CONSUMER POWER, ATOMIZING SUPPLY CHAINS, AND VERY SMALL FIRMS—IS HERE.

"It is not the employer who pays the wages. Employers only handle the money. It is the customer who pays the wages."
—Henry Ford

CONSUMERS—A LITTLE HISTORY

Something is going on in markets today. Change is afoot like we've never seen before. The shift is seismic, and the implications are huge.

For thousands of years, the rules of commerce were stable and changed little. Buyers and sellers came together in the bazaar, or along thoroughfares in small towns and cities. As today, most buyers relied on sellers for expertise—on the quality of fish, apples, animal pelts—or how to repair a shoe. Most towns didn't support much competition—there was just one cobbler, blacksmith, or banker. And even with multiple sellers (those hawking fresh fruits, vegetables, and meats), buyers developed relationships with their favorite vendors.

Back then, marketing was simple too. Manufacturers, distributors, vendors, and service providers didn't have to do much to attract a local clientele; word of mouth was usually enough. If you needed a blacksmith, there was usually one around; you simply had to find him. (The blacksmith didn't advertise much). In the bazaar, it was important, of course, to have a great location, a larger space, and the loudest barkers—all early forms of marketing as we understand it today—but the customer could cover all of this ground in short order. What mattered most were product quality, price, and relationships.

But with growing complexity in our society, things began to change. Early technological developments (such as offset type and the printing press) ushered in an explosion of new information. It became more difficult to know all there was to know about everything. Rapid growth of cities brought more manufacturers and service providers together and more competition between them. Specialization of labor and assembly line production, ramping up at amazing speed with the Industrial Revolution, also brought a specialization of *knowledge*. Workers became divorced from the products they were making, and soon there was simply too much to know. Buying and selling relationships increasingly were defined by an individual buyer on one side and a *corporation* on the other.

Over time, the importance of one-way, *asynchronous* conversations grew. Conversations became *messaging*—not just answers to questions asked, but answers to questions that sellers *wanted* asked. Providers began *pushing* these messages out in increasing frequency and volume. A review of early advertising from the 18th and 19th centuries reveals a great deal of marketing acumen back then (and an unabashed, sometimes shameless, promotion of products and services). Not much different from our world today.

With the advent and growth of new media forms in the latter 19th and early 20th century (telegraph, telephone, radio, and television), the tools and techniques of communication became more powerful, allowing companies to reach ever-larger audiences of potential customers. Marketing as a discipline was reborn, with new strategies employed. Marketing became less personal, and in an increasingly complex, interdependent society, creating and maintaining *trust* became the preeminent issue.

One interesting example of this new marketing was the soap opera. These ongoing daily shows were created (both sponsored and produced) by leading soap manufacturers such as Procter & Gamble, Colgate-Palmolive, and Lever Brothers, beginning on radio in the 1930s and then on television by the 1950s. These companies took advantage of television to reach a much larger target audience (housewives) with interesting, innovative, and engaging (at least for the time) content—along with, of course, important messages about soap. This market was so lucrative that soap companies could justify inventing, creating, producing, and airing daily television shows to engage their core constituents! In 1976, *Time* magazine labeled American daytime television "TV's richest market," and noted that loyal soap opera fans justified the expansion of many half-hour programs to a full hour to capture additional advertising revenues.[1]

In the second half of the 20th century, this mass marketing juggernaut proliferated. Success was widespread as America, Western Europe, and much of the world enjoyed tremendous postwar growth. The rise of a large American middle class provided a mass market for virtually everything—houses, cars, refrigerators, lawnmowers, baby strollers, colleges, credit cards, beer—and on and on and on. Americans sat in front of televisions for hours, bombarded by commercial messages from manufacturers, producers, and services providers. Advertising was sometimes clever, but all too often was dull and unimaginative. But most of all, advertising was *pervasive*—it was everywhere. Targeted catalog marketing (baby boomers remember the Montgomery Ward's and Sears's toy catalogs of youth) evolved into direct mail of everything, and then eventually to poorly executed *junk mail* marketing—your mailbox stuffed each day with meaningless offers to switch to a new credit card provider.

SOMETHING BIG THIS WAY COMES

Now something very big has arrived. The Internet (not so obvious at first) has transformed markets, relationships between buyers and sellers, and the very nature of marketing itself.

This transformation of markets and marketing is occurring through at least four major trends: (1) the availability and transparency of information; (2) new opportunities for asynchronous, on-demand viewing of everything; (3) sharing customer and life experiences through social media; and (4) highly customized target markets and communities.

First, the astonishing global penetration of the Internet has paved the road for an explosion of information sharing. This information has impacted markets everywhere. Frankly, it's surprising now to understand how much the pre-Internet economy depended on just the opposite: the lack (or even obfuscation) of relevant information. In a highly specialized, technical, and complex environment, buyers and sellers often took cover (and the easy way out)—choosing to stay with an existing supplier, even though there were closer, cheaper, or better options. The winners often were the largest, loudest, or most well known. Incumbency mattered a lot.

Today's buyers are moving. Everywhere, they're learning more about products and services, quality and value, and alternatives. The Internet is the conduit for this information. Want to find the same product at a lower price? Simply scan the product code into your smartphone and find a better deal elsewhere (maybe even in the store you're at). This new practice of "showrooming" highlights both the opportunity and challenge of this fundamental change.

A second important change is the rapidly growing opportunity for on-demand viewing. Driven first by the VCR in the mid-1970s, audiences began to change their TV and movie watching habits. (Prior to the VCR, the provider controlled almost all scheduling.) VCR tapes were followed by DVDs, Blu-ray, and most recently by online digital streaming and the now-ubiquitous digital video recorder (DVR). Matched with this technology is a proliferation of

Internet-based content management and delivery services (iTunes, Netflix, and Hulu are popular examples). Time shifting of viewing has not only provided the consumer with scheduling control, but has also offered the chance to skip the advertisements that pay for the programs. (Ouch, that's a problem!) Today, only two types of people still watch commercials: those who enjoy them, and those who can't figure out how to operate their DVR! With new original programming now offered online (outside of the boundaries of traditional broadcast television), there is a further disassociation of content and scheduling, synchronous viewing, and connection with (and efficacy of) commercials. Advertisers are, of course, adjusting to the new reality. New forms of online, Internet-based advertising spring up daily, along with other innovations, such as commercial messages embedded in the programming.

Third (and perhaps one day soon the most important trend of all) is the power of social sharing. The first-generation Internet was primarily about sharing existing information, but Web 2.0 is focused largely on the *creation* of new stuff, much of it by amateurs outside of the traditional media and advertising establishment. Today, a lot of what's shared is the personal experiences of consumers, using an incredibly powerful (and sometimes dangerous) open platform for global word-of-mouth. Harnessing this new information requires that advertisers more fully engage with the market *interactively*, to speak *with* rather than *to* customers. All of these lines—between providers and consumers, pundits and listeners, professionals and amateurs—are rapidly blurring. Today, everyone has joined the party.

Fourth, today's Internet-based economy supports thousands of new, highly customized and targeted 21st-century market sub-segments. From the beginning, the Internet has been about smaller and highly cohesive communities—people sharing and collaborating around specific areas of interest and passion. Early examples of these formed on Telnet and Usenet even before the World Wide Web. Today, similar communities are found in forums and other sites across the net. In early groups, transactions focused largely on information, but commerce wasn't far behind. The eBay website was created in 1995 and changed how everyone viewed the Internet marketplace. Today, thousands of highly focused communities meet online, some explicitly for buying and selling, others for information, and some commerce. Specific and focused market segment groups—that's the new rule.

A WHOLE NEW GAME

Marketers are finding today that the old ways of marketing just don't work very well. And it's likely that they will work even less well in the future. This means changing the approaches of messaging, communications, and connectivity.

Consider this example: The personal referral has long been the gold standard of marketing, in both business-to-business and consumer markets. Personal referrals engender the greatest trust, and result in the highest rates of conversion (prospect to sales). But anecdotal research suggests that in more than 75 percent of these referral cases, prospective customers still do their homework—with personal, independent research (on you and your firm) before they make the call. They'll search for the company online, browse the website, and check social media channels. (Remember this personal referral is the gold standard, the best of prospecting tools.) Still, even these "highly inclined to buy" customers are influenced (for good or bad) by what you and your organization are saying (or not saying) online. What matters today is not just information, but that the *customer is in control.* More and more, the consumer decides when, what, and how to interact with the provider. So, the important question today is what is your message, and what does it say to me when I find it?

> This is a radically new era for commerce. Customers will decide what to look for, where to find it, and when to shop.

They'll do their research in a sea of readily available information sources (along with lots of noise). Amateur voices will mix with (and often drown out) the professional experts. Amateurs will themselves become experts in nontraditional ways.

> This isn't an incremental change: it's a major disruption, a significant tear in the fabric of our society.

This shift will demand that all manufacturers, distributors, service providers—everyone on the producer side—operate within a radically different paradigm. To paraphrase sales expert Jeff Gitomer, customers want to buy, not be sold.[2]

In the early 1990s, author Seth Godin began calling this "permission marketing."[3] His thesis was simple—that providers must ask for the prospective customer's permission—first to engage, before advancing to a next step in a conversation or relationship. This was the opposite of outward-focused, push-oriented, interruption-based marketing (advertisements, direct mail, spam e-mail, and cold calling).

Brian Halligan, CEO of the Internet communications firm Hubspot, calls this "inbound marketing," a methodology focused on *earning* the attention of prospective customers, making the firm easy to find, and drawing interested prospects *toward* the organization. Halligan and others argue that this is best accomplished through the sharing of valuable *content*—webpages, blogs, podcasts, videos, e-newsletters, white papers, e-books, and social media. Content is a foundational building block of inbound marketing.[4]

Inbound guru David Meerman Scott describes the methodology as "earning [your] way in," and contrasts this with the outbound approach of "buying, begging, or plugging one's way in."[5] Halligan and Meerman suggest that inbound marketing is particularly effective for smaller businesses; for those with high-value, high-dollar sales; a longer selling cycle; and for products or services based largely on knowledge (for example, professional services). In these situations, a prospective customer is much more likely to want to know more first, to conduct some personal research, and to come to his or her own conclusions before advancing.

In the permission-based paradigm, it's clear that *relationships* with potential customers must come first. So inbound marketers focus on delivering content that is interesting, useful, relevant, thought provoking, and change oriented. *Content must be valuable.* These inbound marketers *go first*, offering value before anyone asks for it. (This is one of my basic "laws" of business development success, *to go first, add value, and expect nothing.*) That inbound marketers go first without expectation of immediate reward doesn't mean that they don't expect results. Neither does it suggest that they're not into measuring progress—quite the contrary with web-based, analytical platforms. Instead, it means that progressive marketers are focused first on relationship results, not on transactional results. Expecting an immediate return (Okay, I did it, now it's your turn) means that going first is not a gift. Inbound marketing is about the client, not about the marketer.

Relationships simply cannot be rushed. Everyone understands this conceptually. I can count on a predicable response from audiences when comparing marketing to personal relationships. You simply can't rush into a bar 30 minutes before closing, find someone interesting, and ask him or her anxiously, "Will you leave with me?" It doesn't work in bars, and it doesn't work in business. Relationships of value require time, investment, risk, and trust.

Seth Godin reminds us that the customer's permission must be *real*. He describes it this way: "If you stop showing up, people will complain, they'll ask where you went." Hmm. Do you suppose your customers would call in to find out what happened to your last e-newsletter? (Seems like a high expectation.) But that would indeed mark a valuable relationship. In practical terms, permission marketers ask customers to opt in to test commitment and engagement. Those who aren't interested opt out—there's no spamming for true inbound marketers. The goal is to develop a "tribe" (a Godin term) of high-quality relationships, instead of a much larger, but less engaged, list. A community of invested, interested, and engaged prospects who themselves *participate* in the conversation is the real objective, the Holy Grail of inbound marketing.

Godin claims that marketing to these clients is a *privilege*, not an entitlement. It's an opportunity to offer useful, relevant, and *anticipated* messages to a receptive audience. And in a world where consumers have new powers to avoid or ignore old, interruption-based marketing approaches, increasingly it is the only marketing methodology that makes sense. In the Fast Future—when information and noise only grows—these high-quality, permission-based relationships will become incredibly valuable.

Traditional outbound marketing is mass marketing. Inbound permission marketing is customized, even personal, one-to-one relationship based. Inbounders report that this focused approach can deliver real results: response rates to messages of 5 percent, 10 percent, or more. By contrast, well-executed mass market direct (snail) mail today might earn a response of rate of ½-1 percent, and often lower. And e-mail? It's estimated that of the nearly 2 billion emails sent each day, 90 percent are unsolicited spam, with astoundingly low (but apparently still attractive to someone?) effectiveness.

We've come a long way in a short time. I vividly remember as a kid the Sears Christmas Toy catalog, and the excitement I had pouring over its dog-eared pages. Later, the mailbox was stuffed with interesting catalogs of all sorts (inexplicably, they were relevant though never asked for). Still later came all that junk—a mailbox stuffed with meaningless catalogues and magazines, direct mail letters, credit card offers, timeshare vacation announcements, and such. Direct mail became ineffective because marketers were unfocused, targeting the masses rather than interested customers. Marketers became less engaging themselves, less willing to do the hard work of building relationships. Today, the Internet provides infinite opportunity, but it is nothing more than a new platform. The underlying value of relationships and human engagement still apply. And so today we have both targeted, permission-based Internet marketing efforts, and also outrageous amounts of junk (spam).

Indeed, we've come a long way. But there's a long way left to go in this new age of the consumer.

WHERE WE'RE HEADED

Many of the newer Web 2.0 businesses today really understand this new marketing paradigm. These firms are constructed more socially, with an inbound marketing approach built into the business model. But you can also find many old-line firms across the economic spectrum embracing (or struggling with) these new methods. Most are still experimenting, and haven't fully grasped the new marketing opportunity. But who really gets it all yet?

The professional services fields have always lagged behind the curve in marketing. Professionals are by nature skeptical of sales and marketing, and most (frankly) haven't had to do a lot of it for success. But this is changing, and the new opportunities and threats of the global Fast Future will demand that professionals engage more fully in permission-based, inbound marketing. Professionals do appreciate the idea of *thought leadership*, the value of gurus. They're just not keen on overt promotion of themselves. The idea of providing intrinsically valuable content to prospective customers makes sense. The real challenge is rebalancing the firm's focus away from an almost-singular attention to production (productivity and utilization in the delivery of client project work) toward investing in creating content, building relationships, and other marketing-related activities. It's common in many professions for staff to be 70–90 percent billable on project work. On the road ahead, many of these organizations will need to reengineer their business models to include a higher level of marketing effort—perhaps a 50–50 split in time (production versus marketing). Additionally, these marketing activities must shift away from downstream, sales-oriented efforts—and toward upstream, conversation- and relationship-building work.

Marketing the firm has always been important. This basic fact hasn't changed—only the strategies and tactics necessary for success are shifting.

Fundamentally, the difference between old-line marketing and new are (1) the customer's control of the permission-based system (timing, schedule, direction, and tone); (2) the explicit focus on delivering valuable, relevant, and interesting content in a pay-it-forward, without short-term expectations manner; and (3) the opportunity to manage marketing efforts with the new analytics possibilities of the web—quite different from the touchy-feely, squishy management approach of the past.

So, what is it that the 21st-century firm should be doing to create growth, profit, and sustainable success? Marketing is indeed undergoing a revolution today, and most everyone is wrestling with the need to think and act differently. The old ways aren't working, but the new ways are still largely unproven. There are no real guarantees. It's confusing, challenging, sometimes overwhelming. Time to jump in.

SO WHAT?

Here are a few ideas, some of the basic components of this new approach, which progressive future-focused firms must embrace:

- ▶ using a website as the hub—a center of activity and information sharing in the organization, the chance to (as

Patrick Schwerdtfeger implores) "webify [the] business," connecting what's happening in the firm to the website;

▶ creating and sharing *content* on a regular and real-time basis, involving more experts in the organization, and delivering the message across multiple platforms (blogs, social media sites, e-letters, videos, etc.);

▶ active participation in groups of like-minded souls, those with similar interests and passions, energy, enthusiasm, and engagement;

▶ a comprehensive array of products and/or services that allow for progressive consumer engagement—stepping up the curve of cost, effort, and trust;

▶ an operational delivery system supporting step-change improvement in customer experience;

▶ capturing customer feedback to improve service delivery and product quality, development of new products and services, and significant word of mouth, third-party promotion;

▶ a relentless focus on the aspirational vision of the firm, and appreciation of the changes, implications, and opportunities of the Fast Future.

This is admittedly a short and simple list—there are many operational details and decisions wrapped up in each point. In the future, firms will invest more time and effort to break through the noise and clutter of our hyper-competitive business environment. And this marketing will be more intimately integrated into company operations.

Finally, we must admit that this revolution is just now starting, still developing. The battle is engaged. It's not clear where it will end. As with other parts of the Fast Future, change will continue at an ever-accelerating pace. Ten or twenty years out, our notion of the role of the Internet and social media will be different. Today's largest social media playgrounds (Facebook, Twitter, LinkedIn, YouTube) will likely be much different—or perhaps altogether irrelevant. At the core of this profound shift—from sellers to buyers, producers to consumers, providers to clients—is the notion of *choice* and *control*. We'll continue to see and experience change—beyond tools and tactics, content creation, and ultimately *value* creation—driven in large part by consumers themselves. This change will then fuel a still more radical transformation of markets and marketing around the world.

SUPPLY CHAINS—THE CHANGE IS APPARENT

Perhaps nowhere in business is the transformation of the global Fast Future more obvious than in the rapidly evolving global supply chain—that is, how things get done, where they get done, and who does them. Particularly in the last half century, we've witnessed dramatic shifts in the supply chain—think Japanese (and later Korean) automobiles and electronics, Venezuelan oil production, Mexican labor, and Chinese manufacturing and export of everything. Of course, these changes aren't new—supply chain flux has been with us all along. From the inception of early agriculture (and perhaps before) came the first associated trade, as humans took advantage of regional production differences (some crops grew better in certain localities). Later, the Industrial Revolution dramatically shifted the balance of production between global regions and primarily toward the West, but also within countries. For example, the new industrial tools of agricultural (e.g., tractors and threshers) worked much better on the flat and fertile expanses of Iowa than in the small and rocky patches of Vermont. In short order, this development precipitated a large migration of the population out of New England, into the Midwest states. Eventually, these same technology trends (the tractors and the farms got really big) led to the decline and virtual disappearance of the local family farm.

Today, our world is in a constant state of supply chain flux, as capital and people search for better ways of production—smarter, faster, cheaper—promising both enormous opportunity and significant challenge, and likely much more of each than we've ever seen before.

GOOD GUYS AND BAD GUYS ALL WEAR GRAY HATS

As the 21st century unfolds, it is clear that it will embrace a new supply chain paradigm, one more complex and nuanced than that of old. In the "good old days," a generation (or perhaps just ten years) ago, the competitive order was drawn up in black and white. Competitors were competitors. Our team versus them—good guys and bad (and no mixing allowed). This was in many ways easier for all of us—leaders, managers, staff, suppliers, and clients. And frankly, for many this model still makes the most sense. There's a general sense of agreement that the supply chain is changing dramatically, but that doesn't mean it's easy to shift our own attitudes, values, and beliefs.

Here's an example of the new normal, from one of our recent clients:

Smith Engineering, Inc. (SEI) is a mid-market, multi-discipline provider of civil and structural services to several Midwest markets. The firm has enjoyed a half century of success, and has developed a great reputation and strong client relationships. There are other, similar firms who are themselves strong providers and worthy competitors, but SEI has always received its fair share of the business from clients in the region.

In the past, SEI was almost always the prime consultant on large projects. The company contracted niche specialists for the project team when necessary, and often outsourced some of the field-related construction management work when its own crews were booked up. Later, as regulations (and clients) necessitated, the company added other firms to the projects team to satisfy disadvantaged business set asides. But SEI always called the shots.

Today it seems that much of that has changed. It's more common for SEI to find itself partnering with one of its staunchest competitors—just to get the work. Sometimes SEI is the prime, in the lead for a new piece of business, but sometimes the other firm is prime, and SEI is a sub-consultant. Then, to complicate matters, the two firms will be back at each other, competing head-to-head on another project in short order. Recently, the company was brought in by a small minority owned firm and asked to be the prime, even though the primary client relationship would be with this smaller firm.

The bottom line today for SEI leaders is that virtually anything (and everything) can happen—in terms of supply chain relationships—and the firm's managers must anticipate, and cultivate, these opportunities.

It's enough to make your head spin.

You get the point. In this new order, there will be myriad (nearly unlimited) possible combinations between partners and competitors. And there doesn't appear to be an obvious singular path of development. One very big exploration and experiment. More collaboration and also less, horizontal change and vertical globalization and retrenchment. It's confusing, but this is the way it is and will be. No longer black and white, gray is the color of the Fast Future supply chain, and gray the color of the hats worn by all.

LET'S GET SOMEONE ELSE TO DO THAT

Let's start with what should be obvious: outsourcing work to others is a well-known and proven business practice. Outsourcing has been highly successful in many businesses, though it remains controversial to some. That's because, as with other practices that bring about economic efficiency, outsourcing is rarely good for all participants. In all cases, there are both winners and losers.

Most professional services fields (doctors, lawyers, engineers, accountants, consultants) are behind in leveraging outsourcing. Efforts to improve the efficiency of the business are resisted tooth and nail. The reasons for this are several, including pride of ownership, loss of control (creative and managerial), and how professionals define their work and value. Let's take a brief look at each of these.

Professionals view their work as craftsmen or artists. Pride of ownership in the quality of their products, services, and solutions is of preeminent importance. Personal significance and meaning is often attached to their accomplishments. So it's particularly difficult to delegate work to others, or to outsource the business to other firms. All facets of the job are considered (often incorrectly or irrationally) to be of core importance. And even though this is to a degree understandable, this pride of ownership is under intensifying attack by a less personal and sentimental, no-nonsense, bottom line-focused marketplace. In reality, what matters most is the *pride of the client* in owning the finished product.

Professionals care deeply about quality, and about doing things right on behalf of their clients—often much more so than anything else (including profit). For many, the secret to quality is explicit control of everything—the project, solution, client relationship, project staff, method of design, pace of execution, and on and on. Loss of direct control and authority requires a different model of business—interdependent and inter-organizational collaboration. This is challenging for firms used to doing it all themselves.

How professionals define themselves and their work is another impediment to outsourcing. Most are taught on the job in craftsman-apprentice-like relationships, mentored by elders who are inclined to perpetuate the status quo. So professionals are biased to think of themselves like those who have come before (much like shoe cobblers, doing craftsman work as they have for centuries). And most professionals are comprised of some mix of brains and brawn—highly cerebral design or analysis, and also hands-on field or production work to bring their ideas to life. Architects have design and production, and engineers design but also do field surveys, materials testing, and/or construction management. Environmental scientists conduct both brainwork and on-site testing. Changing the beliefs of these professionals about the definition of their work and value is outlandishly difficult, but it's not new. Most other industry sectors have had to face directly the globalizing pressures, to look more objectively at where the real value of their effort is. Still, this paradigm of self, along with the pride of ownership and need for control, are together much of the reason why so many professionals struggle today with the opportunity in outsourcing.

There are thousands of small firms that exist now in fields like accounting, law, medical, architecture, science, engineering, and consulting. These are professionals acting largely independently, with a partner or two, or in firms of fewer than five or ten employees. Professionals often *want* to do the work, to do all of the work, and to do it all their way. (I know—I'm one of them.)

In larger economic terms, it's hard to argue against the global benefits of outsourcing, and practices focused on the premise of economic efficiency through the specialization and mobility of labor. Outsourcing is fundamentally about using others who can accomplish the work either better, cheaper, or (increasingly) both. Outsourcing is controversial when one adds the economics or politics of nations and regions—when the benefits and costs cross geographic boundaries, or when real costs (like the loss of jobs or tax revenues) are experienced.

There are many motivations for outsourcing. As I've suggested, one of these is letting go of lower-value-added tasks in favor of focusing on the value core. But outsourcing might also help the firm to better employ functional experts in certain areas of operations—like IT support, accounting, legal, marketing, sales, or human resources expertise. Outsourcing also includes leveraging niche experts as sub-consultants where the firm might be able to do the work, but can get it done better through others. And, frankly, outsourcing needn't be limited to economic efficiency or leveraging expertise. With today's scarcity of talent in many professions, it just makes sense to look hard at who's doing what, and to make sure that talent is used wisely. Others can be enjoined with the organization to get the work done faster, or to do more of it. This refocusing of talent both inside and outside the firm will likely be a key factor of future sustainable success.

Larger organizations (with larger staffs and multiple offices) have an "inside outsourcing" opportunity in their ability to shift work around to other teams and individuals. However, even in this relatively safe environment, outsourcing isn't all that easy. Professionals are reluctant (without incentive or coercion) to share their work or resources—even if they need to. There's always some friction in any collaboration—skills and expertise don't match up perfectly, learning is necessary, knowledge is lost at the handoff. It's been this way in every organization I've worked with. *Within* the team collaboration is high, but *outside* of these well-defined teams, work sharing is much more difficult.

This is why I say that the hardest part of globalization is the *first three feet*—the space between offices or cubicles, between human beings. Once one overcomes this challenge, then sharing across the office, or across the world, becomes almost trivial.

These are the main reasons why many professionals shy away from outsourcing—pride of ownership, desire for control, and beliefs about the scope of their profession. That said, the rapid developments of the Fast Future will demand a change, and it will become increasingly unacceptable (and unwise as a business practitioner) to avoid rethinking operational effectiveness and efficiency from this perspective. Successful organizations focus first on client needs and wants, and only *then* on how to accomplish those objectives as effectively as possible.

THE TALENT OVER THERE

Beyond domestic outsourcing, a next step is *offshoring,* or out-sourcing overseas. And if outsourcing is controversial, then offshoring is downright immoral! Economically, offshoring is simply leveraging the cost and specialization of labor, and competitive advantage, across the scale of nations. Politically, it's often about lost projects, jobs, tax revenues, and pride. Most economists support this approach built on open markets, free trade, and frictionless movement of inputs (labor and capital) across boundaries, though, again, it's understood that this system produces both winners and losers. Offshoring work is more difficult than domestic outsourcing because of distance, time, language, and cultural differences. Smaller and domestically focused organizations (including most professional firms) lack significant international focus and experience, and they're usually constrained by time, money, and management bandwidth. Many US firms believe that with substantial opportunities at home, international business is simply too risky, not worth the effort. In this context, and with the common provincialism and resistance to change often experienced, it's easy to understand why offshoring hasn't been pursued more enthusiastically. But this will change.

In 2007, my colleagues and I investigated the state of offshoring in the AEC (architecture, engineering, and construction) industry through a comprehensive survey of business owners and leaders.[6] At that time, offshoring of design and production in this market sector was still in its infancy. Only about 10 percent of survey respondents had actually pursued any offshoring, and of those who did, most had simply transferred work in-house to an overseas affiliate. Our investigation found that much of the offshoring had indeed produced mix results. Common issues cited included communication and language barriers, mismatches in time zones and work schedules, and differences in work habits and contracting practices—all of which provided considerable difficulty for these offshoring pioneers. And yet (very enlightening), our research found that *those with actual offshoring experience were more optimistic about its potential than those with no experience.* That is, despite the very real obstacles and challenges, and in most early cases subpar results, leaders saw important opportunities to improve their businesses through offshoring. One CEO claimed that although the level of project rework (and cost) approached 30 percent, overall labor costs were 50 percent cheaper. In other words, despite the missteps, this firm still came out ahead financially, all the while learning important lessons to use in future offshoring.

In his book *The World Is Flat*, Tom Friedman shares a similar tale of offshoring in the professional *accounting* industry, specifically the outsourcing of the individual federal income tax returns of US citizens to accounting firms in India. In the beginning, many accounting professionals reacted skeptically (or worse) to this development. Nevertheless, according to Friedman, just 10 years later, a rather large part of the number-crunching on these tax returns is, in fact, completed by outsourcing firms in India and elsewhere. Friedman says the Indian firms are very advanced technologically (it's a requirement for competitiveness). Of course, there have been winners and losers. Losers include those domestic CPAs who refused to acknowledge the threat and change appropriately. Winners are those who embraced the new reality, and the opportunity to further focus their own efforts on the highest-value services they provided, such as tax planning and advisory.[7]

HERE COMES THE CROWD

With the advent of the web and related technologies, and the rise of a truly globally connected marketplace, offshoring is rapidly evolving to a whole new scale. Outsourcing to a very large, global group of providers is today being used in a variety of businesses, and while still nascent, promises to become ever more prominent and useful on the road ahead. As an example, Amazon's *Mechanical Turk* allows computer programmers (known as requesters) to post new task orders (called human intelligence tasks) to a global pool of potential workers (providers), who then browse and choose among existing opportunities, and complete these for direct compensation. [8] By definition, most of these scopes of work are small and well defined, and are better done by humans than machines. Examples of the work sought include writing product descriptions, identifying performers from photos on music CDs, choosing between options in photographs, and such. Other similar services transcribe audio recordings into print, converting podcasts or speeches into drafts of new books. These specific projects aren't earth shattering, but their implications are a big deal, promising a potential step-change in both productivity and global collaboration.

Amazon has had mixed results with Mechanical Turk, experiences both good and less good. Still, it's not hard to envision a rapid development and growth of this highly collaborative and cost-efficient virtual marketplace. And there's no question that costs of services will come down in a highly competitive global-sourcing environment. In fact, one criticism of the Mechanical Turk model is that it supports a sort of global, virtual sweatshop, where providers have little to no market power. Nevertheless, it's interesting to consider the tremendous access that professionals may enjoy (regardless of where they're physically located), and the astounding potential for improving the quality and value of products and services delivered. The promise is real, and it's big.

A CHANGE OF PHASE IN THE SYSTEM

As we've said before, what is unique and different about the Fast Future ahead is not change per se (that's been happening all along), but the pace, intensity, and magnitude of the transformation afoot. In the supply chain, we've also witnessed ongoing evolution. In fact, it's not new to use the phase-change analogy and imagery—we've long spoken of the supply chain becoming "more fluid." The old way—structures, rules, and paths crystallized into hard and inflexible solids—gave way to a moveable, dynamic, and constantly changing fluidized system. Right?

And yet, today, this flowing liquid image is itself becoming restrictive, anachronistic.

The truth is that today the supply chain is morphing and evolving at a rate faster than the fluid model suggests. Some have begun to speak of a gaseous form, the supply chain fully "atomized" into its individual molecular components.

This is an appropriate and helpful analogy, forcing us to look at the supply chain as it becomes more completely disassociated— or disaggregated. Imagine breaking down the business of the firm into much smaller subparts—all of the individual systems, processes within those systems, and tasks within each of those processes.

And then (similar to the Mechanical Turk model) each of these tasks is evaluated and optimized for efficient execution—better, faster, cheaper. In many cases, it will mean outsourcing that task to someone else—even off-shoring the work to the far corners of the globe (distance and geography more or less irrelevant).

It's a radical notion for many industry segments, especially the professions, but it's right on our doorstep today, and already creeping into many businesses.

Expect the creep to accelerate, and soon overtake, the supply chains of all business.

A FEW IMPLICATIONS

Business owners must now look at the rapidly changing supply chain—first as a reality, and second as an opportunity. Professional services firms, which have been mostly protected from globalization pressures, must now look more broadly at what's likely to happen to their business as new global forces seep in. Firms of all sizes, whether independent individuals working alone, small teams of two or three, organizations of five to twenty employees, and even global organizations with thousands of staff—must increasingly look to operate in this new world of gray.

All companies will need to seek out and develop new associations and collaborations with others—even those long thought of as competitors. Often, this change will require that leaders get out of their own way, subvert their oversized egos and the win-at-all-cost mentality, and think instead about innovation, and winning in the long run. Firms don't have to do everything themselves to drive forward the project and client relationship.

Likewise, professionals must begin to more readily discern the difference between "could" and "should." It's usually easier to believe that the firm can do it—a matter of competency and initiative, than to decide that the firm *should* do it—a matter of strategy and priorities.

Sometimes, professionals gravitate specifically toward that which they've never done—tackling the new challenge. This motivation is understandable, but it's not always good for the business. Robust strategy is more often about deciding what *not* to do rather than what to do. After all, out on the cutting edge is where all the cuts are. With increasing opportunity ahead (along with vastly increasing distraction), focus will itself become a critical competency for many firms.

Most businesses should today devote as much energy to building relationships with supply chain partners as they do in looking for new clients. These teaming partners, sub-consultants, and niche specialists will increasingly be a key to cost-effective, just-in-time comprehensive delivery of products and services. Today, very few firms are doing this to the degree they should (the opportunities are important but not urgent). Staid, inflexible, and non-changing providers may quickly find themselves marginalized, replaced by those more creative, innovative, and nimble. Fluid will beat solid, and gaseous will prevail over both.

Finally, today, individuals and firms both large and small should consider (and experiment with) outsourcing, offshoring, and even crowd-sourcing. It will take some time and energy to sort through these opportunities. But this is an investment worth making, in looking for the step-change advancements in productivity and quality that will come from technology, information, and globalization. Again, rarely will this progress be linear and clean, or without both winners and losers along the way. Small businesses have long utilized outsourcing (accounting and legal expertise, administrative support, marketing resources, and graphics design) not necessarily for strategic reasons, but simply out of pragmatic needs—lack of talent, bandwidth, or other resource constraints. Business owners *could* do these things, but usually *shouldn't*—and instead should focus more productively on real strengths.

Fast Future organizations will almost certainly be vastly more virtual; built mostly with temporary, project-oriented, ephemeral combinations of providers; born of both pragmatic and strategic motivations; and focused on the flexibility, nimbleness, and agility necessary for success.

SMALL FIRMS: "HERE COMES EVERYBODY." (CLAY SHIRKY)[9]

Out on the horizon, just barely visible now, a tidal wave of talent and capability is gathering momentum. It's headed our way, and when it arrives it will permanently reconfigure the shoreline of current labor markets.

A tsunami doesn't always tower in height, but it is deep, thick, and powerful. There's an enormous volume of water displaced, and it keeps coming and coming—eventually pushing over everything in its path. That's an accurate picture, I think, of what's ahead.

In the future, small will be very big! Sure, much of global commerce will remain driven and controlled by mega-national firms and brands, but additionally (and increasingly), millions and millions of very small (fewer than five employees) firms—a tsunami of entrepreneurial talent—will also participate and win in global markets.

The secrets to Fast Future success for very small firms are three: technology, information, and globalization. These three forces are reshaping the playing field, diminishing the traditional advantages and economies of scale, reducing barriers to entry and competition in global markets, and opening up new opportunities for new players. (Literally) millions of aspiring professionals operating as freelancers, independent consultants, and small group entrepreneurs are about to step up onto this global stage, and to compete much more effectively against the big boys. And the results (depending what side of the battle you're on) may be ugly.

Technology is at the core of this change. First it's the web itself, and its transformative global connectivity. The fiber-optic infrastructure (a vast network of undersea pipes connecting continents at nearly the speed of light) has conjoined almost all of the Earth into a true global network. In addition, there's been a nonstop proliferation of new hardware and software products for business applications. (It's hard to keep up with the change, much less the implications.) It's clear that individuals and small firms will much more readily connect through this grid to reach a global audience that's hundreds, thousands—or millions—of times larger than it otherwise would be.

Here's an example of how technology has rapidly reshaped the game in business. Just a few years ago, the online presence of an independent professional or small firm was greatly constrained by cost. Even a basic website (essentially an online brochure) could cost $50,000 or more. Even more problematic, updating that site required professional intervention, and might cost an additional $1,000–$2,000 each time. Most small firms couldn't justify this expense, so online footprints were limited. Today, the situation is completely different. A small firm can usually manage its own website using a third-party content management (CMS) system, and keep the space up to date with useful, relevant, and interesting information—all for $5,000 or less per year. (In fact, those a bit more adventurous can accomplish this for free.) Hardware, software, and Web 2.0 technologies have truly delivered on the promise of inexpensive, effective, global connectivity.

> *At J. Doehring & Co. we use a content management system (CMS) provided by Hubspot, Inc. (Cambridge, Massachusetts). This software hosts our website and blog, and provides related technical, marketing, and creative support. The platform is about as simple as basic word processing or PowerPoint presentation creation.*

The nature of business is also changing in another critically important way, through the de-emphasis of *location*. Where suppliers and customers reside is becoming less

important. This will become a very big deal, diluting a long
history of emphasis on the local provider.

Of course, developments here will be mixed, faster or slower
in different markets. Perhaps it won't change much at all in some
segments. (With some products, location matters very much because,
for example, the products are bulky or heavy, and much of their value
is tied up in moving them nearer to the point of consumption. Other
products or services require personal attention, or a closer physical
connection between provider and client.) In the Fast Future, we'll
see much more of this *disconnecting of place*—between provider and
client, or between manufacturer and customer. Quality and value
will matter most, location of origin much less so.

At times, it's the technology itself that's important. (Perhaps
you'd like to conduct your webinar from Bermuda, or Turks and
Caicos, where Internet bandwidth today is more than sufficient.) But
often, it's the *implications* of new technology that drive the change.
Most important of these is the resulting availability and transparency
of information and knowledge. Today, information flow is already
helping customers to find new products and new providers. There
are thousands (or millions) of additional, high-quality professionals—architects, engineers, doctors, lawyers, accountants—ready to
serve. Of course, you won't fly to India for an annual dental checkup,
but your dentist may very well ship your dental digital x-rays overseas
for analysis or a second opinion. That's already happening today in
medicine, accounting, engineering, and architecture.

Producers around the world (again, many of them very small
firms) want to find and capture new customers. Before long, talented
professionals in India, China, South America, and elsewhere will
break through traditional barriers to entry (for example, state pro-

fessional licensure) to successfully win projects here in the United States. Soon, we'll see more Australian engineering firms leading on domestic environmental work, or Chinese companies managing construction efforts on a major infrastructure project. This is happening already, of course, but what's ahead will define this as the norm—and with very small firms joining the party, too. It's imperative that domestic professional firms tune in, and begin both to defend their current markets and to pursue new global market opportunities themselves.

New technology supports information flow, and that leads to the globalization of everything. This transformation is neither positive nor negative—it just is. Change will be both fast and slow, unevenly distributed, messy—and often unfair. There will be winners and losers. Many opportunities will be created in the developing world, in nations with large populations of trained professionals (and millions of citizens). As they prosper, these developing countries will grow their own internal markets (providing new opportunities for both domestic and foreign providers). Western firms who change and develop themselves will also succeed, some on a very large scale. All nations have challenges—political, educational, social, religious, and economic. Still, many in the developing world will achieve rapid progress against these, and will put considerable competitive pressure on the current economic world powers.

Today, many domestic U.S. markets are somewhat protected from the global onslaught—by constraints real, perceived, and even contrived. Real barriers include geographic distance, language, and culture. Perceived barriers include prejudices about foreign providers (which might be accurate, but often are not). Contrived constraints comprise a surprising variety of social, economic, and political constraints designed (sometimes inadvertently and sometimes on purpose) to keep some in and others out. These include institutions (for example, private universities built expressly for selectivity and exclusion), licensure and certification (bar exams, state licensure, professional certifications), and regional business practices (favoring the selection of local providers). Again, I'm not suggesting that these institutions, structures, or practices are bad, or intrinsically wrong— just that in the Fast Future world they will be increasingly assailed, as new information and knowledge allows both sellers and buyers to look elsewhere.

Licensure (say, for practicing engineers or lawyers) makes perfect sense—for quality assurance and control, and to support growth in local markets. But what about the thousands (or millions) of capable providers outside of the region, often available at considerably lower cost? When is the opportunity to do or try something (or someone) else worth the risk?

As options become more visible, some customers will try out new relationships. Very small firms will join in this growing and developing change. Existing relationships will weaken. The establishment, the insiders, those at obvious risk—these will undoubtedly cry foul and will play the familiar cards: protectionism, nationalism, prejudice, and fear. We'll hear a lot more argument about the evils of outsourcing and offshoring, and of the importance of buying domestically and locally. There is nothing wrong with buying locally(!), unless the local provider is delivering poor quality, higher cost, or less value.

It's true that when all things are equal, most sellers and buyers prefer to deal locally, with people they know and trust. In the Fast Future, the winning strategy is to ensure that all things are not equal.

HOW TO GROW?

The preeminent challenge of the 21st century will be differentiating oneself—standing out in an ever-noisier crowd. As John Rockefeller once said, "Next to doing the right thing, the most important thing is to let people know you are doing the right thing." Breaking through this clutter has always been a primary issue of marketing, and all the more so today, with millions of players on the global scene. In truth, only a handful of mega-national companies have achieved any global brand recognition. Perhaps a few hundred more firms have earned significant regional recognition. Thousands and thousands of organizations large and small remain, battling it out for market visibility and viability.

Add to that now the millions of additional, new, locally based (but globally focused) competitors—small and very small firms—each with something of value to offer, and something to say on the main stage. For these firms and professionals, *marketing* is job one: differentiating themselves, and making sure that *all things are not equal* in the customer's eye. When buyers see the firm as substantively unique, different, and better, then it doesn't matter *who* the competition is, and it won't matter *where* they're from.

In the Fast Future, few initiatives will be as important as
this—and none harder to achieve.

Many professionals are (frankly) lousy at promoting themselves
and their businesses, preferring instead to "let their work do the
talking." In the past, when there was enough work to go around,
this turned out pretty well. On the road ahead, this strategy leads
to nowhere—except perhaps bankruptcy court. Very small firms
will have new opportunities in the global milieu, but they'll have to
do something (marketing) to break through the noise and clutter.
Otherwise, their opportunity will come—and go to another firm
that is equally proficient, but better at promotion.

But of course, it's not just about marketing. Indeed, successful small firms must execute other proactive, strategic efforts toward
building their global business. The best defense is often good offense
and this is true with globalization. If thousands of small foreign firm
competitors are amassing today to assault US shores, then thousands
of domestic US firms should be likewise preparing their own assault
on the opportunities that lie beyond the confines and comforts of
local markets. Let's face it: US providers have long been spoiled by
a very large, safe domestic market. Until now, it hasn't made much
sense to risk this, to venture out beyond the fence line. But this is
changing. American companies will become more like those abroad,
where local markets often aren't large enough, or where local professional talent can't meet local demand. Foreign firms in these areas
have been forced (by opportunity and by expediency) to think and
act more globally. Today, they've got a leg up on those who don't yet
enjoy this important experience and perspective.

Small firms and independents are constrained not only by
comfort, but also by resources—in particular managerial and lead-

ership bandwidth. Pursuing global opportunities requires a significant investment in knowledge, travel, building infrastructure, and nurturing relationships. All of this must be accomplished while operating and maintaining a base business (often alone or with a partner or two). It's a daunting task, and it simply won't occur without a strong mix of vision, strategy, and action.

CASE STUDY: FIRM SIZE IN THE A/E INDUSTRY

One professional segment that will change a lot with the Fast Future ahead is A/E–the group of architects, engineers, environmental scientists, drafting and CAD professionals, interior designers, field surveyors, and others involved in the design, engineering, construction, and environmental assessment and remediation businesses.

Like other professional fields, the A/E segment is highly fragmented and geographically dispersed, composed of thousands of firms, with most of them quite small. Small firms are characteristic of professional services: barriers to entry are low, and professionals appreciate doing things their own way, in control of projects, clients, and the business itself.

According to data from the US Census Bureau Business Database (2007), there are nearly 25,000 architecture firms in the United States, and almost 50,000 domestic engineering firms. Additionally, the sector includes approximately 6,000 landscape architecture firms, 8,000 environmental services organizations, and more than 13,000 interior design firms. Add in a few other specialty services and the total tops 120,000 organizations.[10] (Figure 6-1)

FIGURE 6.1: US FIRMS, PROFESSIONAL SERVICES (NAICS 54), DESIGN,
CONSTRUCTION, ENVIRONMENTAL RELATED

Type	No. of Firms
Architectural Services	24,283
Landscape Architectural Services	6,088
Engineering Services	47,714
Drafting Services	3,146
Building Inspection Services	5,673
Geophysical Surveying/Mapping	729
Surveying and Mapping (Ex Geo)	9,567
Interior Design Services	13,492
Environmental Consulting Services	8,274
Total (Within NAICS 54, AEC and Related)	**118,966**

Source: U.S Census Bureau, Business Database, 2007.

Not only highly fragmented, this sector is highly skewed towards very small firms. As Figure 6-2 shows, nearly 60 percent (about 72K) of companies have fewer than five employees, and almost 80 percent are comprised of fewer than ten staff. Moreover, 90 percent of all firms report a total staff of less than 20, so together, more than 100,000 of these firms are in the very small range. Only about 4 percent of all A/E organizations operate in the medium- to large-company category.

FIGURE 6.2: SIZE DISTRIBUTION OF US FIRMS, PROFESSIONAL SERVICES (NAICS 54), DESIGN, CONSTRUCTION, ENVIRONMENTAL RELATED

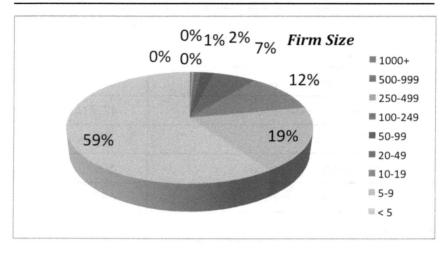

Source: U.S Census Bureau, Business Database, 2007.

Rapid market change will bring new advantages and opportunities to small domestic firms, through improvements in technology, increasing information and knowledge, and wider geographic reach. Some of these small firms will compete more successfully on larger regional, national, and global platforms. Of course, others won't be as fortunate, overwhelmed by the tidal wave of global connectivity.

At the other end of the A/E industry spectrum, there are about 100 firms in the large category, those with annual revenues of more than $100 million (staff size 800-plus). Of course, many of these companies are still relatively small organizations; only a few boast staff of more than 10,000. Nevertheless, while much fewer in number, these larger consulting firms wield considerable market power, and together account for a large and disproportionate share of A/E industry work. These large companies are much more likely to already enjoy global scale, and they're better positioned to reap some of the benefits of the Fast Future world. Most are involved in international business, and some have considerable international experience. These relatively large firms also possess considerable technical and managerial bandwidth. They are the closest representations in the sector of a true "full service, one-stop-shop" (though executing well on the promise of the one-stop-shop is most challenging).

Larger A/E industry firms are more likely to tackle the bigger, structural issues of the design and construction industry. Chief among these today is the challenge of project funding. Everywhere, there is much infrastructure need, but usually too little money to pay for it. Funding is an impediment for all projects, but it's a tall barrier for small companies. (Frankly, it's not that the larger organizations have the answers today, just more likely that they are asking better questions.) Larger firms are often better positioned to take advantage of changing conditions in markets.

If there are new opportunities for both small and large A/E organizations, what does this say about the middle market? Today, this middle ground is comprised of companies with between $13 million–$10 million in net revenues, or about 100 to 800 employees. In the United States, there are about 1,800 firms of this size. These organizations are clearly distinct from both small and large firms. As middle-market players, they face similar Fast Future opportunities and challenges, and some that are unique to their size and position. These organizations have traditionally enjoyed historical success and strong recognition in regional markets. They're seemingly well positioned for continued success, and it's at times hard to see their shortcomings. Still, these companies often overestimate their importance, significance, and future market sustainability. They're relatively big fish in their chosen ponds, but certainly not "too big to fail." Radical change doesn't seem obviously necessary.

Many of these organizations are in a sense too good to risk becoming truly great on the road ahead. But the cold, hard truth is that none of the organizations in this sector—none of the more than 100,000 in the industry—are too big or too important to fail. Most are, frankly, insignificant in the global order. None would be long missed if they suddenly disappeared. Very small professional organizations usually understand this viscerally—they're almost always operating close to the edge of ongoing sustainability (or survival). And in companies of all sizes, it's the professionals themselves who are the real assets of the firm. As Henry Ford suggested, "Whether you think you can, or think you can't, you're right." Success is at least partially a self-fulfilling prophecy. Small, medium, and large firms must grab a hold of the Fast Future, and with a special mix of paranoia, proactivity, and creativity, prepare their organizations for the opportunities and challenges that lay ahead.

SO WHAT

There are many important implications of these changes in the marketplace, and the uber-trends of consumer power, supply chain evolution, and the rise of very small firms. In fact, there's much more here than most firms can easily process. Nevertheless, here are some general questions to help frame out initial thinking:

- ▶ How are our customers changing today—in their buying patterns, habits, and behaviors?
- ▶ How are our markets changing, and our competitive landscape shifting today, and which of those developments are short term (economy related) or long term (structural evolution)?

▶ What technologies are most important to the changes seen in our markets (and our customers) at present? What will these opportunities, platforms, and tools (Internet, social media) look like in five years?

▶ Are we prepared in the organization to change our thinking and acting in response to very large shifts in our markets and business? For example, what if customers demanded products and services be delivered 50 percent faster, or 30 percent cheaper (or both)?

▶ How are we gathering and utilizing information today to allow all for a deeper and more meaningful connection and relationship with our individual customers (as opposed to targeting mass-market segments)?

▶ What are we doing now to get more of our organization involved in thought leadership, content creation, social connection, and inbound relationship marketing?

▶ How would our business (and industry) need to change if we were required to expend considerably more effort in marketing and business development than we do today? Half again more? Twice as much? Three times?

▶ How are our supply chains (providers, partners, competitors) changing and evolving now, and what will this community look like in five years? In 10 years?

▶ What are the major implications of a business environment in which customers can see much more transparently into our operations, and specifically to view where our major value-added occurs?

▶ Is outsourcing a portion of our business a viable opportunity and business strategy? How about offshoring (outsourcing overseas)? Perhaps we should also consider the reverse—that is, taking a previously outsourced effort back in-house?

▶ How prepared is our firm for the inevitable onslaught of new competitors, very small firms, often from elsewhere? How will we compete; what is our response strategy?

▶ If competition is increasing in our own target markets, then how can and should we repay the favor elsewhere? Specifically, where should we go ourselves to take advantage of new customers, supply chain shifts, and the rising power of consumers?

▶ How can we prepare our organization for greater agility and adaptability, as pervasive change continues in the future?

7

Urbanization, Mobility, and the Power of Infrastructure

CITY LIVING WILL BECOME EVER MORE ATTRACTIVE TO (NEARLY) EVERYONE, AND THOSE WHO BUILD TODAY WILL RULE THE WORLD TOMORROW.

"Stadtluft macht frei," "City air makes you free."
—(Proverb from the Holy Roman Empire)

IN THE BEGINNING

There's nothing really new about urbanization. Cities have been with us since the Neolithic revolution, when hunter-gatherers first began to settle into agricultural societies.

This transition occurred simultaneously in several locations around the globe about 8,000 to 10,000 years ago.[1]

The advent of new farming techniques encouraged hunter-gatherers to abandon their nomadic lifestyle, and to settle near others also living through agricultural production. The population density increased considerably, and this concentration encouraged still more to join in agriculture. Most early communities focused specifically on farming, but others developed around natural resources (obsidian was an early example) or trade.[2] Early traders sometimes used fruit and vegetable seeds as currency, and this helped to disseminate both the seeds of the fruit and the seeds of opportunity for additional agricultural communities.[3]

Some of the earliest cities of the world first developed in Mesopotamia, the land between the Tigris and Euphrates rivers (in modern-day Iraq), including Eridu, Uruk, and Ur. A bit later, around 7500–5700 BC, other communities developed in Catalhoyuk (modern Turkey) and in Syria. Still later, urban communities sprang up in China, the Indus Valley (Pakistan), and Egypt. In the ancient Americas, early cities were founded in the Andes (Norte Chico) and in Mesoamerica (Maya, Zapotec, and Teotihuacan).[4] Thus, early on, there were urban populations of significance in nearly every region of the world. And from the beginning, these earliest settlements often employed recognizable urban strategies.[5]

FIGURE 7-1. EARLY SETTLEMENT CITIES ALONG THE "FERTILE CRESCENT" OF MESOPOTAMIA, THE "LAND BETWEEN THE RIVERS"

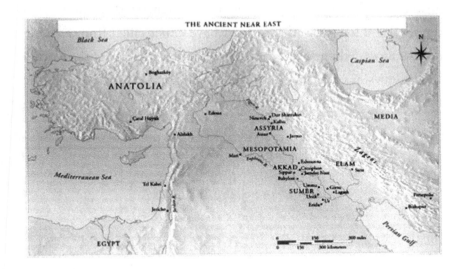

Success with agricultural, natural resource exploitation, and growth of commerce supported the further development of cities, and eventually urban centers with a half a million or more citizens existed around the globe—in Alexandria (Egypt), Carthage (Tunisia), Constantinople (Turkey), Rome, Pataliputra (India), and Chang'an (China).[6] Many of these early cities shared recognizable urban attributes—such as grid plans for development, systematic drainage, flush toilets, and sewage systems—but they were also a diverse lot. Some were for their time quite large, others much smaller. Some cities focused on trade or commerce, while others served as political or religious centers. As is true today, cities were both similar to one another and unique.

Urban centers developed simultaneously around the world, but, of course, not all survived, or even thrived, through the ages. Some shot up but then quickly waned. Others have remained relevant for a thousand or more years. Which cities have endured is a complex story of history—inputs and outputs, endemics and idiosyncrasies, collaboration and conquest, strategy and fortune. As Figure 7-2 demonstrates, a few of the urban centers have remained in the world's top ten for a long period, but most have either fallen from an early rank or ascended more recently. Along the way, the size of the world's largest cities has exploded to include today more than ten times the number of people of just two centuries ago.[7]

FIGURE 7-2. TOTAL POPULATION IN THE TOP TEN CITIES THROUGH TIME

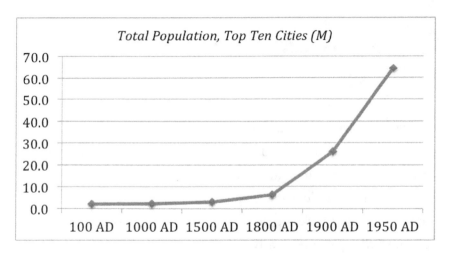

Four Thousand Years of Urban Growth: An Historical Census, 1987, St. David's University Press, at http://geography.about.com/library/weekly/aa011201a.htm.

FIGURE 7-3.: TOPTEN (BY POPULATION CITIES) THROUGH TIME (X)

100 AD

Rank	Name	Population
1	Rome	450,000
2	Luoyang (Honan), China	420,000
3	Seleucia (on the Tigris), Iraq	250,000
4	Alexandria, Egypt	250,000
5	Antioch, Turkey	150,000
6	Anuradhapura, Sri Lanka	130,000
7	Peshawar, Pakistan	120,000
8	Carthage, Tunisia	100,000
9	Suzhou, China	n/a
10	Smyrna, Turkey	90,000

1000 AD

Rank	Name	Population
1	Cordova, Spain	450,000
2	Kaifeng, China	400,000
3	Constantinople (Istanbul), Turkey	300,000
4	Angkor, Cambodia	200,000
5	Kyoto, Japan	175,000
6	Cairo, Egypt	135,000
7	Baghdad, Iraq	125,000
8	Nishapur (Neyshabur), Iran	125,000
9	Al-Hasa, Saudi Arabia	110,000
10	Patan (Anhilwara), India	100,000

1500 AD

Rank	Name	Population
1	Beijing, China	672,000
2	Vijayanagar, India	500,000
3	Cairo, Egypt	400,000
4	Hangzhou, China	250,000
5	Tabriz, Iran	250,000
6	Constantinople (Istanbul), Turkey	200,000
7	Gaur, India	200,000
8	Paris, France	185,000
9	Guangzhou, China	150,000
10	Nanjing, China	147,000

1800 AD

Rank	Name	Population
1	Beijing, China	1,100,000
2	London, United Kingdom	861,000
3	Guangzhou, China	800,000
4	Edo (Tokyo), Japan	685,000
5	Constantinople (Istanbul), Turkey	570,000
6	Paris, France	547,000
7	Naples, Italy	430,000
8	Hangzhou, China	387,000
9	Osaka, Japan	383,000
10	Kyoto, Japan	377,000

1900 AD

Rank	Name	Population
1	London, United Kingdom	6,480,000
2	New York, United States	4,242,000
3	Paris, France	3,330,000
4	Berlin, Germany	2,707,000
5	Chicago, United States	1,717,000
6	Vienna, Austria	1,698,000
7	Tokyo, Japan	1,497,000
8	St. Petersburg, Russia	1,439,000
9	Manchester, United Kingdom	1,435,000
10	Philadelphia, United States	1,418,000

1950 AD

Rank	Name	Population
1	New York, United States	12,463,000
2	London, United Kingdom	8,860,000
3	Tokyo, Japan	7,000,000
4	Paris, France	5,900,000
5	Shanghai, China	5,406,000
6	Moscow, Russia	5,100,000
7	Buenos Aires, Argentina	5,000,000
8	Chicago, United States	4,906,000
9	Ruhr, Germany	4,900,000
10	Kolkata, India	4,800,000

Four Thousand Years of Urban Growth: An Historical Census, 1987, St. David's University Press, at http://geography.about.com/library/weekly/aa011201a.htm.

As is true today, early urban development brought to society both good and bad. Cities concentrated people—producers, consumers, and traders—and reduced the transportation costs of goods, services, and natural resources. This concentration resulted in the development of new markets and also increased diversity in the community, with a significant uptick in the exchange and sharing of knowledge and ideas. The new challenges of a larger population stoked the fires of innovation—leading (for example) to the development of running water and sewage disposal.[8] Later, during the Middle Ages in Europe, urban cities helped to break the power of local lords who ruled over the rural countryside.

Within the Holy Roman Empire, many cities had no lords at all (other than the emperor), leading some to claim that *"stadtluft macht frei,"* "city air makes you free."[9]

Of course, these new urban concentrations also brought the negative social costs we're familiar with today—increase in crime, mortality, cost of living, pollution, and congestion. But on balance, early urbanization delivered on the promise of increasing economic opportunity for many. In his *City Economics*, Brendan O'Flaherty argues that these urban settlements survived because their advantages offset disadvantages. O'Flaherty says that the economies of scale and return on effort tied to the efficiency gained by higher throughput and lower costs are the primary economic advantage of cities.[10]

ASCENDENCY IN THE WEST

Beginning with the Renaissance in the 17th century and accelerating with the Industrial Revolution in the 18th century, development and growth in the industrial society gave rise to many great new cities, first in Europe and later in the United States. Centers of science, technology, and new manufacturing sprouted, often close to the raw materials and other inputs of this burgeoning new commerce.

And then by 1850, the railroads began to radically transform everything—connecting producers and customers, accessing raw materials, reducing transportation costs, and supporting new emerging manufacturing centers. The railroads offered a virtual time machine for societies that operated at much the same speed in the early 1800s as they had a thousand year earlier.

Stephen Ambrose wrote about the completion of America's first transcontinental railroad:

... for the people of 1869, especially those over 40 years old, there was nothing to compare to it. A man whose birthday was in 1829 or earlier had been born into a world in which President Andrew Jackson traveled no faster than Julius Caesar, a world in which no thought or information could be transmitted any faster than in Alexander the Great's time. In 1869, with the railroad and the telegraph that was beside it, a man could move at 60 miles per hour and transmit an idea or a statistic from coast to coast almost instantly. Senator Daniel Webster got it exactly in 1847, when he proclaimed that the railroad "towers above all other inventions of this or the preceding age."[11]

Almost immediately, the importance of location— natural resources, labor populations, and local markets— changed radically. Everything was mobile, and could move quickly to wherever the opportunity was. New cities exploded (seemingly overnight)—especially in the United States, where so much new land offered so many new opportunities.

Certainly the early megacities of the Western world were no Shangri-La. By all accounts, the urban centers of Europe—London, Paris, Rome, Moscow—were unhealthy, dangerous, and ultimately deadly places to exist. Later Boston, New York, Philadelphia, and others were no better. Most inhabitants were poor, and working conditions were by today's standards horrendous. Environmental concerns were magnified with industrialization—mountains of trash, highly contaminated water and air, and a plethora of communicable diseases. Still, largely because of the jobs and economic opportunity, these cities flourished in both the old and new worlds.

The Industrial Revolution brought with it a rollercoaster of economic progress, a time characterized by repeated boom and bust, overheated markets and economic collapse. There were plenty of bad actors in business and finance, and no shortage of shenanigans to go around.

The fortunes of many cities rose and fell with these economic ups and downs. Virtually all world urban areas were laid low by the Great Depression of the 1930s, since all had become increasingly inter-connected in a new global marketplace. World War II revived the economies of the West and, afterward, those in Europe and Asia destroyed by the war. Urbanization continued, but in the United States with a twist. Increasingly, city residents headed for the suburbs, enjoying the economic benefits (employment and concentration of resources) of urban life, but with room to spread out and build a local community. Suburban centers were first popularized in places like Long Island outside of New York City, where in 1947 William Levitt and his firm Levitt and Sons created the new hamlet of Levittown with nearly 50,000 inhabitants. Considered by some the new suburban prototype, Levittown became one of the first mass-produced suburban developments.[12] Around the country, these developments drew their share of critics, but they were well received by a postwar population hungry for new economic opportunity near (but not in) the big city.

In the modern era, cities continue to grow along lines both similar to and distinct from one another. Older urban areas with limited space (in Europe, the American Northeast, and many parts of Asia) have continued to concentrate on densely packed footprints, sometimes growing primarily vertically. Examples include New York's Manhattan Island, Hong Kong, Shanghai, and Singapore. In other cities, development has spread out over a much larger (and sometimes more disorganized) area, creating large "exurbs" or "edge cities." In the United States, Los Angeles, Houston, and Atlanta come to mind as examples.

Today's modern urban centers continue to deliver both positives and negatives to inhabitants. On the downside, managing waste, water and air pollution, and the spread of disease remain key concerns around the globe. Higher rates of crime, traffic, congestion, and commuting time are problematic issues as well. Today, large cities also create enormous centers of heating, with large areas of concrete and asphalt replacing natural vegetation and soil—along with the heat generated by manufacturing, transportation, and residents themselves.

On the positive side, the proximity and density of inhabitants continues to facilitate the sharing of information, knowledge, and new ideas; innovation; and greater work collaboration. Cities create a diversity of perspectives, beliefs, and cultures, and much opportunity bubbles up out of this diversity. Urban concentration also helps the global environment (though somewhat counter-intuitively), by concentrating human activity into a smaller space, by improving the efficient use of space (skyscrapers), and by reducing the environmental impact on areas outside of the city.

URBANIZATION AHEAD

Worldwide, the percentage of urbanites eclipsed the 50 percent level in 2009, and today the world is slightly more urban than rural.[13] There are large areas of the world—especially in Africa and Asia— where populations remain largely rural (here it's still about 60 percent rural), but cities continue to grow and develop most everywhere. Of the world's 400+ largest cities (with populations of greater than 1 million), about three-quarters of these are located in the low- to middle-income countries of the developing world.[14]

But the global map of urbanization is dynamic and evolving rapidly.

Urban populations today live in towns and cities of a wide variety of sizes. Figure 7-4 reveals the regional distribution of the 100 largest cities in the world, nearly half of which are located in Asia. But, these top hundred metropolitan areas account for only about 10 percent of the world's total population.[15] Globally, the urban landscape is characterized by a lack of concentration (people are spread out), and by a significant diversity of size (cities are both small and large), and this landscape will remain to 2025 and beyond.

FIGURE 7-4. GEOGRAPHIC DISTRIBUTION OF THE WORLD'S LARGEST 100 URBAN AREAS

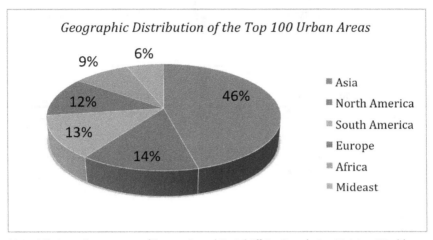

Geographic Distribution of the Top 100 Urban Areas

United Nations, Department of Economic and Social Affairs, Population Division: World Urbanization Prospects, the 2011 Revision. New York, 2012.

According to the United Nations, by 2050 the world's population will reach 9.1 billion—an increase of 2.3 billion people. During this period, urban populations are expected to grow by 2.9 billion, absorbing more than all of the world's total population increase. Much of the urban growth will occur in cities of the developing world, particularly in Asia. About 60 percent of the growth will come through natural increase (more births than deaths), and about 40 percent will come from rural migration into urban areas.[16]

As Figures 7-5 and 7- 6 indicate, the amount and pace of change in urbanization is quite uneven around the world, and this variability will also continue. Urbanization has already penetrated deeply in the Western world regions of North America, South America, and Europe, where today some 70–80 percent of people live in urban environments. In the developing areas of Africa and Asia, the urban population stands at about 40–45 percent, though it's in these regions that city growth will be the fastest.

By 2050, some 86 percent of the population of developed regions, and 66 percent of developing regions, will call the city home. At that point, the global urban community fraction will be 69 percent.[17]

FIGURE 7-5. URBAN POPULATION, PERCENT OF REGION TOTAL

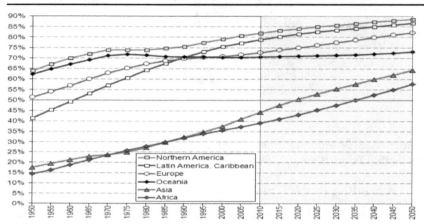

United Nations, Department of Economic and Social Affairs, Population Division: World Urbanization Prospects, the 2011 Revision. New York, 2012.

FIGURE 7-6. URBAN POPULATION, PERCENT OF GLOBAL TOTAL

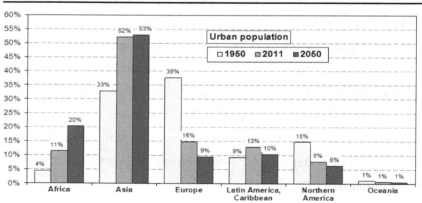

United Nations, Department of Economic and Social Affairs, Population Division: World Urbanization Prospects, the 2011 Revision. New York, 2012.

In United Nations estimates, urban zones of all sizes will grow and develop in the future, as Figure 7-7 suggests. In 2025, some 4.6 billion folks will reside in urban environments. Of this total, 42 percent will live in cities with 500,000 or less total population. Over three-quarters of the world's urban dwellers will live in urban areas with fewer than 5 million total inhabitants. Only about 14 percent will call home the very largest cities—those with populations of 10 million or more.[18]

FIGURE 7-7. URBAN POPULATION GROWTH PROJECTIONS BY URBAN AREA SIZE

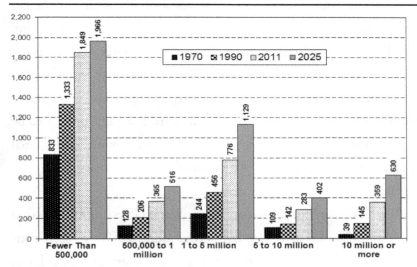

United Nations, Department of Economic and Social Affairs, Population Division: World Urbanization Prospects, the 2011 Revision. New York, 2012.

As was described for the United States in Chapter 2, in some regions urban growth will lead to a coalescence of previously separate urban areas into much larger regional urban centers. These "megaregion" urban centers will further change the size, scale, and nature of urban environments in many areas of the world.

INFRASTRUCTURE RISING UP

The business of building the world is booming, and across the globe the results are astounding. Notwithstanding the 2008 global downturn (which stalled temporarily development most everywhere), the race continues at a brisk pace. Consulting firm IHS Global Insight calculated the 2010 global construction spend at almost $5.5 trillion USD, and forecasted steady growth to more than $8 trillion USD by 2019.[19] It's clear that the developing world sees value and need in infrastructure, and there is a keen interest in building it fast. Across Asia (in mainland China, Hong Kong, South Korea, Singapore, and Australia), in the Middle East and Arab Gulf States, and in other locales, governments and/or private concerns are busy transforming their countries with new buildings, roads, bridges, and other transportation and trade related infrastructure. Indeed some appear to be playing a game of "the biggest, most, and fastest wins." The global opportunity is now, and the race is joined.

But not in the United States.

Yet, this is not entirely true. Certainly the US economy has been astonishingly robust over the last several decades. We've seen considerable growth in the private sector, a large boom (and bubble) in commercial and residential development, and loads of investment across economic segments including health care, energy, biotechnology, pharmaceuticals, and military. And we're just now crawling out of a deep recession in which the US government spent three-quarters of a trillion dollars for economic stimulus, and a similar amount for bank and corporate bailouts. We've financed two overseas wars at an astronomical cost (and it seems to me with very little success). And with an eye-popping debt that now threatens the whole ship, it's hard to say that the United States is not spending money. Unfortunately, all of this only makes the lack of sustained investment in infrastructure that much worse.

If those nations who build infrastructure today will lead the world tomorrow, then it quite simply won't be the United States leading. We've fallen behind in investments in most areas—not only the tangible infrastructure of roads, bridges, airports, and marine terminals, but also in other important areas, such as education and health care. What's happened to our belief in global leadership, to our sense of "manifest destiny" in conquering all for good? (Not that it was ultimately, of course, all for good, or good for all.) Is the American Dream no longer supported by Americans, and instead co-opted by others around the globe? Or is it simply someone else's turn to lead—to grow, develop, and rise to preeminence on the world stage?

LOOKING BACK AT INFRASTRUCTURE IMPORTANCE

In the early years of the Industrial Revolution, Americans set out to capture, subdue, and exploit their new country (including taking it away from those who were already there).

Central to this early expansion were the railroads, at that point the largest infrastructure development in the history of the world. And a familiar pattern emerged: economic development occurring alongside of infrastructure.

The railroads needed people and people needed the railroads. Coal was both the fuel firing the locomotive *and* the major commodity of the line. Development opened up new coal resources and new customers still farther away. The same happened with farm produce, oil and gas, mining and steel, and goods of every type.

From the beginning, development of infrastructure and the economy were intertwined.

And it happened fast. From about 30,000 miles of track nationwide in 1860 (the United States having just crossed the Appalachians to tap new resources in the Midwest), total track miles exploded to 254,000 road miles by 1916. For the next two decades the railroad system dominated transportation, accounting for about 65 percent of total US freight shipments, and essentially all of the long-haul traffic. And from the turn of the century, the lines were fast too. For instance, each day, fresh milk from northern Vermont farms began an early morning journey, from the cow to five-gallon can, from the farm to local station, and then onto fast priority trains bound for New York City or Boston, ultimately delivered to customers that very same day.[20]

After the railroads came still larger investments in the automobile and the infrastructure required to move millions—both people and goods. The US interstate highway system (as we understand it today) was first conceived in a 1939 report to Congress, offered by Thomas MacDonald and Herbert Fairbank of the US Bureau of Public Roads. Their ideas of "free roads" led eventually to congressional approval of the Federal Highway Act of 1956, signed into law by President Dwight Eisenhower.[21] (During World War II, Eisenhower had been impressed with the quality and importance of Germany's well-engineered Autobahn network). The program eventually established nearly 50,000 network miles, built at a cost of $128.9 billion (not including the turnpike toll roads.) Cities were connected to one another as they had never been, and the entire nation was joined into a system of communication and commerce. Interstate trucking grew rapidly to challenge and then overtake rail transport for most goods and services. Large urban areas benefited from highways and beltways that better organized traffic, while opening suburban and exurban areas to further development. Large suburbs offered the promise of home ownership and social connection for a nation of new families.

Building on these investments, tremendous economic growth helped cement the United States as the world's preeminent free economy superpower—a position the country enjoyed for most of the latter twentieth century.

Today, we're experiencing a third phase of large-scale infrastructure building—though this time involving the *technological* and *information* infrastructure of the global Internet. This new platform includes many components—computers and networks, switches and routers, fiber-optic cables crisscrossing the oceans, and such. And there's no question that this infrastructure will be even more important to global connectivity and commerce than the infrastructure that has come before. Also, there's no question that the United States has played and will continue to play a preeminent role in the investment and development of this transformative technology.

Still, this third wave of infrastructure is different. Whereas the tangible infrastructure of railroads and highways (and everything built around them) greatly benefited the local, regional, and national US economy (as did similar investments elsewhere)—investments in the Internet are global, in both nature and benefit. Investments made in global technology benefit users around the world, and deliver less competitive advantage to the local country.

REACHING UP AND OUT

To get a sense of the global change afoot, let's take a look at the world's tall buildings. Tall buildings are, of course, only one example of infrastructure development. Sometimes these skyscrapers have questionable benefit, and they're often controversial (both in general terms, and in the context of a specific project). Nevertheless, tall buildings have historically been viewed with national pride, as iconic symbols of economies and cultures. So I think they're a fair proxy for the larger trends of infrastructure.

The tallest 300 buildings in the world are catalogued and reported by the Council on Tall Buildings and Urban Habitats (CTBUH).[22] Today, almost half of the tallest buildings are in Asia, with another quarter in the Middle East. Only about 20 percent are located in North America, and less than a quarter of the tallest buildings have homes in the developed regions of North America and Europe (including Moscow).

On a country basis, the figures are further revealing. Mainland China leads the list with 76 of the world's tallest, about one-quarter of the top 300. Hong Kong adds another sixteen, so China's total today is 92—30 percent of the list. In Asia, China is followed by South Korea (14), Australia (10), and Japan (8). Others are located in Singapore, Malaysia, Thailand, India, Indonesia, Vietnam, and North Korea.

In the Middle East, the small but wealthy nation of the United Arab Emirates now boasts 57 of the tallest buildings, about the same as the United States, with 55. In the West, it's Panama behind the United States, with 9 tall structures, more than any other in the Western hemisphere.

These numbers tell a part of the story, but the age of these buildings yields still greater insight of the trend.

In the United States, 75 percent of the 55 buildings were constructed before 1999. About 20 percent have been built in the last ten years. By contrast, the oldest building in the UAE was completed in 1999, and 60 percent of this nation's tallest buildings have topped out in just the last three years.

That's phenomenal. The same is true in Asia, where 72 percent (106 structures) were completed in just the last ten years. It's clear that (at least with the tallest buildings) the United States and the West have fallen far off the pace of new global trendsetters. Many Westerners say that tall buildings don't matter anymore. Are they right?

What about other components of infrastructure—roads, bridges, and tunnels; dams and ports; airports and trains? According to the American Society of Civil Engineers (ASCE), America's infrastructure is in poor shape. In fact, in their *2009 Report Card on America's Infrastructure,* ASCE delivered 11 Ds and 4 Cs for US infrastructure.[23] The problems are acute in virtually every area—water systems (dams, levees, and water and wastewater pipes), transportation systems (roads, bridges, tunnels, rail, and airports), and waterways transportation (rivers, ports, and harbors). Everywhere, the story is the same: not enough investment to keep up and maintain existing systems, or to build new systems to support continued growth, development, and quality of life. In fact, this report claims that the United States spends about 2.4 percent of GDP on infrastructure investment. By comparison, Europe spends twice that amount—5 percent of GDP, and China spends even more, at about 9 percent of total GDP.

The ASCE study repeats itself again and again in suggesting that the primary constraints to infrastructure improvement are not related to technology or innovation, but simply to a lack of will, commitment, and/or money.

What is needed to turn this tide, to get America interested in infrastructure investment? Clearly the United States is a different market, economic, and political system from the others (particularly those in the developing world). With 9 percent of GDP spent on infrastructure, China leads the way. But China is coming from a very different place, racing to catch up from a position far back in the pack—perhaps where the United States was a century ago. And, of course, China's culture and political structure is radically different too, driven largely by central planning (with a much more unquestioned authority). China's needs are great, with an enormous population that is growing both in size and in expectations, and migrating in astonishing numbers toward the urban centers of opportunity. But China faces considerable challenges in continuing to grow as it has. Many experts believe that the country cannot invest its way out of its structural problems. China relies too heavily on global export, and must now develop a much larger and stronger base of domestic consumption. In this way, the country is the opposite of the United States. In China, there may soon be too much infrastructure per capita GDP, while in the United States there is too little.

In the Arab Gulf States, we see yet a different context, fueled by the enormous wealth of these nations, relatively small populations, and (today) stable governments. Notwithstanding the recent recession, this region boasts infrastructure development on the grandest of scales. The Arabian subcontinent boasts many of the world's tallest buildings (all of them new), as well as some of the very largest developments in commercial, hospitality, and retail. Growth continues, fueled by big projects and big dreams, such as Qatar's hosting of the World Cup in 2022.

Even more interestingly, the success enjoyed here with traditional infrastructure development has further emboldened regional leaders, who have now turned their attentions to still-larger objectives. According to area management consultant Oliver Patar, now that these Arab leaders have demonstrated their capacity to build the world's largest shopping malls and hotels, they're now determined to create even higher-level infrastructure—for instance, a world-class, world-leading university.[24]

This is a perfect example of the power of infrastructure. As with the United States in the last 200 years, investments in infrastructure pay off not only in the return on those assets, but also in furthering the capabilities, dreams, and ambitions for more.

It's never the case that a particular investment will be perfect, intrinsically good, or a safe bet (there are no guarantees). But the building of infrastructure often leads to good, and will likely position investors and nations at the forefront of the Fast Future transformation.

It's clear that unless the United States gets busy (very, very busy) over the next 10 to 20 years, it's almost certain that we'll fall considerably farther behind the rest of the world in tangible infrastructure—and perhaps increasingly in economic productivity, worker happiness, and global economic influence. The United States will continue to participate in world development—as a nation of global bankers and investors, but maybe without much infrastructure improvement at home.

IMPLICATIONS OF URBANIZATION

Across the globe, urbanization is accelerating alongside the demands and opportunities of a rapidly globalizing society. Significant economic integration—between countries and across regions—and an insatiable quest for economic competitiveness, is both driving urbanization, and affected by the urbanization achieved.

Though the details for specific cities will always remain somewhat uncertain (witness the change in fortunes of New Orleans, Louisiana, after Hurricane Katrina, or in northern Japan after the 2011 Earthquake and tsunami), several larger-scale implications resulting from the trends of global urbanization seem evident.

Since most of the world's population growth will occur in urban areas, it's likely that most of the new economic opportunities will also occur in these urban areas. This isn't true for all businesses, but it is for most. Economic demand comes through people, and, thus, much of it will come from where the people are. As urban centers develop and grow, new businesses will grow alongside these customers. In the developing world, this growth will coincide with the rise of a significant working class (and perhaps middle class), with considerably more economic power than the populations of these regions enjoy today.

The global power base will shift as a result of differential population growth, and much of the urbanization from now until mid-century will occur in the *developing* world—in countries that have (or will have) considerable talent and skill in their people. Connected ever more tightly to the global network, these rising urban centers will increasingly set the tone, agenda, and rules of global growth. There will be big winners—and big losers—as the centers of economic power shift around.

New and developing cities will provide powerful opportunities for rethinking how urban populations live and succeed together. A convergence of many new technologies, new urban planning and development models, and newly evolving political, economic, and societal frameworks will (all together) result in an explosive array of innovation in urban life. Of course, this will also take place alongside a very sizable upheaval, disruption, and conflict with the existing status quo.

City development will continue to mash together highly diverse populations—just as it does now. Opportunity and challenge will remain linked, though many traditional measures of diversity (such as ethnic, racial, or national norms) will likely become much less important in an integrated, homogenized, global community.

It's likely that we'll continue to see distinction in our urban areas. Today, cities areas are often known for certain specialties: New York and London for finance, Silicon Valley and Bangalore for technology, Las Vegas and Macau for entertainment. Perhaps new urban specialty areas will develop: in finance, entertainment, medicine—or who knows what? Where will we go for virtual reality vacations, or for cheap but high-quality medical care?

Interestingly, the rapid evolution of technology, the explosion of information availability and transparency, and the convergence of these with burgeoning social media communications may counter (in important and even shocking ways) the strong global forces of urbanization. Specifically, the opportunity to disassociate work from place—what is done verses where it is done—may soon provide millions of world citizens the opportunity to live wherever they want—in urban or rural environments to suit their individual tastes—while still exploiting the power of urban concentration and connectivity.

The reality (opportunity and constraint) of this emerging development is not yet clear, but its promise is potentially transformative, and may be outrageously significant. We'll see.

SO WHAT?

Urbanization is a longer-term, global demographic uber-trend, and it's sometimes difficult to connect its importance to our industries and businesses—especially over the shorter haul. And even the important infrastructure projects that will contribute to reshaping the urban built environment often require considerable time and resources to develop to fruition. Nevertheless, we can and should be asking some general questions about the impact of these trends on our organizations today, including:

▶ What are the major implications of urbanization on our customer base? How will our clients and customers change (for example bigger or smaller, more affluent or less affluent, more educated or less educated, more ethnically diverse or more ethnically segregated, etc.)?

▶ How will the changes of urbanization affect our industry, and the industries and businesses of our clients and customers?

▶ What new and developing geographic markets should we be looking at today—either domestically in the coalescing mega-regions areas, or internationally in developing urban markets?

▶ What about the counter-trend of disassociation of work and place (telecommuting, work from home, high-quality Internet access, independent contractors, etc.)? How will this impact our business, and what opportunities should we pursue even now?

▶ What are the new business opportunities or market segments that are likely to develop in more concentrated, urban environments?

▶ Will the rise of massive urban centers around the globe— and particularly in the developing world—shift the power base or center of focus of our industry, or our core markets, elsewhere?

▶ What does the United States' lagging posture on infrastructure development and replacement mean for our economy, industry, and company?

▶ Where are the nascent, developing infrastructure-related opportunities for our firm at present, and what are we doing about these right now?

8

Embracing Diversity, and the Ascending Global Meritocracy

WHAT ONE *DOES* WILL SUPPLANT WHO ONE *IS*—IN A MORE DEMOCRATIC, MERIT-BASED WORLD OF INCREASING OPPORTUNITY.

"In a democracy the poor will have more power than the rich, because there are more of them, and the will of the majority is supreme."
—Aristotle

A GROWING DIVERSITY

In the Fast Future, we will all think much differently about diversity. Over the next several decades, differences in race, ethnicity, and gender will become much less important than they are today—particularly in business. I say this not because I'm an idealist (though I suppose I am). Instead, I believe that economic forces both pragmatic and primordial will drive most business culture (and society in general) toward a new more egalitarian paradigm—one in which identities of individuals and communities will be defined more by commonality of ideas, passion, collaboration, and consensus on important objectives.

Our majorities will be defined more by our alignment, and less by the old demarcations we've focused on for millennia.

Of course, the diversity of humanity (ethnicity, language, and culture) has been with us since our beginnings. As early human populations spread out across the Earth (from wherever it is that humans first appeared), each group developed important differences in identity—racial, ethnicity, culture, beliefs, and such. Interestingly, while our differences were (and are) real, these original populations were often quite similar to one another. Most societies were comprised of small and local villages, and most early citizens were subsistence farmers and hunters. Trade was usually limited and local. Many jobs and roles in the group were recognizable from culture to culture—just as they are today.

This social and economic pattern remained unchanged for many thousands of years, but in the last few millennia we've witnessed a steady, serial ascendancy of unique civilizations, from South America, China, the steppes of Asia, Greece and Rome, and the Islamic world. Individual European states eventually grew out of the chaos of the Middle Ages, and soon carried a new colonial imperialism around the globe. This shifted the political and economic balance of the world toward the West. Many became involved in a new sort of globalization (though certainly not all enjoyed the economic benefit equally). Later, the Industrial Revolution accelerated Western ascendency, and rapid growth of various nations. This trend, along with two global world wars, then shifted into our current order—an increasingly globalized society, the Western world still ascendant economically (but with the East rising rapidly), with English spoken as the first language of global business, despite being the first language of only 5 percent of the world's population.

So global diversity isn't really anything new. But just how diverse are we, considering the more familiar dimensions—like race, ethnicity, nationality, gender, religion, and such?

These questions are surprisingly hard to answer with precision. Accurate and reliable global statistical data is not easily accessible, and probably for a variety of reasons. First, definitions of race and ethnicity are not completely clear and consistent themselves, and so not always useful in statistical analysis. Citizenship in a particular country isn't the same as "nationality," which is (not uncommonly) tied more closely to ethnic identity rather than to a particular geographic boundary. Finally, it's often difficult to proceed *objectively*— attempts to simply describe the lay of the land involve our perceptions, judgments, and prejudice.

Of course, it's obvious that there are many different ethnic and racial groups that comprise the global society, and that many of these groups are large and significant in population size. These ethnic groups include southern Asians, eastern Asians, southeastern Asians, people of Middle Eastern origin and descent, Native Americans, blacks of African origin, white Anglos and Caucasians, Hispanic and Latin peoples—and on and on. In my view, the Fast Future significance of global diversity is likely to be positive, not negative. While the history of humanity has unfortunately included a great deal of bad associated with our differences, in the future it's likely that these differences will become much more important as *opportunity*—both in bringing together a diversity of opinions and ideas, and in appreciating and exploiting our differences more positively, in a truly global economy.

One dimension of our diversity that we can objectively measure is *language*, which itself illuminates the diversity of the world. Any guess where English ranks today in global language? It's spoken nearly everywhere, and is indeed widely recognized as the language of global business. But as Figure 8-1 demonstrates, English is not the most widely employed *first* language of the world.[1] In the top spot is Mandarin Chinese, with about 875 million speakers. Indian Hindi is second with 366 million native speakers, while English and Spanish are tied for third, claiming about 340 million speakers each. Some 207 million speak Bengali, in both India and Bangladesh. There are also 176 million Portuguese speakers, 167 million Russian, and 125 million Japanese. Nearly 100 million count German as their first language, and 78 million speak Korean primarily. A combining of the 15 major variants of Arabic yields 200 million total Arabic speakers. Indeed with respect to language, the world is clearly a very diverse place, and most certainly not as Anglo-centric as one might imagine.

FIGURE 8-1. LANGUAGE DIVERSITY IN THE WORLD

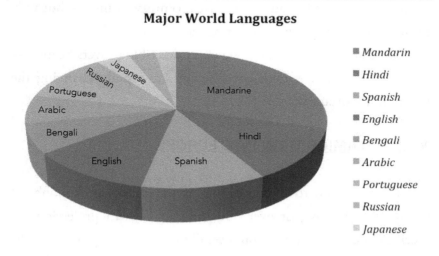

Source: *Ethnologue: Languages of the World, Seventeenth Edition, 2014*

Today we're beginning to see much more change in diversity—and with likely profound consequence. This change involves a very large, global-scale migration—from the rural countryside into urban centers, and from countries of less opportunity to those with more. There is a strong sense of economic democratization at work in the global society—the "meritocracy" we'll consider next.

Globalization promises to spread the wealth around (at least a little more), and away from the powerful West toward the developing regions of South America, Africa, and Asia. But, of course, it's also driving the enormous migration (and emigration) we also see today. Not only are goods and services traveling around the globe, but so too are the makers, providers, and workers of those goods and services. Through this migration, many nations will become much more ethnically and culturally diverse. This won't happen overnight—complete global assimilation will take a century or more—but we'll see it occurring at an ever-increasing pace.

Here are just three short vignettes describing diversification—examples of how the forces of diversity are rapidly changing the world in important ways.

MUSLIM IMMIGRATION INTO EUROPE

In 2011, the total population of the European Union's 27 member states was just over 500 million. Growth projections in specific countries are varied, but overall the EU will grow very slowly, at an annual rate of just 0.64 percent between 2011 and 2060.[2] Slow indeed.

Movement within the EU continues in recognizable patterns. First, citizens are migrating from the industrialized areas of the North (Benelux, Britain, and Germany) toward "sunbelt" destinations in the South (Spain, Portugal, France, and Italy)—much as is occurring in the United States. Second, migration continues from the relatively poorer countries of Eastern Europe to the relatively wealthy nations in the West.

Third, the European Union boasts a net positive influx of immigrants from other world regions. In 2010, 47 million people (about 9.4 percent of the population) classified themselves as immigrants. Of these, about two-thirds were born outside of the EU, while one-third were originally from another EU state. Immigrants come from all corners of the globe, but primarily from Africa, the Middle East, and Asia. Many of these immigrants are Muslim.[3]

According to projections by the Pew Research Center's *Forum on Religion and Public Life*, the world's Islamic population is expected to increase in the next 20 years by about 35 percent, from some 1.6 billion today to 2.2 billion in 2030.[4] Muslim community growth is about twice the rate of non-Muslims, an average annual growth rate of about 1.5 percent for Muslims, and 0.7 percent for non-Muslims. Surprisingly, this expansion in the Muslim world actually represents a slowing in the rate of this group's growth—from an average annual rate of 2.2 percent between 1990 and 2010.

About 60 percent of Muslims live today in the Asia Pacific region, and 20 percent live in the Middle East and North Africa. Muslims are a small minority population in Europe and the Americas, but their numbers will grow (relative to the total population) in both of these regions as well.

In Europe, the Islamic population will expand from about 6 percent of the total (2010) to 8 percent by 2030. In absolute numbers, European Muslims will increase from 44 million today to 58 million in 2030. Within the EU, the largest increases will occur in western and northern Europe, where Islamic groups may approach 10 percent or more of the total population in some countries.[5]

What's the significance of this migration? Indeed, Islamic migration into Europe poses several challenges for European society. Overall, the EU is religiously diverse, though it is dominated by a Judeo-Christian heritage that includes Roman Catholicism, Protestantism, and Eastern Orthodoxy. Of course, today many European nations are not religious, having rejected the theocratic history of the continent. Some countries, including the Czech Republic, Estonia, and the Netherlands, report that a majority of their citizens claim no religious affiliation at all.

In this context, with theism on the decline, the influx of believers of Islam, Hinduism, Buddhism, and Sikhism does create cultural diversity—but also considerable tension. Of course, Christian-Muslim tensions in Europe are not new; it's a storyline tracing back a thousand years. But large-scale immigration into the EU today is forcing this tension to the forefront. Many Muslims want a closer association between religious and government authority. Differences of race, ethnicity, language, and culture further exacerbate the situation, and impede the pace of cultural assimilation.

In recent years, EU fertility rates have increased slightly, from a low of 1.45 children born per female in 2002, to 1.58 in 2012. Though this increase was noted across most EU member countries, it still represents a level below the population replacement rate (roughly 2.1 children per female). Based solely only on natural births, the EU population will decline in real numbers. Retirement-aged workers cannot be replaced (in numbers) by a younger generation. The EU (like other Western societies) faces a Fast Future of eventual economic decline, increasingly comprised of older, retired citizens, without enough younger workers to sustain (notwithstanding a marked uptick in productivity) the economic vitality of the past.[6]

Robust immigration into the EU of a large Muslim population could mean economic salvation for the region. This immigration could offset the intrinsically low birthrate of Europeans (particularly those of Caucasian ethnicity). Additionally, these immigrants display a much higher natural birth rate within their group (closer to that of their country of origin than to their country of arrival). Many European nations have a relatively welcoming immigrant policy today, and they will continue on this track. On the other hand, rising tensions in some EU countries, the inevitable clash of cultures, and the rise of militant Islam on the world stage—all threaten to darken this opportunity for bolstering European diversity and economic growth. How this will all shake out over the next 50 to 100 years is unclear. EU politicians (like politicians worldwide) today seem remarkably unwilling to grapple with these difficult issues and opportunities. Nevertheless, the implications of this change undoubtedly will be far reaching—in economics, education, housing, labor, welfare, the arts, and religion—in virtually all aspects of human endeavor.

LATINO-HISPANIC EXPANSION IN THE UNITED STATES

The US population is changing, and perhaps nowhere more profoundly than with the growth and development of the Latino and Hispanic community. (Though overlapping and often used similarly, the terms Latino and Hispanic don't mean the same thing. *Latino* refers to those of Latin American descent, and *Hispanic* to those of Spanish-speaking descent.)

The US population of Hispanics is growing rapidly, as shown in Figure 8-2. According to the US Census Bureau, about 9.1 million US residents were listed Hispanic in 1970. By 2011, the number had grown to 52 million. The Hispanic group is expected to grow rapidly to 86 million by 2030, and 133 million by 2050. Today, about 16.7 percent of the US population is Hispanic. By 2050, the group will represent more than 30 percent of the country's total.[7]

FIGURE 8-2. PROJECTED HISPANIC POPULATION GROWTH IN THE UNITEDSTATES

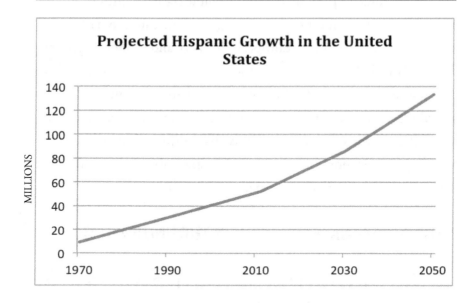

Source: U.S. Census Bureau

Over the last 10 years, more than half (55.5 percent) of the total population growth in the United States came from Hispanics. Within this community, nearly two-thirds of the expansion came through natural increase—that is, new births inside the country. About one-third came through immigration of additional Hispanics into the country.[8]

US Hispanics are a young group compared to the overall population, comprising about 24 percent of the people under age 18; 16 percent of those between the ages of 18 and 64; and just 7.2 percent of residents aged 65 and older.[9]

Geographically, the Latino and Hispanic community is concentrated in the nation's South and West. Hispanics account for more than 25 percent of the populations of the southern areas of California, Arizona, New Mexico, and Texas. There are more than

14 million Hispanics in California alone, nearly 10 million in Texas, almost 4.5 million in Florida, and 3.5 million in New York—along with another 20 million dispersed across the other US states. California, Texas, and Florida lead the nation in absolute numbers, but as a percentage of existing population, the Hispanic community is rapidly growing in many areas.[10]

In the United States, Hispanics are overwhelmingly Latinos, and primarily of Mexican origin and descent—32 million total, or about 62 percent of all Hispanics. Other ethnic backgrounds include Puerto Rican (4.6 million), Cuban (1.8 million), Salvadoran (1.6 million), Dominican (1.4 million), and Guatemalan (1.0 million). Mexican ethnicity dominates the Hispanic population in most US regions; exceptions include the Cuban population in Florida; Puerto Ricans in the northeast states (New Jersey, Pennsylvania, New York, and southern New England); and those of Salvadoran background in the mid-Atlantic region around Washington, DC.[11]

Hispanic immigration into the United States is an important and controversial issue in our national dialogue, similar to that of Muslim immigration into the European Union. There are important economic benefits from immigrant labor and vibrant new markets, but also the challenges of cultural assimilation and accommodation. The recent recession has cooled the issue somewhat, with a reversal and net outward migration from the United States (in particular, back into Mexico, where that nation's economy has grown more rapidly than that of the United States).

Barring a radical shift in the pro-immigration policies of the United States, this trend of rapid growth in the Hispanic community will continue and likely accelerate—a consequence of the robust US economy, and the proximity of neighboring Hispanic countries in Central and South America. Additionally, US Hispanics will continue to grow rapidly in numbers through natural births, regardless of immigration policy. Much as was the case with US immigration in the last two centuries (mostly from the European countries of Ireland, Italy, Germany, and others), the influx and growth of Hispanics will continue in American society throughout the 21st century. Overall, racial, ethnic, cultural, and economic diversity will increase in the United States, and that change will bring with it both significant challenges and opportunities.

A CHINESE CONSUMER CLASS

It's obvious that China's economic star is rising fast, and this will continue in the Fast Future (though not forever, and not without struggle). Chinese capital today is flowing to all corners of the globe, to projects and prospects of all sorts. Back home, the Chinese government has used astoundingly large investments in infrastructure, both to rapidly develop the nation and to provide for an enormous economic growth machine underpinning the entire economy. Many economists argue that this path is unsustainable, and that China must significantly overhaul its economic model for future sustainability. The country must increasingly move away from its near-sole reliance on export markets, and instead build up a considerably larger domestic market for consumption. China needs a middle class.

This is good news for millions of Chinese, who are indeed ready to join this middle class. The country today is quite an enigma—rapid growth and development, a growing global economic juggernaut, and still with hundreds of millions of citizens living at or below the poverty line. Most of these Chinese poor live in far-away rural villages not significantly different today than they were 200 (or 2,000) years ago. But the country is also moving rapidly to change this. Today, there are more than 100 large cities dotted across the landscape, each with a population of 2 million or more, and many of these less than 40 years old.[12]

A lot hangs in the balance of these developments, and many questions remain unanswered. Chief among these is whether the Chinese model—a mix of political authoritarianism and (increasing) economic freedom—can itself survive in a rapidly changing, globally connected world. How far Chinese citizens will agree, pursuing economic freedom and opportunity while submitting to continued central authority, remains to be seen.

Assuming some continued growth in personal freedoms, we're likely to see not only a more economically successful Chinese middle class, but also a significantly more mobile and globally involved one. Some will remember the onslaught of a newly mobile Japanese tourist wave (and tremendous outpouring of Japanese capital) in the late 1970s and early 1980s. At that time, it seemed as though the Japanese might buy up everything—companies, commercial real estate, fancy vacation homes. This newly mobile society (rebuilding after World War II) was suddenly everywhere.

But by comparison, Japan is a small country, with (today) 128 million citizens. In contrast, China boasts about 1.34 billion residents, more than 10 times as many. Imagine an increasingly wealthy, mobile, Chinese tourist class of 300 million–400 million! Developments like these—and we might consider India, Brazil, Nigeria, and others in a similar vein—will certainly boost diversity all over the Fast Future globe.

THE MERITOCRACY IS COMING

One really important developing uber-trend seems clear. In the Fast Future, we're headed (though certainly not in a straight line) toward a meritocracy—a world much more open to opportunity, and with millions more participating in new and exciting ways.

Indeed, I've been called a dreamer (but as John Lennon wrote, "I'm not the only one"). Of course, it won't be easy; those forces controlling the status quo today don't want to let go. But as we've seen with other global trends, the pace, intensity, and sheer magnitude of the change ahead (in technology, information, globalization) will overwhelm this status quo.

The gates are beginning to open, and there'll be no turning back the masses of the enthusiastic and talented.

There are many examples today—of this change in progress in politics, economics, and society around the world. Few are complete, and none are perfect. Still, these developments are pushing us ever faster toward a more *meritocratic* outcome. As examples, let's look briefly at a few of these.

POLITICS AND GOVERNMENT

Pause a moment and consider the arc of history over the last 500 years. Much has changed. Modern civilization grew first out of local, feudal societies and into a succession of global empires driven by technology (ocean-navigating ships, for instance), and a hunger for natural resources, wealth, and power. Important experiments in democracy were conceived in France and America, and later in other nations rejecting monarchial government. World War I substantively ended the reign of kings and queens, ushered in a modern era, along with new political forms in Soviet and Sino communism. World War II firmed up the battle lines, and the subsequent Cold War itself provided a choice (between democracy and communism) for all nations around the globe. A lot of change—still, the change continues.

USSR

As recently as the early 1980s, the Cold War issue was still in doubt, though a rapid unraveling of the Soviet Union and its control on Eastern Europe subsequently spelled the end. Failure in the Soviet Union grew out of the challenges of economic inefficiency, leadership transition, and the difficulty of sustaining political control. But ultimately, communism failed in large part because of global change—the uber-trends of technology, information, and globalization. As author Tom Friedman has argued, this was the time of new personal computers, complete with first-generation desktop publishing software, which together allowed those outside of the political and media establishments to begin communicating (with home-published newsletters and fax machines).[13] And just as is happening again today, this mix of technology and a public hungry to express itself proved a powerful force for change.

Recognizing the transformation in progress, Mikhail Gorbachev began initiating radical new initiatives in the USSR: *glasnost* (openness) and *perestroika* (restructuring). Perhaps he knew (but maybe he didn't) that these very programs, creating openness and transparency in government while restructuring bureaucratic systems for a new era, would further accelerate the demand for change, and lead even to the government's ultimate collapse. Gorbachev took the top leadership post in 1985; by December 1991, the Soviet Union itself was dissolved.[14]

The Soviet Union's demise freed many nations formerly under communist control. These countries have taken various paths since. The Baltic countries of Lithuania, Latvia, and Estonia were quickly assimilated into the European Union, as eventually were several others in Eastern Europe. Others, such as Belarus, and parts of Georgia and Ukraine, have remained closely aligned with Russia. Still others under communist influence, notably Cuba, Syria, and even North Korea, have become even more isolated and, without Soviet support, weaker economically.

ARAB SPRING

On December 17, 2011, a Tunisian municipal inspector confiscated the fruit stand wares of an unemployed and frustrated citizen Mohamed Bouazizi. Later that day, Bouazizi doused himself with gasoline and set himself afire. His death galvanized a people unhappy with their economic and political situation, setting off the Tunisian Revolution and larger Arab Spring movement. Beyond Tunisia, fervor swept the Arab world and led to the overthrow of regimes in Egypt, Libya, and Yemen. Significant protests and/or civil uprisings also occurred in Bahrain, Algeria, Iraq, Jordan, Kuwait, Morocco, and Oman, with lesser protests occurring elsewhere.[15]

The results of these protests have varied across the region; most were met by violent government response. Many protesters employed civil resistance (strikes, demonstrations, and marches), but some used violence themselves. In many instances, the use of new social media platforms to communicate, raise awareness, and organize internally clearly defined these actions as distinctively 21st century.

IRAN

During the 2009 presidential election in Iran, protests flared over the disputed reelection of Mahmoud Ahmadinejad, and in support of opposition candidates. Some refer to this event as the "Twitter Revolution" because of the protesters' reliance on Twitter and other social media sites for communication and sharing. Widespread election fraud was claimed by both opposition parties. Protest activities escalated, and government authorities responded with violence. Protests erupted again in February 2011, alongside the other movements of the regional Arab Spring. Still, Iranian protests have not to date resulted in a significant change in government within the country.[16]

MYANMAR (BURMA)

Myanmar, an extremely isolated Asian country controlled by military junta for the last 50 years, has recently initiated some promising efforts at political and economic change. Pro-democracy leader Aung San Suu Kyi was released from house arrest, a National Human Rights Commission was established, and general amnesty was granted to political prisoners. Institution of new labor laws allowing for worker organization and relaxation of some censorship has also occurred. These reforms surprised some in the international community, and in support of these changes the regional economic group ASEAN approved Burma's bid for 2014 Chair. US Secretary of State Hillary Clinton visited Burma in 2011 (the first visit by a US Secretary of State in more than 50 years). Though there is much more progress to be made in Burma, these changes—likely the result of Fast Future pressures at work—are welcomed by the international community.[17]

CHINA

Any discussion (even abbreviated) of global political and economic trends must include the juggernaut that is China. China is today the world's second largest economy (third, if the EU is counted as one), and it may become the largest by 2050.[18] Importantly, China has also emerged as a new, alternative political and economic model for the world—a mix of political communism with an increasingly capitalist economy. It's unclear how successful this Chinese system will be (since economic freedom often creates with it a desire for political freedom, as well). As with Gorbachev's *glasnost*, it's possible that opening the Chinese economy will lead also to greater political and social change. But perhaps not. Chinese society is clearly different from others—like Russian and American. Still, economic opportunity appeals to all peoples around the world.

EUROPE

With all of the worldwide upheaval at work, it's possible to overlook important political developments in the Western world that are also transformative in scale and meaning. The European Union, as a political and economic experiment, continues, despite the large current overhang of financial risk in several member states (Greece, Portugal, Ireland, Spain, and Italy). There is talk at times of disbanding of the Euro, the common EU currency, though simultaneously others call for even greater economic integration and cooperation.

Europeans face other challenges of governance (together and separately), including importantly how to deal with large-scale immigration from outside of the EU, often of Muslim peoples from

Africa and Asia. Today, Europeans are largely nonreligious, and many European nations strongly desire "freedom *from* religion." So it's not surprising that they are uncomfortable with the rapid influx of the religious, conservative, and even theocratically inclined. This is an enormously important issue for Europe, and a key challenge for the region ahead.

DOMESTIC

The United States is today experiencing something of a crisis in the nation's two-party system of governance. Over the last several decades, America has (it seems) become almost evenly split between left-leaning liberals and right-leaning conservatives. And while there are many more moderates in the mainstream of American society, loud voices on either the left or right often control the conversation (bolstered by the many new forms of communication, such as cable-television). Significant change in the financing of politics has also changed the game, further discouraging moderation and compromise. As a result, the US system has become increasingly dysfunctional and paralyzed in action, at a time (it might be argued) when the need for policy leadership is as important as ever. Global competitiveness, investment in education, rebuilding infrastructure, and a vision for the nation in the 21st century world—all of these are largely missing today in US politics. The United States is admired for its history, principles, and systems, but its future as a world leader is frankly much less certain today.

ECONOMIC AND SOCIAL

The distinction between politics and economics is increasingly arbitrary.

The world is ever more interconnected, affecting economic, political, and social systems simultaneously. Financial capital flows with greater fluidity, and investments impact all dimensions of society. In the Fast Future, it will be challenging to retain political isolation while participating in economic opportunity, or alternatively to participate in global political affiliations without economic connectivity. Nations, societies, and cultures are (both good and bad) forced to decide: all in or not.

Most nations have joined, though a great many struggle to manage the rapid changes of global change. Only a few of the world's nearly 200 countries remain deeply isolated, and largely outside of the worldwide network (e.g., North Korea, Burma, Cuba, and Haiti).

Of course, there is today a great disparity in the sharing of the world's resources (among countries and peoples). Most are poor. According to the World Health Organization, some 23 percent of the world's population lives on less than $1 U.S. per day, representing in low-income countries about 43 percent of their citizens. By some estimates, nearly half the world's population (3.5 billion individuals) exists on less than $2 each day.[19]

The gross national income per capita of nations varies widely. In the Americas and in Europe, this amount (2012) is about $24,000 per person per year. In the eastern Mediterranean, and in South and East Asian regions, that figure is about $3,600–$3,800, more than six times less. In Africa, the amount is $2,400, 10 times less than that of North America and Western Europe.[20]

This disparity isn't new—we've long had both haves and have-nots economically. What is different (and what will be big news) is that this is *beginning to change*, and will so more likely in the decades ahead. Of course, this change won't be frictionless (the current haves won't give up without a fight), but it will change—as we progress toward the *meritocracy*. Change will happen because more and more are becoming cognizant of what's possible.

The notion that one can work to improve economic and social standing is relatively new—and, until most recently, uniquely *American*. For much of history, this simply hasn't been true. For most, each generation expects to follow the previous generation: where to live, what to do for work, what aspirations for success and survival—these are formed largely on the basis of past experience. Things didn't change much from year to year, or from generation to generation.

But, of course, America *was* different. Our new nation was born during the unprecedented growth of the Industrial Revolution, and Americans cultivated a much different belief—namely that they might pursue a different path from fathers and mothers, and live in different places and circumstances. Americans could become whatever they wanted. We've come to think of this concept (imperfect as it is) as the American Dream.

But (very importantly), this ideal is also attractive elsewhere *around the world*—and it's catching on fast. Through the power of technology and information, and a rapidly shrinking, globally interconnected world, many hear this message, and are discovering what's possible. (It's not that all will want to chase the same dream (that is, to become exactly like Americans); *it's much more powerful than that.*

It's the notion that each of the world's 6.5 billion citizens might create their own *unique* dreams, to grow far beyond current obstacles and constraints. Powerful indeed, and potentially transformative, both economically and socially.

Meanwhile, as more and more of the world's population begins to see, understand, and pursue this idea of economic and social success, all is certainly not well on the American home front. Indeed, the tremendous growth and success of a wealthier class over the last 30 to 40 years—concurrent with the erosion of progress in the middle class—has led to rapidly rising American pessimism. Repeated surveys confirm that Americans are quite concerned about their future, and the future of their children (and even before the recent recession). Many are falling farther behind in job security, financial stability, and career satisfaction. Health care and education costs have spiraled up, retirement pensions have disappeared, and with the recent financial collapse, both housing and retirement values have tumbled. It's increasingly difficult for many Americans today to remain confident in the American Dream. The concurrent rise of a visible uber-wealthy class (the so-called 1 percent) hasn't helped perceptions much.

I've been asked about this repeatedly. As the question goes, if we're really headed toward a global meritocracy, then what about this one percent (or really 0.1 percent) at the top of society's wealth, and their continued increasing abundance? Yes, there is something going on here (particularly in America), and I think it's rotten to the core. (See Figure 8-3 for a view of the changes in American CEO pay versus the average worker.)

The uber-wealthy are becoming ever more so, and often strikingly disengaged from reality. *Wealth itself is not the issue*—in fact, it's central to the American (now global) Dream of individual success. The issue as I see it is not wealth, but *undeserved wealth*, and success that is unfairly taken from others on an unleveled playing field. [21]

FIGURE 8-3 RISING DIVERGENCE IN AMERICA–COMPENSATION OF AMERICAN CEOS AND WORKERS

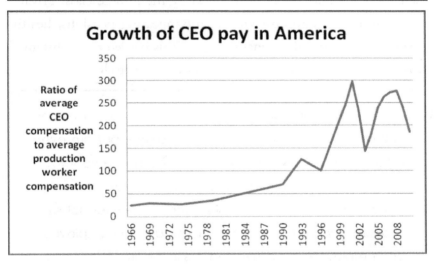

Source: Mishel, Bernstein, and Allegretto, The State of Working America 2006-7

Behind this trend is a combination of forces. First, there's been a broad movement in the United States toward a right-leaning, conservative philosophy (with Republican Party ascendancy, and a strong push toward policies that favor a pro-business political environment). Secondly, significant innovation in the financial services sector has been largely unchecked by government. The financial industry has successfully shifted much of its downside risk (market and business failure) to the public sector (government subsidizes the "too big to fail" risk), while simultaneously retaining the upside of increasingly complex and risky bets. Finally, changes in political campaign financing have greatly increased the influence of wealthy individual donors and political action committees, and have turned the focus of both major US parties (Republicans and Democrats) toward uberwealthy constituent supporters.

Meanwhile on the business front, much of the pain and suffering resulting from the constant pressures of global competitiveness have been borne disproportionately—first by the working class sector, and then (over the last couple of decades) by the middle class. Private-sector employees have lost ground (disappearing pensions, health-care benefits curtailed, stagnant wages). This has led to a substantial erosion of power and growth of the middle class itself.

Finally, there are important changes in American culture that have affected the workplace, but are even bigger in scale. Over the last half century, we've seen a rather pronounced drift away from "*corporate community*" toward one more individually (and sometimes selfishly) focused. The corporation has invested less in employees, and employees have invested less in the firm.

Unfortunately, many have become increasingly disconnected from the employer organization, and from one another—shifting instead to an "each for himself/herself" view. The recent (2011-13) experiences of the *Occupy Wall Street* movement I think demonstrate the point. Protesters in both America and around the world clearly tapped into a latent unhappiness (even anger) over growing economic disparity. Still, protesters often seemed to lack organization and focus, and a substantive power base from which to operate.

What united participants was their protest of the status quo—and at times little else. But the forces of the global meritocracy will eventually coalesce, and press the established powers—those that support and protect the top 1 percent in America and elsewhere.

Again, I'm not attacking wealth per se. In the meritocracy, enormous inequalities will remain. A meritocracy is not a socialist system; meritocracy rewards those who perform best with wealth and success.

And, hopefully, we will become better at distinguishing between those who have earned their success (for instance, value-creating entrepreneurs like Apple Computer founder Steve Jobs) from those who have not (but who are enjoying a 1-percent lifestyle based on position and role).

CHANGE IN THE WORKPLACE

Much has been said about the multiple generations in the workforce today. This is a new and decidedly different environment, but one we will have with us now for good—as individuals remain engaged with work through much longer lives, and as younger individuals become more important to organizations earlier in their careers. In the United States today, there are four generations working simultaneously (including the Silent generation, Baby Boomers, Generation X, and the Millennials [Y]). The titles and labels and time brackets (simply stereotypes) are less critical than are the larger concepts. What's important is the handoff of power occurring between these generations. Management and ownership is today transitioning away from the Silent and Baby Boomer groups, and to the new X and Y generations, who view work much differently. Painting with the broadest brush, today's younger folks desire a more balanced life, with work important but not the only important thing. Many Gen X and Millennial workers are impatient with career development—less willing (it seems) to invest in the longer term, or to commit to a specific organization (as their parents did). Instead, these folks want to do important stuff today, to be involved and participate, and even to lead—right now.

This is a particularly important point for how companies must rethink work and organization, to take advantage of and utilize these new workers. Today, innovative companies are creating much flatter, decentralized, and *democratically* focused environments where all staff are more equal and participative. To be sure, this sort of thinking doesn't automatically resonate with Baby Boomers (me included), who can view these changes with cynicism. Still, a number of firms are now moving rapidly to embrace new democratic models that not only work better for staff, but also provide new competitive advantages in the global, meritocratic marketplace.

"Democracy" often connotes politics—pundits, mindless campaigning, partisan gridlock. But the principles of democracy extend far beyond politics, to more generally describe how humans interact with one another in all facets of life (including work).

At work, organizational democracy considers a system based on *freedom*, rather than on fear and control. It's a way of designing an organization to amplify the possibility of human potential—and the organization as a whole.

One organization devoted to the development of democracy in the workplace is Worldblu (www.worldblu.com). WorldBlu is a global network of firms whose collective purpose is to "unleash human potential and inspire freedom by championing the growth of democratic organizations worldwide." Worldblu's vision is to enable business leaders to design, develop, and lead the most successful democratic organizations around the world, with a goal of 1 billion people working in free and democratic workplaces.[22]

Worldblu founder Traci Fenton argues that the command and control management models of the industrial age don't fit well with our future, and that this democratic organization is better suited to the challenges and opportunities ahead. Tracy says that leaders' reluctance to change stems from (1) ego (letting go of power and the limelight), (2) ignorance (of what organizational democracy is and entails), and/or (3) fear (of what will happen or won't). So, Worldblu asks leaders to consider the question, "What would we do if we were not afraid?"

Figure 8-4 outlines the 10 principles of organizational democracy most important in the view of Worldblu, those that must be implemented and supported by a successful, democratic organization.

FIGURE 8-4 THE WORLDBLU TEN PRINCIPLES OF ORGANIZATIONAL DEMOCRACY™

1	**Purpose and Vision**	A democratic organization is clear about why it exists (its purpose) and where it is headed and what it hopes to achieve (its vision). These act as its true North, offering guidance and discipline to the organization's direction.
2	**Transparency**	Say goodbye to the "secret society" mentality. Democratic organizations are transparent and open with employees about the financial health, strategy, and agenda of the organization.
3	**Dialogue + Listening**	Instead of the top-down monologue or dysfunctional silence that characterizes most workplaces, democratic organizations are committed to having conversations that bring out new levels of meaning and connection.
4	**Fairness + Dignity**	Democratic organizations are committed to fairness and dignity, not treating some people like "somebodies" and other people like "nobodies."
5	**Accountability**	Democratic organizations point fingers, not in a blaming way but in a liberating way. They are crystal clear about who is accountable to whom and for what.
6	**Individual + Collective**	In democratic organizations, the individual is just as important as the whole, meaning employees are valued for their individual contribution as well as for what they do to help achieve the collective goals of the organization.
7	**Choice**	Democratic organizations thrive on giving employees meaningful choices.
8	**Integrity**	Integrity is the name of the game, and democratic companies have a lot of it. They understand that freedom takes discipline and also doing what is morally and ethically right.
9	**Decentralization**	Democratic organizations make sure power is appropriately shared and distributed among people throughout the organization.
10	**Reflection + Evaluation**	Democratic organizations are committed to continuous feedback and development and are willing to learn from the past and apply lessons to improve the future.

Source: WorldBlu, at http://www.worldblu.com

In practical terms, Worldblu argues that organizational democracy is about focusing on the business in a participative and collaborative way, with decentralized networks of individuals sharing control, leadership, and strategy. This approach supports the goals of business: creating profits and wealth, meaningful work, and talented and satisfied employees. Some democratic companies focus today well beyond the basic business metrics, on what the organization calls the "quadruple bottom line" of financial, community, external environment, and internal environment.

WE ARE HUMAN

To be sure, it's not *idealism* that I'm suggesting here, an expectation that the Fast Future will be a purely egalitarian society.

What I see instead is the brute and brutal force of competition, economic opportunity, and global expediency, pressuring the status quo infrastructure in favor of something more diverse, globally connected, and productive. Peoples around the world will coalesce around new ideas and goals—and less so in tribes based solely on race, ethnicity, or national origin. Of course, this transformation won't be smooth (how can it be, given the significant disagreement, strife, and warfare present today?). No, the change will be messy, interrupted, and nonlinear—and, as always, the Fast Future world will see both winners and losers.

Those with legacy control will struggle, and some will fall. Those who haven't enjoyed the fruits of success (but who possess key resources—people, education, raw materials) will in some cases rise and win. In general, our world will benefit from this global change, diversity, collaboration, and interconnectedness. (Now that does sound idealistic!)

Against this backdrop, perhaps we should also consider some basic thoughts on human nature. First, we shouldn't apologize for what is natural. Social scientists call it *homophily*—our basic instinct and desire to affiliate with others like us (that is race, ethnicity, nation, gender). This is a part of our nature, our desire to congregate, socialize, interact, collaborate, trust, and love those with whom we most closely relate. Historically, this has defined our tribal identities. When other forces (for example, authoritarian government) are removed, these tribal instincts quickly reemerge. We've seen a great deal of this around the world in recent years—in the Balkans, Afghanistan, Iraq, Syria, and Arab North Africa. It's the rise or resurgence of tribalism and ethnic strife in place of dictatorship.

Second, most humans are *provincial*—that is, locally focused and centered. We tend to place ourselves and our environment at the center of the picture, and we overestimate our relative importance in global affairs. We know less about other peoples, other places, and other ways. We're often blinded to economic opportunity in a global world because it's outside of our focus and comfort zone.

Third, as humans, we all have *prejudices*, though often these are inaccurate, anachronistic, or even irrational. But keep in mind that prejudice, too, is a part of our human nature, our mechanisms for *pre-judging* others and our surroundings, and helping to make sense of an environment of overwhelming complexity. What's needed is to fine-tune our mechanisms through higher self-awareness, constant (and more objective) testing, continual learning and unlearning. Of course, it's not true (for example) that a person with a different skin color is intrinsically more dangerous or less educated (and even when these factors are correlated, they're not causal). The same is true of a prejudice against a professional who speaks a different native language. Sure, many non-native speakers have difficulty in communicating in new settings (wouldn't you?). But to dismiss all prospective candidates from a region simply because of this difference is damagingly short-sighted, and misses understanding the fundamental opportunities and benefits of a diverse team, organization, and society.

SO WHAT?

There are many questions—and many angles—to consider in looking at the relevance and importance of growing diversity, and the rising meritocracy, in our business and life. Here are a few:

- ▶ How is rising diversity in our local and regional population changing our business? Our industry? Our clients' business and industry?
- ▶ What opportunities do we see, or may be emerging today, relative to new diversity—new projects, new products and services, new markets?
- ▶ What new threats do we see, or are emerging today, relative to new diversity—changes in our business landscape, new products and services, new competitors?
- ▶ What are we doing now in our organization to increase the diversity of our staff and team?
- ▶ What perspectives, paradigms, and prejudices do we have today that might be holding our company and/or industry back?
- ▶ Does it make sense for us to focus more of our US-based business on the rapidly growing Hispanic community? Why? How?
- ▶ Does it make sense for us to focus more of our US-based business on international markets and opportunities? On international talent?
- ▶ How can we make our organization and our company more democratic—more collaborative, more participative, more engaging—for our entire staff?

Longevity, Healthy Living, and the Bio-Century

PEOPLE ALL AROUND THE GLOBE WILL LIVE HEALTHIER AND LONGER LIVES.

"I don't want to achieve immortality through my work. I want to achieve it through not dying."
—Woody Allen

A LONGER LIFE

View the arc of human progress over the last century and it's clear that peoples all around the globe are living longer (and for the most part) healthier lives. Of course, there are plenty of issues that remain, problems today in the business of life and living. And true, many of the challenges of health, economics, politics, and society won't resolve quickly or easily.

Nevertheless, the trend toward longer and healthier life—born primarily of advances in science and medicine, along with (though it doesn't always seem so) a reduction in the scale of world violence—holds great promise for the future.

Data collected over the last 50 years demonstrates this increasing longevity in virtually all countries. Total life expectancy (as measured at birth) is rising virtually everywhere.[1] Figure 9-1 provides comparative data from several nations for 2012. Average life expectancy does very considerably with region and country. Nations with the longest expectancy include Japan (83.9 years), Australia (81.9), Italy (81.9), Canada (81.5), and France (81.5).

FIGURE 9-1. LIFE EXPECTANCY FROM BIRTH, SELECTED COUNTRIES

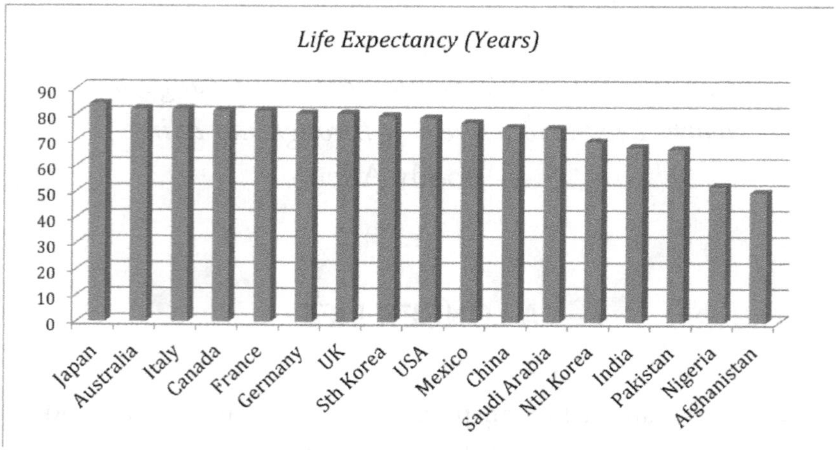

Source: Central Intelligence Agency, World Factbook 2012.

The United States now enjoys an average life expectancy of 78.5 years (number 51 in the world). And while the nations of the developed world dominate the top 50 spots, a number of countries in the developing world—including Mexico (76.7), China (74.8), Brazil (72.8), India (67.1), and Pakistan (66.3)—also expect relatively long life (and a significant increase in recent decades). There are also some aberrations in the trend lines—notably in Russia, where life expectancy today is 66.2 years, a decline from the 68.1 years measured in 1970. Another trend buster is Nigeria, which (like much of sub-Saharan Africa) has grown rapidly over the last 50 years in total population, but with only modest gain in life expectancy, to a current figure of 52 years. A few nations have lost ground, including North Korea (64.1) and Haiti (62.5), due in large part to their political and economic isolation.

As Figure 9-2 suggests, country by country, the data is varied, but overall the trend is clear: People virtually everywhere are living longer lives.[2]

FIGURE 9-2. TRENDS IN LIFE EXPECTANCY FROM BIRTH, SELECTED COUNTRIES

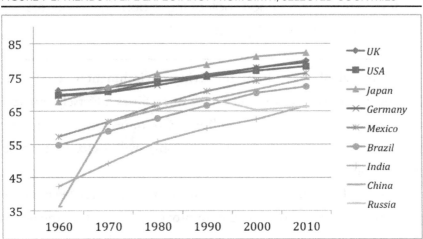

Source: United Nations, World Population Prospects, Department of Economic and Social Affairs, Population Division

Though the future isn't given, it's likely that life expectancy will continue to rise most everywhere. Over the next several decades, this may result in the lengthening of life by an additional 5 to 10 years. Or perhaps, as the Singularitarians suggest, this uber-trend in expectancy will accelerate much more rapidly, and significantly lengthen the lives of some—ever closer toward the promise of functional immortality by mid-century.

LONGER, AND HEALTHIER TOO

There are many basic and significant health issues in the world today.

According to the World Health Organization (WHO), more than one-third of the world's population—about 2.5 billion people—still lack access to basic, improved sanitation facilities.[3] And nearly half of these don't have access to a proper toilet facility of any kind.

Removal of waste from the living environment is crucial to improving human health, and a lack of facilities adversely impacts those still managing in this condition. Continued increases in the population (numbers and concentrations) will exacerbate these negative health factors.

The WHO does report that steady progress has been made (and, in fact, is ahead of schedule) in providing clean drinking water to communities around the world. Having set a 2015 objective to reduce by 50 percent the number of those without access to sustainable safe drinking water, this goal was achieved by 2010. Nevertheless, as of 2010, more than 780 million people still relied on unimproved sources for basic drinking water needs. So, progress—yes, but there is still a great deal to do in providing the basic necessities of drinking water and proper sanitation for all.

The World Health Organization also reports significant action toward reducing global child mortality, though achieving targets in this area are behind schedule.[4] In 2010, 7.6 million children under the age of 5 died (that's nearly 21,000 each day, almost 900 each hour). Improvement in reducing child mortality is geographically uneven, with some regions advancing quickly, and others much more slowly. In fact, 70 percent of the under-5 deaths in 2010 occurred in just 15 countries, and about 50 percent of the total occurred in just five nations (India, Nigeria, Democratic Republic of the Congo, Pakistan, and China).

Over half (58 percent) of these underage deaths are caused by infectious diseases, chiefly pneumonia, diarrhea, and malaria. A majority of these child deaths are completely preventable. (One wonders just how many of these lost young people would have played a significant role in our future.)

HIV/AIDS continues to menace some regions, particularly in Africa and Asia. In 2010 some 34 million people were living with the HIV infection, and in that year 1.8 million people died of AIDS-related illnesses worldwide.[5] (Since the beginning of the epidemic, more than 30 million people have died of AIDS.) Today, Africa remains the most affected continent, with 1.9 million new cases reported in 2010 (70 percent of the total 2.7 million new cases reported worldwide). A great deal of progress has occurred in both treatment (continued advances in drug therapies and in reducing their costs) and prevention. One hundred nineteen nations now report ongoing testing for the virus, with 95 million people tested in 2010. However, progress in fighting back the HIV/AIDS epidemic has been inconsistent, and almost everywhere too slow.

In analyzing global health information, it's clear that population health is often closely tied to an area's prosperity and wealth (much more so than to a lack of progress in science or medicine).

> The strongest forces buffeting healthy living in society are usually a lack of *financial* resources, along with (at times) a lack of *political* will and commitment.

For example, look at the differences in development in North and South Korea (Figure 9-3), separated since conflict on the Korean peninsula ended in 1953.[6] For the first 20 years or so afterward, both of the Koreas grew and developed, with life expectancy increasing in each nation. However, by about 1980, the great divergence in the economic fortunes of each became evident, and reflected in the life expectancy of citizens. South Korea became an "Asian Tiger," with rapid advancement in wealth and living standards. North Korea slipped back, increasingly isolated politically and economically, and with significant impact on the health impact of the people of the North.

FIGURE 9-3. LIFE EXPECTANCY TRENDS IN THE TWO KOREAS

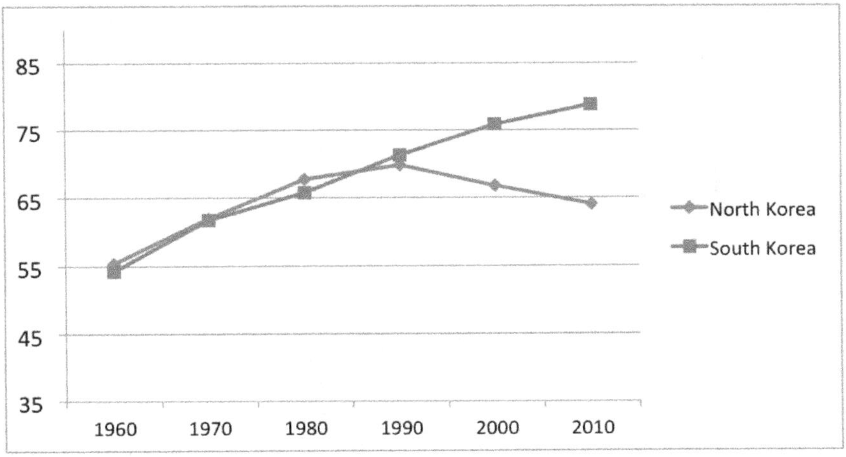

Source: United Nations, World Population Prospects, Department of Economic and Social Affairs, Population Division

Comparing the distribution of wealth worldwide with the average weight of children provides a similar insight on this correlation between financial resources and health. In much of the developing world, a primary challenge is the scarcity of food, resulting in the malnutrition of children. Increasingly, in the developed world it's just the opposite: too much food, and the concomitant rise of obesity and related concerns. The difference in experiences of the regions is striking, as shown in the Figures 9-4 and 9-5 data on underweight child population percentages around the world.[7]

FIGURE 9-4. PERCENT OF CHILD (UNDER FIVE) POPULATION UNDERWEIGHT, SELECTED COUNTRIES

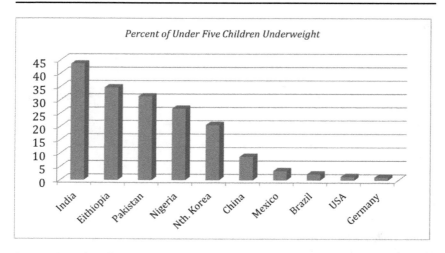

Source: Central Intelligence Agency, World FactBook, 2012

FIGURE 9-5. COMPARING PERCENT UNDERWEIGHT CHILDREN WITH OVERALL OBESITY, SELECTED COUNTRIES

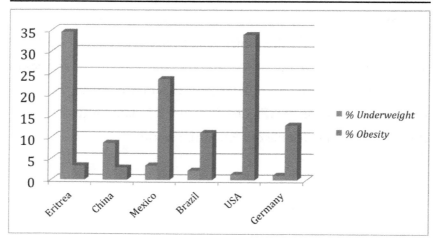

Source: Central Intelligence Agency, World FactBook, 2012

Finally, youth unemployment is another area of concern—and often related to health and social well-being. Across the world today, too many young people can't find stable, steady, and meaningful work. The global recession of 2008 exacerbated the issue everywhere. In many countries, the level of youth unemployment (ages 15 to 24) is alarmingly high—today nearly 50 percent in Armenia, South Africa, Bosnia, Serbia, and in the West Bank of Palestine.[8] In the European Union, youth unemployment ranges (by country) at 18–27 percent. And in North America, unemployment of young people stood at 17.6 percent in the United States (2009); 14.8 percent in Canada (2010); and 9.5 percent in Mexico (2010). Lack of opportunity for youth is unhealthy, a contributor to the disappointment, frustration, and anger that has boiled over in the unrest of the Arab Spring, backlash to European Union austerity, and the various "Occupy" movements in cities around the United States and the globe. Again, it's a lack of economic resources, and/or the sharing of these resources, that has negatively impacted the health of individuals and our society.

Over the long run, longevity and healthier lives is a clear uber-trend, with obvious benefits (and some related challenges) for the world. But in the short term, the path forward will most likely be neither smooth nor straight.

21ST—THE CENTURY OF BIOLOGY

There is so much going on, so much happening in the world of technology, biotechnology, and medicine that many futurists believe that the 21st will be the century of biology—and in particular *synthetic biology*.

Randall Mayes, technology trend analyst and author of *Revolutions: Paving the Way for the Bio Economy* (2012), puts it this way:

> Biology + Engineering = Synthetic Biology. As biology becomes a true engineering discipline, bioengineers will create genomes using mass-produced molecular units similar to the microelectronics and computer industries. [9]

In Mayes's view, our current focus on genomics—the study of genetics, genomes, and the synthetic manufacture of new DNA parts—promises to radically reshape much of our business and life (manufacturing, sustainability, health care) in the not-too-distant future. Indeed, there are significant challenges remaining—the complexity of natural biological systems, and the need for a lot more computing power are two of the most important. Still, biotech developments will soon bring forth enormous potential benefit to our society (along with some real and substantive threats). Mayes sees progress ahead in areas that include avian flu vaccines, new malarial drugs and treatments, 3-D printing of human tissues and organs, new solutions in bio-fuels and bio-plastics, developments (and threats) in bio-weaponry, and new advances in bioremediation. Not everyone is, of course, excited about all of this acceleration in the biotechnology arena. In fact, many concerned activists are working to slow or stop research and development in these markets. Public discourse is divided on the subject; again, there are both important pros and cons to consider.

Nevertheless, it's likely that development will continue with astonishing speed and acceleration—with business, governments, society—and all of us—together struggling to keep up.

Futurist Bertalan Mesko follows technological and social development in the field of medicine, and sees many significant transformations either already here, nearing fruition, or not far off in the distance.[10] Mesko notes that today, for instance, we *already have* new online information systems that are curating correct and reliable medical information and records, rising digital literacy in medical education, virtual dissection, digestible and wearable (smart watch) medical sensors, personalized genomics, real-time operating room diagnostics, medical robots, telemedicine, virtual research trials, and artificial intelligence (computer support) in medical decisions.

Developing technologies *in-progress* include microchips with onboard human cells in clinical trials, DIY biotechnology, embedded sensors, medical tricorders (like Star Trek), semantic (continuously improving) health records, augmented reality (Google Glass), robotic nurses, wearable sensor skins, 3-D printed biomaterials and drugs, artificial organs, adherence control (rewards and consequences for therapy follow-through), evidence-based mobile health, and much more meaningful use of social media (digital brain). Technologies *on the horizon* but not quite here yet include gamification-based wellness, holographic data input, multifunctional radiology, remote touch, humanoid robots, blood-borne nanobots, redesigned hospital experiences, virtual reality applications, functional cyborgs (machine-augmented humans), and even virtual or digital brains (also postulated by Ray Kurzweil in *The Singularity Is Near*).

Mesko offers his own prescription of sorts—how to prepare for the future of medicine (as both medical professionals and patients), suggesting that parties work to (1) follow the main trends and keep up with the technological discussion; (2) remain vigilant for new solutions that improve business and practice; (3) embrace digital technologies more comfortably, and use them to make life and work easier and more efficient; (4) watch trends outside of the medical field as well; (5) beware of the hype and remember that digital solutions will require considerable evidence and data; (6) work to influence decision-makers, spreading the word via social media for solutions that make sense; and (7) remember that, ultimately, a significant part of successful medicine is the human touch provided in the doctor–patient relationship.

LONGER AND HEALTHIER LIVES— SO WHAT DOES IT MEAN?

One implication of longer and healthier life is obvious: There simply will be more of us, and a lot more of us will be older.

In developed countries, growth in the older age segment will be the only growth seen (with new births at an all-time low). In contrast, in most rapidly developing nations, this increase in longevity will affect the population more modestly, while a very high natural birth rate will dominate population demographics, and result in a much younger society overall (and with a likely loss of institutional and cultural knowledge, memory, and wisdom). Taken together, these developments suggest a divergence of experiences in the developed and developing world, and a growing importance overall of the developing countries.

Older citizens have different objectives and priorities, and will, of course, want and need different products, services, and activities. An aging population will demand more of the health-care system, and continue to drive health-care-related spending. In the United States, this will increase the need and value of health-care management and reform. Technological development will also continue—at a breakneck pace—and will deliver important solutions to challenging health issues, but will bring new problems along as well (affordability, long-term care, bio-ethics, etc.).

Beyond its direct impact on health, increasing life expectancy will affect other areas of life. Education is an example. In fact, it's likely that our basic paradigm of education will evolve substantially in just a few years. We've long utilized a model that focuses on learning in the first 15 or 20 years of life. This made more sense when we lived for 40 or 50 years total. One spent roughly the first half of life learning how to do something, and the second half doing it. But now, with many living longer, healthier lives to 70, 80, or 90 years of age (and soon even longer), it makes sense to reevaluate. Why stop learning, and the learning process, in your mid-20s? Given the rapidly changing character of virtually everything around us, continued lifelong learning seems necessary and important. On the road ahead, we'll see many new developments in ongoing, continuous, lifelong education, with education more seamlessly integrated into everyday life. In many countries, our older populations are already demonstrating this, enjoying lifestyles of physical effort, sports, hobbies, travel, and continued education much more so than the generation before. In the Fast Future, this will accelerate as older citizens pursue a more blended mix of leisure, work, community involvement, and education.

Another issue related to the aging of the world is a growing, structural, and probably *permanent unemployment* in the developed world. In some sectors of our economy, there are simply fewer jobs available, along with many older folks who'd like to continue working. These trends cut to the heart of a question of expectations. Specifically, is "meaningful employment" a *right* that all citizens are entitled to, as many do believe? If so, what will we do with a system that doesn't "need" all of its citizens to be working? Significant change is on the way.

In the United States, this situation began in the 1970s and 1980s, as old-line industrial sectors (textiles, steel, automotive, agriculture) proved increasingly uncompetitive on the global stage. Factory shutdowns became familiar around the country, though concentrated in the industrialized north. This led to a new kind of long-term, structural unemployment. There were few jobs for former factory workers, but the damage was limited then primarily to the blue-collar workforce. Then, in the 1990s and 2000s, this structural unemployment broadened into the ranks of white-collar professionals as well, as computing power, information technology, and accelerating globalization rapidly shifted much of the environment of business around the world. Today, these forces are accelerating, and we'll experience big changes in the employment (and unemployment) of many market segments, perhaps affecting most those who are experienced, higher paid, and older. As people live longer, some will find it difficult to remain engaged in the work economy, with implications both short-term and far-reaching in our society.

Longer and healthier lives—nearly everywhere. Some developed regions will obviously age, but very high birth rates in the developing world will leave these areas younger overall. Those who enjoy the growth of their "gray hair" population will also likely struggle to keep these folks engaged and involved. Will long-lived individuals engender the respect, admiration, and esteem that has been historically bestowed on the wise, or will these older generations be viewed as a cost, and an unfortunate drag, on a much younger global population? It's hard to say, but it's clear that in the Fast Future there will be a lot of older folks around, as peoples all around the world enjoy longer and healthier lives.

SO WHAT?

Again, while trends in longevity, healthy living, and the rapidly developing century of biotechnology are clearly important and likely transformative to our world—that doesn't mean it's necessarily easy to connect the dots between this future tomorrow and our response today. Nevertheless, we must continue to ask relevant, pertinent, and challenging questions such as these:

▶ What are the implications of people living longer (even much longer) on our existing markets?

▶ How will important increases in longevity affect our clients' businesses and industries?

▶ How might longer and healthier living affect our current staff, and the pool of prospective employees we'll face in the future?

▶ What products and services are likely to increase in demand? Which will have lesser demand, or even become obsolete in the future?

▶ What must we do now to position our company for these changes ahead?

► How will changes in development and health, health care, and medicine affect our business—markets, products and services, geographies and customers served?

► Having more, older citizens around will likely change the balance of many issues in our society. What potential threats can we expect from these developments? What opportunities are likely to emerge? What should we do now to prepare for either (or both)?

10

Climate Change, Environmentalism, and Energy

**ALTERNATIVE ENERGY AND THE ENVIRONMENT WILL
RISE—BUT PETROLEUM WILL STILL BE KING.**

*"I don't know much about climate change. But
I'm pretty sure we better figure out what to do to
lessen its impact—at least its health impact—
and that's not going to happen unless you have a
lot of young talent interested in these topics."*
—Paul Farmer

CLIMATE CHANGE—WHAT'S THE REAL DEBATE?

The ongoing discussion over climate change and global warming is a familiar one—and the battle lines are clearly drawn today. Perhaps, like many, you've already made up your mind and you'll be difficult to convince. That's okay—I get it. Still, I think it's helpful to step back and consider not just *what* you believe, but *why* you believe it. Many of us locked in to a position on this subject early on, and we haven't paid close attention to the discussion since. Perhaps it's time for a reassessment.

When the issue of global warming first appeared, I was a geologist at Exxon, one of the world's largest oil companies. Big Oil (and Exxon, in particular) took an aggressive stance against global warming and its obvious threat to the petroleum industry. Changing minds in the petroleum industry has progressed only slowly over the last 20 to 30 years. Despite the fact that oil companies are generally comprised of scientists and engineers who appreciate data and deliberate, evidence-based theory, it's been extraordinarily difficult to shift away from the entrenched fortifications. Still, many in the industry, and in the business world over all, have come around to look more objectively at the potential threats—and the opportunities—of global warming, sea level rise, and climate change today.

Frankly, it is hard to parse the rhetoric, and to separate the reality of climate change from all of the garbage tossed around on either side. Fundamentally, it seems to me that measuring absolute temperature around the world (land, air, and sea) would yield reasonable, objective, and absolute data. Based on this data, it seems that indeed the Earth is warming. More complicated then is the question of our *involvement* in this trend—whether human activity and industry is ultimately to blame—in whole or in part—for the rising heat. Then, third is the question of *action*—whether or not humans can (through changing their habits) reverse these climate effects, and if so, how urgent the situation really is—how fast we must act. The answers to these last two questions are less clear to me, though certainly each seems worth asking.

Overall, my perspective is summed up well by the following parable, written by Thomas A. Moore, PhD, Director of the Center for Bioenergy & Photosynthesis at Arizona State University (Dr. Moore credits the original story to a comment offered by Arnold Schwarzenegger to author Tom Friedman)[1]:

COMPARING CLIMATE CHANGE TO YOUR SICK CHILD

A parent with an apparently healthy child takes the child to the doctor for annual checkup. The doctor consults with the parent after the checkup and, looking worried, explains that the child has unusual levels of CO2 in blood, nitrogen in urine, maybe a low-grade fever, and a remarkable lack of diversity in the intestinal microorganisms so necessary for metabolism and essential micro-nutrients. The doctor goes on to say that the laboratory measurements were so unusual they repeated all of the measurements on fresh samples of blood, urine, and stool. Same results. The doctor says she has never seen anything like this in many years of practice.

The doctor says she doesn't know exactly what this means, since it has never been seen before, and notes these measured levels are consistent with certain of the child's activities. The doctor strongly recommends immediate steps be taken to lower the levels and reestablish biodiversity.

The parent says. "My child appears healthy. I'm getting a second opinion." The parent does that and in the end takes the child to 100 doctors and 100 different labs do the workup. All the measurements come out the same.

Ninety-nine of the doctors recommend immediate action to lower the levels, even though they do not know exactly what would be the consequences of doing nothing.

One of the doctors looks at the same measurements and says is could be a natural part of growing up for this particular child and recommends waiting to see if something bad happens.

Now, suppose you're the parent. What would you do?

As with many other important debates in our society today, there are visible, distracting, and irrational perspectives on both the left and right. Climate change deniers have irrationally dismissed a great deal of scientific work and information, and instead have gravitated (apparently) toward an anti-capitalism-driven conspiracy theory. On the other side, those positioned aggressively against business and industry interests, capitalism in general, and the differential wealth and success of some, see the climate change dilemma as a weapon for their own agenda.

But it's time now for both progressive and conservative leaning leaders to reject all of these outlandish arguments, and instead to look more objectively at both their own perspectives and beliefs, and at the opportunities and threats of the future ahead. Many business, industry, and government organizations are today doing just that. And it may just be that our future depends on it.

A QUICK LOOK AT ENERGY

In the interest of transparency—a confession: when it comes to energy and environmental matters, I'm opinionated, and far from unbiased.

I studied biology and geology in college, and worked as a petroleum geologist for many years at Big Oil. I then spent several years managing that company's environmental clean-up efforts across about half of the United States—dealing with myriad environmental, regulatory, legal, and other outside interests. And I was born and raised in Texas, in the center (at least we thought) of the global petroleum economy. So, admittedly, I'm far from objective.

Even beyond Texas, it's easy to see that *energy is huge*. Energy is big business, and it's important in the businesses and lives of all of us. Energy has always been a crucial commodity for humanity—and right from the beginning, as suggested by Figure 10-1. And as with other Fast Future trends, the importance of energy is growing and accelerating.

FIGURE 10-1. THE HISTORY OF PRIMARY ENERGY SOURCES

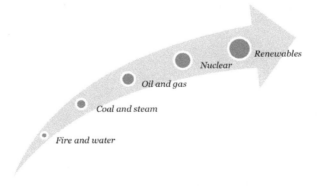

Renewables

Nuclear

Oil and gas

Coal and steam

Fire and water

Energy is one of our economy's largest and strongest sectors, both in the United States and globally. Moreover, the business of energy (particularly that of the fossil fuels of oil, gas, and coal) has been remarkably robust, with sustained economic growth and profit for more than 100 years.

The global energy sector is largely controlled by some of the world's largest organizations—either multinational corporations or governments—with considerable bank accounts (and vested interests) in both energy's present and future. The energy industry will, of course, continue to change and evolve, but it's also likely to remain strong, powerful, and critically important in the Fast Future ahead.

Domestically, Americans use a variety of energy sources for needs both commercial and personal. Leading the list of sources are the petroleum products of oil and natural gas, followed (in order) by coal, nuclear electric power, and various renewable energy sources (hydropower, wood, biofuels, biomass waste, wind, geothermal, and solar).[2] (Electricity is not a primary source of energy, but a secondary source that is generated from one of these primary forms.)

Here's the breakdown for US energy sources as reported by the US Energy Information Administration (EIA):

FIGURE 10-2. US ENERGY CONSUMPTION BY ENERGY SOURCE, 2011

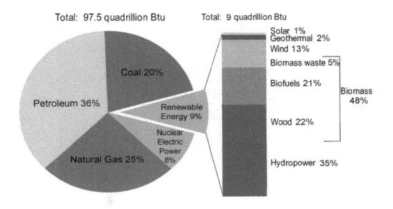

Source: U.S. Energy Information Administration, Monthly Energy Review, March 2012

Each of these sources of energy is distributed over a variety of uses, with each employed differently in various applications. Figure 10-3 further details the relationships. Note, for example, that about 71 percent of all petroleum (oil) energy is consumed in the transportation sector, while 93 percent of the energy of transportation comes from petroleum oil. Similarly, while 91 percent of coal is utilized in the making of electric power, that coal represents just 46 percent of the total energy input used in the production of electricity. (In other words, almost all coal makes electricity, but less than half of electricity comes from coal.)[3]

As the data shows, most of our oil is used in either transportation or industrial applications, while most coal is targeted for electric power generation. All of the US nuclear power is used for electricity. But other energy sources, including natural gas and renewables, are more broadly distributed to various economic uses.

FIGURE 10-3. PRIMARY ENERGY CONSUMPTION BY SOURCE AND SECTOR, 2011

(QUADRILLION BTU)

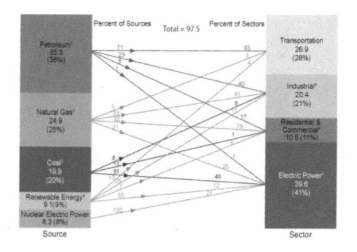

Endnotes:
1 Does not include biofuels that have been blended with petroleum—biofuels are included in "Renewable Energy."
2 Excludes supplemental gaseous fuels.
3 Includes less than 0.1 quadrillion Btu of coal coke net exports.
4 Conventional hydroelectric power, geothermal, solar/PV, wind, and biomass.
5 Includes industrial combined-heat-and-power (CHP) and industrial electricity-only plants.
6 Includes commercial combined-heat-and-power (CHP) and commercial electricity-only plants.
7 Electricity-only and combined-heat-and-power (CHP) plants whose primary business is to sell electricity, or
  electricity and heat, to the public. Includes 0.1 quadrillion Btu of electricity net imports not shown under "Source."

Note: Primary energy in the form that it is first accounted for in a statistical energy balance, before any
transformation to secondary or tertiary forms of energy (for example, coal is used to generate electricity).
• Sum of components may not equal total due to independent rounding.

Source: U.S. Energy Information Administration, Monthly Energy Review, April 2012.

Figure 10-4 highlights the changing trends in US energy consumption over the last 50-plus years.[4] Oil consumption has risen strongly through this period, with brief drops during the embargos of the 1970s and 1980s, and (importantly) during the latter half of the last decade (partly the result of a global recession and party due to a large shift toward natural gas). Coal use has also gained steadily during this period, most of it surfaced mined, and nearly all of it deployed for power generation. Coal consumption has dropped quickly in the last few years, a victim of cheaper and readily available natural gas for power plants.

Natural gas production is up strongly, and prices are down, and this trend is expected to continue. Renewable sources are gaining modestly, but their development is hindered by low gas prices. Nuclear energy has plateaued in the United States, and though it seemed poised for a rebirth prior to the Fukushima accident in Japan in 2011, it's not likely now to see appreciable growth in the coming years.

FIGURE 10-4. US PRIMARY ENERGY CONSUMPTION ESTIMATES BY SOURCE, 1950-2011 (QUADRILLION BTU)

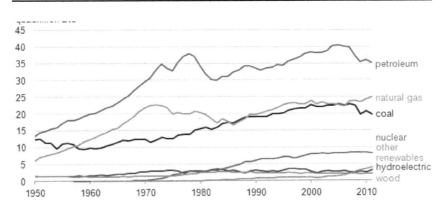

Source: U.S. Energy Information Administration, 2012.

Though energy production from the three major fossil fuels—petroleum, natural gas, and coal—has dominated the US energy mix for more than 100 years, the energy sector has seen continuous change. Some of the changes since 1949 (according to the EIA's *Energy Perspectives*) include these:[5]

- The share of coal produced from surface mines increased significantly: from 25 percent in 1949 to 51 percent in

1971, to 68 percent in 2011. The remaining share was produced from underground mines.

- In 2011, natural gas production exceeded coal production for the first time since 1981. More-efficient, cost-effective drilling techniques, notably in the production of natural gas from shale formations, led to increased natural gas production in recent years.
- Although total US crude oil production has generally decreased each year since it peaked in 1970, it increased by 3 percent in 2010 from 2009, and about 4 percent in 2011 from 2010. These increases were led by escalating horizontal drilling and hydraulic fracturing, notably in the North Dakota section of the Bakken formation.
- Natural gas plant liquids (NGPL), hydrocarbons separated as liquids from natural gas at processing plants, are important ingredients for manufacturing plastics and gasoline. Propane is the only NGPL that is widely used for heating and cooking. Production of NGPL fluctuates with natural gas production, but their share of total US petroleum field production increased from 8 percent in 1950 to 28 percent in 2011.
- In 2011, total renewable energy consumption and production reached all-time highs of 9 quadrillion BTU each, due mainly to relatively high hydroelectric power generation and continuing increases in biofuels use and wind power generation. In 2011, biofuels production was about nine times greater than in 2000, and wind generation was about 20 times greater than in 2000;

PETROLEUM IS (AND WILL BE) KING

Here's the bottom line on oil: Despite what some claim, and what many may desire, the world is not about to run out of petroleum. It's just not going to happen anytime soon.

There is a huge supply of oil in the world (proven reserve estimates from the US Energy Information Administration range from about 1 trillion to 4 trillion barrels), and even with rising consumption in developing countries, these reserves will power much of the world's needs for decades to come. Global economists disagree in predictions of the future point of *peak oil* (that moment at which half the world's oil resources will have been reached and exploited. After peak oil is reached, the total supply of oil will shrink, and supply will fall rapidly relative to demand, with consequent rise in price). While some believe that the peak oil inflection point has been already reached in the United States, estimates for *global* peak oil generally range from about 2020–2050. The US EIA predicts that peak oil could be reached as early as 2020, or as far out as 2121.[6] Historically, the world's geologists have been conservative, and have often underestimated (sometimes grossly) the world's total petroleum reserves.

Not only are there considerable oil reserves remaining, but also (as with other natural resource commodities) the amount of petroleum available is closely tied to its price. As the value of petroleum products rise, so does the amount of the resource available, and the effort some will be willing to risk to extract it. This is the nature of commodities. Scarcity increases value, and value reduces the scarcity. Higher prices (especially after the peak oil inflection point) will drive new technologies for extraction and other innovation in the global supply chain. We're not likely to run out of oil anytime soon.

Admittedly, a great deal of the world's oil resides in unstable geopolitical regions, and there is little guarantee of a continuous and uninterrupted supply. We'll most certainly see continued volatility of petroleum pricing tied to production uncertainty, and likely interruptions of various magnitudes and degrees. Because of this risk, politicians have spoken for the last half century or more about the need for energy independence. But, until recently, this was almost always empty rhetoric. Now, new US production of both oil and gas from domestic shale formations offers a real opportunity to achieve this goal—to reduce (or eliminate) US dependence on foreign oil supplies.

This new oil and gas production from domestic shale formations points out another reason why we won't run out of petroleum anytime soon—new technologies come through to extend reserves. Today, the technological advance is horizontal drilling through the shale formation, combined with hydraulic fracking (not a new technology per se but used in a new application here). These technological advancements have transformed industry economics, creating a new "boom" for exploration, development, and production. This evolution will undoubtedly continue.

All of this is not to argue that the use of petroleum products is necessarily good, or that extending the reserves of petroleum will ultimately be a net win. But it's just a reality that fossil fuels are more abundant than many think (or would like to believe). We won't run out, but we *may* build up the will to stop using so much petroleum as a fuel in favor of alternatives.

Today, I don't see enough courage to do so, but as evidence mounts on fossil-fuel-related climate effects—and (importantly) as economically legitimate alternatives (such as viable electric cars) do indeed emerge—we'll likely shift more to these alternative energy sources, leaving petroleum for the manufacture of other products that don't have ready alternatives (for instance, lubricants or plastics). Fundamentally, this must include a solution for both *transportation* (electric cars, though the electricity itself must also ultimately come from clean sources) and *power* (reducing the use of coal, through carbon byproduct elimination or sequestration).

RENEWABLES ON THE RISE

The history of alternative or renewable fuels has long been a rocky one—and this will continue.

Energy is a large chunk of the cost of many products and services, and capturing cheaper energy inputs is critically important to business and consumers. It's not that we're blind to the issues of fossil fuel use, it's just that most individuals and companies think and act first with their wallets, second with their ideologies.

Alternatives—like wind, hydroelectric, bio-fuels, and nuclear— have been up and down over the years, gaining or losing relative to petroleum (their economic viability often related directly to the price of oil). Some alternatives, such as solar, will benefit greatly from technological developments yet to occur, driving down costs much further. Others—including both solar and wind—will also benefit from scale as larger energy projects develop, and as a critical mass (tipping point) is achieved with both production and consumption.

Governments can and must play a role in developing these energy alternatives, though experience suggests that investments probably shouldn't be made in specific projects (betting on winners and losers in the marketplace), but instead in setting broad direction and policy through regulation and tax incentives. Of course, even this longer-range investment doesn't always work out well. Over the last several years, we've seen a steep decline in the fortunes of ethanol-based bio-fuels resulting from the end of government subsides. The US government strongly supported development of this industry, but with some unintended consequences. As use of fuel ethanol rose, so did the price of corn (its primary feedstock in the United States), with rising costs then rippling through corn, cattle, and other parts of the food chain. It doesn't make much sense to pay more for food, just so the corn can go into automobile fuel tanks. (Feed the people, not the cars!)

Wind energy production is growing rapidly, and will continue in areas where the wind blows. Wind energy requires capital infrastructure (by now everyone has seen those gigantic windmills in use today), and it takes a while to pay off these investments—especially when the price of natural gas is down. Wind is big business in the Plains states of the Midwest, and in some western US states where more environmentally focused citizens have pushed for alternatives. Recently, wind initiatives have been proposed in new environments, such as the Cape Wind project off the coast of Massachusetts in Nantucket Sound. Other much larger wind farms even farther offshore, out on the Atlantic shelf, have also been proposed, and are gaining some interest. Perhaps, someday, a considerable portion of our energy needs will be met by large wind farms at sea. One constraint relevant to both wind and solar (but important in all energy considerations) is the cost of *transportation* of electricity. There's a lot of wind at sea, and in the upper Midwest; and solar power across large sections of the southern United States (and across equatorial deserts worldwide)—but in most of these areas there are fewer people. Electricity can be generated in these regions effectively, but it then must be transported to the denser population centers for use. That's expensive.

A NEW BREED OF ENVIRONMENTALISM

Admittedly, I've grown up in an Industrial Age paradigm.

In this context, business (commerce) and the environment have always been at war—juxtaposed against one another. In the last century, one had to choose—either to be a capitalist or an environmentalist. But no overlap, no mixing.

This situation is changing, evolving today, though slowly. Our youth are coming of age in a new world order, one that will be more globally focused. Certainly the prospect of an Earth with 9 billion inhabitants will itself change the discussion. Young people are in tune with the goals of environmentalism, though they're also interested in capitalism and the promise of economic opportunity. This generation will more naturally blend objectives and ideals to create a new model of *economic environmentalism*. I don't think it will be easy—business and environmental objectives are often at loggerheads. But led by this new group, we'll all become increasingly more environmentally sensitive and focused. Part of our motive will be self-preservation—our own survival interests. With 9 billion neighbors, we'll need to rely on each other more to do the right thing, and to root out the bad actors in the global environment. Everyone will depend on protection of the Earth's resources and systems.

My background and work experience helped me to understand energy, but probably hindered my objectivity in dealing with the environment. Like other scientists (especially geologists), I've long been skeptical of man's ability to significantly change the Earth directly. Geologists learn that the Earth is old, robust, dynamic, and constantly changing (though slowly). Across this history, the Earth has experienced untold scores of up-and-down cycles in temperature, magnetic polarity reversal, ocean sea level, and such. Over the scale of geologic time, humans have played a very small, mostly insignificant role. That said, the evidence is certainly compelling that something is afoot. Well documented now, there's no question that global temperature is rising. The question is how much of this rise is attributable to human activity, and specifically to the production and consumption of fossil fuels. Much of the heating may simply be related to a natural normal warming cycle in the Earth (though the implications to humanity of warming are the same, regardless of cause). But today, the risk of global warming is simply too great for inaction. If we've caused or enhanced the rise of temperature with our CO^2 production, then we presumably can work to reverse (or mitigate) our impact, as well. In the Fast Future ahead, this will become *much more important*, and much more interesting, to all of us.

Environmental protection will increasingly be driven by economics—and will in some instances become big business itself. One client CEO—an owner-operator of an environmental consulting firm—likes to remind his staff that someday there will be big opportunity with "climate change." When pressed for specifics—"Hey Jim, what do you mean?"—he always says, "I don't know, but it's going to be big." Jim is right. The opportunities ahead, not so evident today, will be big, and will help to define a new trajectory for environmentalism in the Fast Future.

SO WHAT?

Here are a few suggested sample questions, from among the many that you and your organization should be considering today, with respect to climate change, environment, and energy:

- ▶ What is your position on the issue of climate change? How about your firm's position? What if you are wrong?
- ▶ What is the likely impact of climate change on your business and industry in the next few years? Over the longer term?
- ▶ What is the likely impact of climate change on your clients' business and industry in the next few years? Over the longer term?
- ▶ What is your organization doing today to address these issues and opportunities?
- ▶ How would your local (and regional) geography be affected by climate change—increasing storm frequency or magnitude, wider swings in seasonal temperature variations, sustained rising of sea level?
- ▶ How does the current situation in the energy sector affect your business? Are you involved in the fossil fuel energy markets (oil, natural gas, coal)? Should you be?

▶ Are there opportunities for your firm to become involved with renewable energy projects and markets (bio-fuels, wind, solar, hydrothermal)? If so, what's your next step?

▶ Does your firm see opportunities today to become more involved in environmental causes—to improve public relations, community involvement, and/or economic benefit?

▶ How could/would/will domestic energy independence impact your firm? Your industry? The economy in which you operate?

11

The New Look of Community

**CONNECTING TO NEW COMMUNITIES WILL BECOME MUCH
MORE VALUABLE AND MEANINGFUL EVERYWHERE.**

*"What should young people do with their lives
today? Many things, obviously. But the most daring
thing is to create stable communities in which
the terrible disease of loneliness can be cured."*
—Kurt Vonnegut, Jr.

THE NEW COMMUNITY

Do you see community as more important or less today than it
was 20 years ago? Fifty years ago? A century back?

For a long while now the common narrative concerning community has mostly been one of *loss*.

Over the last several generations, we've lost the nuclear family, the local church, and the hometown. Society has become more mobile, transient—even ephemeral. We're all on the move—prospecting for better opportunities, new challenges, a fresh start. And this isn't just an American story: people all around the globe are on the move (immigration policies notwithstanding) from rural farms to towns, towns to cities, cities to even bigger cities. And as people have migrated, we've indeed stretched and torn the fabric of our traditional structures of community—family, farm, town, church, school, company, club, and so on.

Still, this loss of community doesn't mean that human beings have lost their *aspiration* for *living in a community*. We're a gregarious, community-oriented species. We want to be together, to associate and interact with one another, to learn from and teach one another, and to live together in community. So the fact that we've lost our sense of place only means that in the Fast Future, humans will continually long for new communities in which to belong.

Many generations past, humans spread out on the land—first as nomads, and then as farmers. Subsistence living dictated an optimal density for the population. (Of course, it's still this way today in many rural and agricultural cultures.) Small local communities formed where individuals could connect, trade, and support one another. Straightforward.

But continued technological development (especially with the Industrial Revolution) increasingly decoupled the productivity of labor from the land and local area itself. Goods and services were made elsewhere, in factories sometimes far away. Long-distance trade exploded. Local communities fragmented.

Today, our rapidly changing and intensely interconnected world is once again witnessing a major disruption, further decoupling workers of the 21st-century global village. We're living far from our parents (who are themselves living longer), we have children in schools all over, we work for companies with global operations (and job opportunities and expectations everywhere), and we travel the world to see and experience it all (cheap and easy travel is both necessary and quite expected today). Some move about because they have to, others because they can. But we're all moving and mobile, and it's not easy to establish community connectivity (especially for those from faraway places, uncommon clans, cultures, nationalities, races).

So now, into this uber-mobile society comes the Internet, Web 2.0, and social media. A coincidence? I don't think so.

Again, though our 20th-century lifestyle made community engagement much more challenging, it didn't change our ultimate desire (and need) for interaction with others. Social media and other new forms of community are simply the latest 21st-century opportunities to find, connect, and join with one another.

And these new platforms will radically reshape everything again—how we do life together—in communities both local and global, on the farm and in town, and in the developed and the rapidly developing world.

There are all sorts of communities growing through social media (just about anything you can think of). Consider, for instance, games that involve thousands (or millions) of simultaneous players, cooking and recipe swapping clubs, model railroad enthusiasts, community gardening groups, sports fanatics—the list is truly endless. Bolstered by new platforms, and the wide availability of both information and connectivity, today common interest groups with very specific interests can much more easily find one another, regardless of where they're located, and they can connect and create powerful new forms of community. And there's nothing to prevent these groups from later collaborating on something else. One group might first share local gardening secrets, and then later mobilize for social activism. Or perhaps the opposite will occur; for example, a local community formed to support a political cause that then morphs into a support group for disadvantaged citizens.

EXAMPLE: FACEBOOK GETS OUT THE VOTE

A couple of summers ago I witnessed a new community in action in my (adopted) hometown, when a small group of highly concerned and motivated parents (mostly moms) took to Facebook to rally support for a local tax override proposition to fund the school budget. It worked, and the efforts of these few helped to raise awareness and understanding in just enough citizens for the proposition to pass (by just three votes in one of the three participating towns). It certainly wasn't a perfect or frictionless experience—amateur governance never is—but it was a powerful example of a small group of individuals coming together and changing the course of local government. These like-minded moms and dads faced a difficult challenge

in building community in traditional ways (door to door, local rallies). As
we've seen recently in examples the world over, there is immense power
(and implications for change) in the simple idea that those with similar
beliefs and interests can find and connect with each other relatively easily
today, and can then take action either with (or against) those possessing
traditional forms of power. Small actions, heady results.

Facebook is today the largest of these new social media communities. In just its first decade, Facebook reports more than 1 billion registered users, and more than half of these active daily users.[1] This makes Facebook about the same size as the world's two largest countries—India and China. (Just a few years back, Facebook was little more than an interesting but irrelevant information-sharing tool for college students. Who saw this coming, and coming this big and fast?) Today, worldwide Facebook members use the service to share information (including lots of photos; Facebook is the web's largest photo-sharing site by a factor of 10) about themselves and their interests.[2] Additionally, millions of Facebook "pages" (including a few by J. Doehring & Co.) share information and promote organizations, service providers, and brands. And there are thousands of specific interest topic groups (like the local school budget group for moms and dads in my town) who join to share and act. Of course, the service is certainly not without its problems and skeptics. There are important privacy concerns becoming more obvious each day, a growing abundance and annoyance of ads (as the company focuses more on commercial interests), and maybe a growing dissatisfaction with the need to constantly work on "curating" our own seemingly perfect life stories. There are many who don't see the value; that's okay (of course, it was like that at first with telephones too). Still, it does seem that the tide is turning fast. As more social media sites develop a global scale and reach, millions of users are joining in, and (like a crowd gathering down at the local park) they're increasingly figuring out what to do and talk about *after* they get there. The whole social media scene is one great big community experiment (one very large sandbox) where people come together and try new things, connecting, coalescing, and playing. There's more and more collaboration, and according to NYU communication professor Clay Shirky, the value of that collaboration is both rising and potentially astonishing—a mind-blowing global value.[3]

There are other social media sites enjoying tremendous growth and use, including LinkedIn and Twitter, and others like Google+ and Pinterest. Each purports to add something in approach, functionality, or focus to this rapidly developing community landscape. So it's Twitter for near constant information sharing, LinkedIn for business and career, Pinterest for visual collaborators. There are hundreds of different online forums (on Yahoo and elsewhere) that provide community around specific interests. (These aren't a particularly new idea—forums today are the chat rooms and BBS services of the past, and a staple of Internet connectivity. What's new is the popularity and proliferation of these communities.)

EXAMPLE: THIS WONDERFUL THING ABOUT DEMOCRACY

I belong to a number of online groups–on Yahoo, LinkedIn, Facebook, and others. One dynamic of these communities is that they are often considerably more egalitarian than traditional groups. Post and get a response. It matters less (than in the physical world) who and what you are. So it's easier here to interact with the towering technical gurus, famous writers and speakers, and corporate CEOs. Again it's not utopia, and some do act online with their same standoffish, aloof, and arrogant personalities,

but it's often more democratic here than in communities where power
structures are more visible. This suggests that online social communities
may be a good place to begin a conversation (and a relationship)—with
someone you'd like to get closer to.

Change and development of new communities is not limited (by a long shot) to online social media groups. Nearly all communities are being transformed. Higher education is an example, destined now for a complete overhaul. We've long believed that the value of education was unassailable—so much so that families (literally) mortgaged their futures to pay for college for the kids. But in recent years, continued escalation of costs has called this belief into question. Is it really worth it? Is it necessary? Are there any good (or even acceptable) alternatives? Now comes new opportunity, technology driven, to provide high-quality educational content online for mass consumption. Harvard and MIT partnered up in 2012 to create Edx, a joint venture to offer some of these universities popular courses in an online, not-for-credit format. Some 370,000 students from around the globe signed up for the first offerings. These courses, known now as MOOC (massive open, online courses) are rapidly gaining the attention of the nation's best universities, who are partnering with Edx, Coursera (with 1.7 million users), and others as quick as they can.[4] Frankly, it's not at all clear how colleges, universities, and other educational providers will adjust to this new dynamic—what the new business model for education will be. But it is clear that the situation is changing fast. In the Fast Future, most of us will learn through new online tools (high-quality holograms are reportedly not far off). Higher education will become readily available to millions more consumers, with the scale of it likely leading to much lower costs.

Religious communities are another example of rapid change. Today, we're in a period where many traditional denominations have fallen victim to internal division, infighting, and decline. At the same time, new faith communities continue to grow and thrive. How is it that both trends occur simultaneously? It's partly a story of life cycle—some communities are vibrant and alive, whereas others are dead or dying, no longer meeting the needs of their members. Some communities are new, fresh, and relevant—critically important in a world of increasing transparency and choice. And in the larger sense, the value of religious community per se is still apparent, so many continue to search for a meaningful connection.

WORK, WORKPLACE, AND COLLABORATION

Changes in community will also impact the *workplace* in a big way—particularly in (1) the disassociation of work from place, and (2) the rapidly rising class of talented, pseudo-professional amateurs.

Technology, information availability, and rapid globalization of virtually everything are together promulgating an all-new platform for accomplishing work, which will completely redefine both *how* work is done, and *where* it is accomplished. These changes aren't brand new: telecommuting has become almost passé as organizations downsize their physical plants and put workers out into temporary, shared space, or home offices. As online meeting software has improved and long-distance phone charges fallen fast, connecting and collaborating without a local physical connection has rapidly become the norm. This will continue.

Projecting this evolution forward leads eventually to other ideas we've discussed here—including a complete *disassociation* (or "atomization") of the supply chain, and the rising and important opportunity for very small firms.

In other words, once work is disassociated from workplace, it's much easier to consider a more drastic disconnection, so that the firm is producing less and less of its work in-house with its own permanent employees. (This is and will be particularly true for non-core business functions—and in the Fast Future much of the company's work will be considered non-core.) Talented individuals around the globe will compete for these new outsourcing opportunities, and this will lead to a large class of temporary employees, contractors, freelancers, and such.

Small and very small firms, located almost anywhere (and virtually everywhere), will connect together through technology, information, and globalization to accomplish in new ways the work of business.

What will this mean for human community? Clearly, we're in for change, and it won't all be easy. Of course, as technology continues to improve (some suggest we'll soon use super high-tech, virtual-reality systems), these new connections will more closely approximate true physical contact. And with a high degree of globalization, our communities will be much more unique, eclectic, and diverse. That's a good thing. On the other hand, the lack of physical connection (and physical proximity) will likely affect our communities in negative ways, as well. In the last half century or so, most of us spent a good deal of our adult time at work. And it's at the office where we often developed our self-identity, made close friends, and sometimes met and chose our spouse. True, even dating is done today more and more online. Still, it's hard not to expect that something will be lost as we evolve from a local, physical workplace community, to one completely disassociated, global, and completely virtual.

Amateurism, or pseudo-professionalism, is a more recent development that may prove astonishingly important in the years ahead. Again, it's the familiar forces of technology, information, and globalization driving this development and opportunity for millions.

These Fast Future forces are exposing the inner workings of many professions and businesses, and allowing others to see and learn how stuff is done. As a result, those outside of the traditional channels will proceed (and succeed) through initiative, talent, and perseverance—though often without the formal training, college degrees, or professional certifications so important in the past. Think today (for instance) about how technology has changed the world of the professional photographer or newspaper reporter. Virtually anyone with a smartphone can contribute. Not all of it will be good, but some of it will be excellent.

In its earliest form, the Internet served primarily to connect individuals to one another. The World Wide Web and Netscape browser improved the connection immensely, and unlocked a treasure of information for all. Many professions and businesses were constructed originally around the *control* of important information, and, in fact, most institutions of power in business, education, and government were built around control (and often obfuscation) of information, knowledge, and know-how. Today, most all of these are scrambling (or soon will be) to adjust to the new reality, to new competitive forces, and likely to significant transformation of their businesses and industry.

Fast on the heels of connection and information sharing, the Internet also provided a platform for *collaboration*. An obvious first step here was commerce—accomplished in a variety of ways, but perhaps most notably through eBay, which revolutionized the marketplace, creating a nearly global, one-to-one market bazaar. Today eBay, Amazon, and many other e-tailers continue to rapidly remake commerce in virtually all markets. In just a few short years, we'll probably look back with curiosity at our strange history that once involved "going to the store."

And so today we have connection, information sharing, and commerce – and additionally now many new forms of collaboration, including collaboration which creates new information-new types of content, technology, art. Admittedly, our early forms of new information are a mixed bag (and some are truly awful). Lowest on the value spectrum are things like YouTube's trolling comment posts. Pick a YouTube video and page through the comments added by others. In almost every case, this will lead to disgust (and even despair) over the human condition. Conversations devolve into the basest of instincts, and the nastiest, most hurtful opinions you'd believe possible. This is the result of ignorance, misunderstanding, and lack of empathy for others—along with (very importantly) the ability today to post comments *anonymously*. Still, the salient point is not the quality of these comments, but the sheer volume of the contribution. They're not worth much today, but imagine if they were—so many individuals, with their focused time and effort, invested in adding valuable information, perspectives, and opinion. If this were better realized, what would that mean?

A better and more valuable example is the customer feedback comments of services such as Yelp, Amazon.com, various travel sites, and (increasingly) many other individual retail sites. This feedback has become critically important for these providers, and in their online pages this input is *at least as important* as the information offered by the company. So customers are already collaborating with manufacturers and service providers to tell the story. Again, it isn't perfect, and I suspect the loudest voices (either pro or con) are really outliers to the real truth. Still, one can see the potential power and effectiveness of this collaboration.

Further up the value chain are the myriad special interest groups that gather to share information, provide resources, teach and learn, support one another, and create together community. Some of these are commercial in nature, and focused around popular brands like Amazon, Starbucks, BMW, or Nordstrom's. Some are thematic, such as the thousands of Internet forums on Yahoo and other sites, LinkedIn or Facebook groups, and such. YouTube has now become an important platform here, as well. (Pick a subject or problem, and you're likely to find a YouTube video explaining in full how to proceed, do it, and fix the problem—Google searches for answers in text are "so yesterday".) Again, there is an enormous amount of effort involved in this work, and some of it is quite valuable.

More on the "artsy" side are the millions of popular apps and games that people (mostly adults) use in increasing numbers. Some of these games—Angry Birds, Words with Friends, Candy Crush—enjoy millions of enthusiastic users. Others—Second Life and World of Warcraft—have thousands to millions of players interacting with one another in real time-and with lots of effort. Still other collaborative games—yes, even like LOLCats—allow contributors to create new content and then post and share it with others. Facebook,

Instagram, Pinterest, and others do the same, providing an opportunity for individuals to express themselves in new ways. Again, it isn't all great (or even good), but it is all *new*—and, thus, the potential for something much better exists and tantalizes.

This is the basic idea expounded by Clay Shirkey in his book *Cognitive Surplus*.[5] Shirkey argues that we are on a rapid learning curve, and that as collaborators use and develop these 21st-century tools, crude comments and kitschy art will soon give way to higher forms of sharing—commercial enterprise, political activism, community improvement—using the incredible power of connectivity around the globe. Shirkey believes this *cognitive surplus* is already very large, and growing still at a rapid rate. As we harness the collaborative systems for higher value and good, it seems almost a given that the Fast Future world ahead will be profoundly different from our current reality, and potentially unrecognizable in just a couple of decades.

Today, most of us are technology, information, and globalization neophytes. Soon we will be amateurs, apprenticing to something much better in most every field, profession, and business. Some will then become pseudo-professionals, and offer their talents and services to the world—often more effectively or at much lower cost than currently identified professionals. Before long, this rising amateurism will completely change everything.

WHAT SHOULD YOU DO?

Let me be clear. My belief is that *communities* will continue to be important in the Fast Future, *because* communities are intrinsically important to humans.

I'm not advocating for any one particular community or social type. Facebook and Twitter are big today, but there's no guarantee they will be in another decade. (In fact, the rapid pace of technological and cultural change suggests they won't be as popular, supplanted instead by the next big thing.) Only a few years back, social media pioneer *MySpace* dominated center stage, boasting at the time a huge community of more than 200 million users. Fast forward to the present and *MySpace* appears virtually irrelevant (unless you're in the entertainment business). It's likely that this path of meteoric rise and fall will be repeated again by other 21st-century community creators. Volatility and uncertainty will be the order of the day from now on.

If communities are important, and new forms are continually developing, then how should we think about and get involved with community? How does one find the right communities to pay attention to, to join and participate in, to collaborate with and even lead?

HERE'S MY PLAYBOOK FOR TAKING ACTION:

Pay Attention—It's incumbent on forward-looking leaders to pay attention to communities of all kinds, and particularly today to social media communities—and to join and follow these in search of emerging opportunities. I'm a member of (and experimenting with) several—a couple dozen—Internet forums: 25 LinkedIn groups, several professional trade organizations, two university alumni associations, and a handful of hobby groups as well. And, of course, I receive my share of newsfeeds, blog posts, e-newsletters, and such from the thought leaders I follow and interact with. Today, the biggest challenge is not information, but *noise*. There is a nearly endless array of voices out there—and their numbers continue to grow. Part of "paying attention" is continually looking around, investigating, and trying out new thoughts and ideas in a working laboratory. Many of these experiments are dead ends—communities that don't deliver the value expected. That's okay; it's the nature of this exploration. Another factor of paying attention is to have more people doing it (in the workplace, for instance), beyond a handful of managers, and instead involving all of the organization's staff. It's important to make sure that those involved are of different ages and backgrounds, since each generation views community differently. Diversity is a plus.

Visual Map—Create a picture of the various communities you (or the organization) are involved with. Don't worry about a potential lack of connectedness or relevance—quite often today true relevance is hidden, and only apparent in second or third order connections. The point of the visual map is to see and document where one's focus lies in relation to the larger landscape. This may point out where holes exist, or suggest opportunities for additional investigation and discovery.

Involvement—If the first step in community is joining, the second is participating. Of course, a challenge is first deciding where to focus. In practice it's a constant search for new groups, and continual testing out of these over time. Some don't work and are dropped, replaced by other communities. A handful, perhaps a half a dozen or so, will rise to the top. These are the ones to participate in. Don't forget that community is not simply about quantity; the quality of relationships (and value) is important.

Leadership—Beyond joining and participation, leading efforts in some communities (or leading the communities themselves) is tremendously important. Leadership roles bring the potential for enormous visibility and value to the individual and his or her firm. Nothing speaks credibility like a position of community leadership. Of course, this requires considerable investment—in time, effort, and focus. It's often well worth it.

Innovate—It's hard to overstate how important continuous innovation—creativity, flexibility, agility—is in the development of community, and in the opportunities that come forth. As we accelerate into the Fast Future, traditional pathways to success are disintegrating everywhere, replaced by an uncertain and continually evolving landscape. The future will be more transient and ephemeral. In that environment we'll need to do all of these: finding, joining, participating, and leading—and all much more nimbly, at the ready to shift gears and attention as opportunities mutate. If it sounds messy, it is. The role of effective leaders is to find a path and make it work.

AGAIN, SO WHAT?

New forms of community materializing and emerging every day, and this suggests that an experimental approach to change is in order—trying out some of these new opportunities, staying flexible and agile, failing fast, shifting and growing. It's a strategy of action, and of mistakes (omission, not commission). In this environment, leaders should continue to ask key questions. Here are some:

▶ What are the traditional, physical communities that we in the firm are involved in or should be involved in?

▶ What are the new, online social media communities that we in the firm are involved in or should be involved in?

▶ How are changes in traditional community structures affecting our business today? Our industry today?

▶ How are changes in traditional community structures affecting our clients' business now? Our clients' industry now?

▶ How are the developments of new, emerging communities (especially social media) changing the nature of our business, operations, and/or competitive landscape?

▶ How are changes and developments in community affecting today relationships with existing customers?

▶ How are changes and developments in community affecting today our relationships with new, prospective customers (e.g. marketing and business development)?

▶ What are we doing differently today (within the firm) to strengthen our business communities and our community involvement? What should we do more of? What should we do less of?

12

A Future of Change

**THE ERA OF STABILITY AND PREDICTABILITY
IS OVER; VOLATILITY, UNCERTAINTY, AND
CHANGE ARE THE NEW NORMAL.**

*"Because things are the way they are,
things will not stay the way they are."*
—Bertold Brecht

CHANGE ISN'T NEW

The Greek philosopher Heraclitus of Ephesus (535–475 BC) claimed long ago, "Nothing is permanent but change."

Often, we think of change as a more recent phenomenon, but it's clear in looking back that change (often profound change) has been a part of the human condition since the beginning.

What was the beginning?

Speaking scientifically—it's believed that the genus "Homo" evolved directly from *Australopithecine* ancestors nearly 2.5 million years ago. The first example of a new human species, Homo *habilis*, is widely considered to be a direct ancestor of *Australopithecus garhi*. However, this ancestry is not completely proven, and the May 2010 discovery of *H. gautengenis* in South Africa suggests possible early humans even before *H. habilis*. Some scientists expect the discovery of additional "proto-humans" in the near term, the result of improved DNA analysis and of the understanding of likely geographic locations of early habitation.[1]

The big change—the really big deal—with these early humans was the size of their heads! Archaeologists and scientists report an approximately 33 percent increase in cranial size and capacity between the two species (about 450cc in *A. garhi*, and about 600cc in *H. habilis*). Further, cranial capacity doubled again as *H. habilis* evolved through the stages of *H. ergaster*, *H. erectus*, and *H. heidelbergensis* at about 600,000 years ago. By this point, skull size approximated that of modern humans.[2]

This period of early human development (beginning about 2 million years ago) is called the *Paleolithic* (Old Stone Age), referring to the earliest use of tools made of chipped stone. Development of stone tools continued through the lower Paleolithic, later augmented by tools made from antler and bone, along with engravings, sculpted figures, and paintings or engravings on cave and rock walls in many places. During the middle Paleolithic (about 40,000 years ago), early *Homo sapiens* (primarily Neanderthals) improved these core tools of stone and bone. Then, in the upper Paleolithic (around 10,000 years ago), modern *Homo sapiens* developed with more unique and distinctive local cultures, based in part on more skillfully created tools and weapons of various materials. A big change, but unfolding over a rather long period of time.[3]

Paleolithic humans were hunter-gatherers who pursued wild game for meat, and foraged the land for other types of food, firewood, and materials necessary for life. Subsistence and survival were the primary goals of this nomadic lifestyle. Stone tools and weapons, cooking and eating utensils, and discovery and use of fire were the most important change developments.

The Neolithic period (from about 10,000 to 3500 BC) launched the first agricultural revolution. In many areas of the world, these developments precipitated a radical change in lifestyle—away from the nomadic hunter-gatherers, toward a more settled existence involving agriculture. And during this time, domestication of many plants and animals occurred independently in at least six separate locations worldwide. This more sedentary existence involved living in more permanent locations, and resulted in the establishment of villages and towns. Continued evolution in agriculture brought specialization of various crops, sophisticated irrigation, and storage of surplus food production. These changes, in turn, supported even higher density of populations, diversification and specialization of labor, and significantly increased trade. The non-nomadic life also allowed for and supported many new forms of more permanent art, architecture, and culture; centralized administration and governmental structures; and, eventually, new systems of knowledge and knowledge transfer—culminating (eventually) in the first fully developed, complex societies of the Middle Eastern cities of Samaria at the close of the Neolithic period (ca. 3500 BC).[4]

In some parts of the world, humans began melting copper to make new tools as early as 7000 BC. By 3500 BC, this copper was being mixed with tin to form a new alloy—bronze—and the significant human progression of the Bronze Age (roughly 2500–500 BC). Bronze-made tools and weaponry are the primary representations of this period, but much more occurred. For one, since copper and tin ores are not that widely distributed, the appearance of bronze implements around the world suggests a considerable amount of global trade. Additionally, early forms of writing were developed during this time—in Egypt (hieroglyphics), the Near East (cuneiform), and the Mycenaean Mediterranean (Linear B). Various forms of alphabet were created, as were the first wheels for carts and wagons, domestication of horses for many uses, and new forms of boats and ships for seafaring exploration and trade.[5]

The history of early humans also includes considerable movement and development—large-scale geographic migration, intermixing between populations and cultures, and changes in lifestyle and relationships. By comparison, the two other animal species most closely related to humans—the chimpanzees and gorillas of the family *Hominidae*, have each experienced very limited geographic migration, and even today their geographic range remains extremely narrow.

CHANGE IS ACCELERATING

So even a cursory look at early human history demonstrates that change has been with us since the start. Technological breakthroughs: early stone implements, the discovery of fire, and early explorations in agriculture—all brought profound change in the human condition.

But our quick review suggests something more (and perhaps even more interesting and important): that the pace of human change is *accelerating*—and has been for a very long time.

This is evident in comparing the long span of the Paleolithic with the later Neolithic and Bronze Ages that followed. And adding in the subsequent periods from medieval to modern times illuminates this trend further. The pace of change and human development continues to accelerate, and with the result (as Figure 12-1 and 12.2 point out) that the duration of each of subsequent age (as defined by the major developments within) has been shorter than the one before.

FIGURE 12-1. A SUMMARY OF MAJOR AGES IN HUMAN CULTURAL DEVELOPMENT

Human Age	Major Attributes/Developments	Time Period	Time Duration (years)
Paleolithic	Hunter-gatherers, Stone Age implements	2.5M BC–10,000 BC	2+ million
Neolithic	Farmers and ranchers, towns and villages	10,000 BC–3,500 BC	7500
Bronze		3,500 BC–500 BC	3000

Iron	Use of iron and steel, agricultural practices, religions, language, written history	1200 BC–500 AD	1500
Medieval (Middle)	Feudal government, urbaniza-tion, religious preeminence	500–1500 AD	1000
Modern	Nation states, western ascen-dancy, global exploration and discovery, colonization, resource exploitation, global trade	1500 AD–present	500
Industrial	Technology development and innovation, industrialization, urbanization, globalization	1800–present	200
Technol-ogy	Communications and computer technology, information technol-ogy, global communications, social technology	1900–present	100

FIGURE 12-2. DURATION OF MAJOR AGES AND PERIODS OF HUMAN HISTORY

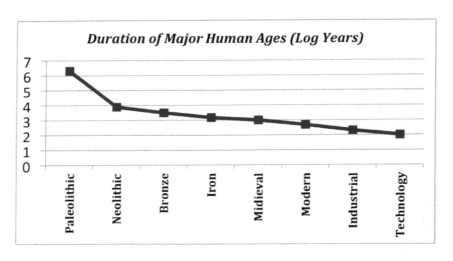

The graph here is plotted on a logarithmic scale, which suggests not only that change is accelerating, but also that the pace of this change is accelerating at an *exponential* rate. Of course, this isn't a highly mathematical analysis. The definition of each era is somewhat arbitrary, and there is overlap in later eras with shorter durations.

Still, the empirical evidence, spanning most of human history, does strongly suggest an acceleration of change.

Closer analysis of development *within* each period likewise demonstrates the accelerating pattern. As Figure 12-3 indicates, there has been a dramatic increase in technological development and innovation through time. And even though the list below is certainly incomplete, the sense of it is clear: there has been a great acceleration of change into the modern age, with considerably more happening in the 20th century than in the 16th century—or before.

FIGURE 12.3: MAJOR INVENTIONS/DEVELOPMENTS THROUGH TIME

Paleo-lithic	3500s BC-1100s BC	1000s BC-0AD	0AD-900s	1000s-1300s	1400s	1500s	1600s
2+ M yrs.	2400 yrs.	1000 yrs.	900 yrs.	300 yrs.	100 yrs.	100 yrs	100 yrs
Fire	Wheel	Homing pigeon	Postal service	Movable type Paper money	Printing press	Pencil	Newspaper
Cooking	Cart	Two-mast ship	Bound books	Magnetic compass	Copyright	Bottled beer	Refracting telescope
Spear	Riverboat				Whiskey	Com-pound micro-scope	Submarine
Spear-head	Ship oar	Crane	Gun-powder	Eye glasses			Adding machine
Bowl	Alphabet	Library					Reflecting telescope
Rope	Cuneiform writing	Crossbow					
	Domestic horses	Catapult					
		Canal					
	Phonetic alphabet	Water wheel					
	Encyclo-pedia	Three mast ship					
		Paper pulp					

1700s	1800-1849	1850-1899	1900-1949	1950-1999	2000-2005
100 yrs	50 yrs.	50 yrs.	50 yrs.	50 yrs.	5 yrs.
Steam engine Dictionary	Morphine	Pullman sleeper Gatling (machine) gun	Zeppelin dirigible	Credit card Video tape	IPOD
Sextant	Steam locomotive Stethoscope Portland cement	Plastic	Air conditioner Tractor	Contraceptive pill	Hybrid car
Carbonated water Spinning frame	Matches	Mail order Telephone	Theory of relativity Cornflakes	Solar cell	YouTube
Telegraph	Typewriter	Carpet sweeper Photography	Helicopter Military tank	Hard disk	Facebook
Flush toilet	Braille	Light bulb Toilet paper Fountain pen Motorcycle Automobile AC motor & transformer Zipper Motion picture	Gas mask Radio tuner Robot	Laser	Twitter
Steamship	Calculator		Television	Audio cassette SpaceWar, 1st video game	LinkedIn
Hot air balloon Power loom Guillotine	Telegraph Morse code Photography		Frozen food	BASIC language	
Bicycle	Sewing machine Anesthesia		Liquid rocket Penicillin Scotch tape	Compact disk	
Gas lighting Cotton gin Smallpox vaccine Soft drink Battery			Jet engine Electron microscope	Handheld calculator	
			Radio-telescope Magnetic recording Photocopier Ballpoint pen Color TV Software controlled computer Aerosol spray can Nuclear weapon	Arpanet	
				ATM	
				Barcode scanner	
			Mobile phone	Floppy disk	
				Microprocessor	
				Pong video game	
				MSDOS	
				IBM PC	
				Scanning tunneling microscope	
				Windows software	
				Digital cellular phone	
				World wide web	

And, even within the current revolution of modern technology, information, and communication, one can see the ongoing acceleration of change and development. Consider the following chart (Figure 12-4), comparing the adoption rate of each major new communications platform in the 20th century (time required to capture an audience of 50 million total users). Radio came first, but it was 38 years before the audience grew to 50 million. Television adoption was faster, reaching 50 million viewers in just 13 years. Internet adoption exploded to 50 million in just four years, though even this velocity has been eclipsed by subsequent technology products. Apple captured 50 million users with the iPod in just two years, and with the iPhone in one.[6] Facebook, Twitter, YouTube, and other social media platforms have grown exponentially since their creation, and today the reach of these platforms far surpasses the 50 million user threshold. In 2012, Apple released its iPad2 and sold some 3 million new units in its first weekend after launch, and the recent iPhone 6 apparently received some 10 million orders in its first weekend.[7]

FIGURE 12-4. COMPARISON OF COMMUNICATIONS PLATFORM ADOPTION (FIRST 50M USERS)

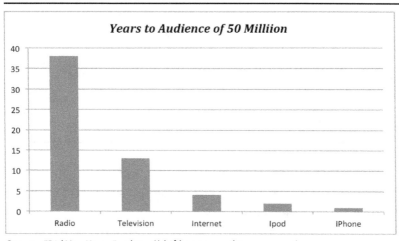

Source: "Did You Know," at http://shifthappens.wikispaces.com/.

Futurist Ray Kurzweil has studied this trend of acceleration in human development. His graph (Figure 12-5) of the "canonical" milestones in the evolution and development of life on Earth show a linear progression on a logarithmic scale, again suggesting an exponentially increasing rate of change.

FIGURE 12-5. CANONICAL MILESTONES IN THE HISTORY OF CHANGE

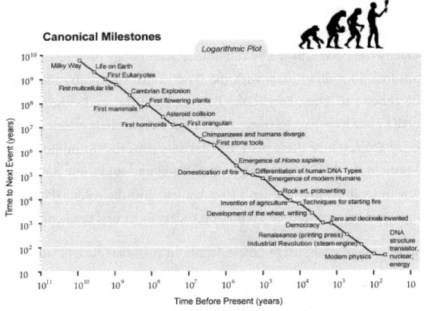

Source: Ray Kurzweil, The Singularity is Near, Viking, 2005.

Kurzweil also provides a comparison of the milestone lists of 15 other researchers (Figure 12-6) to further substantiate this principle of exponential change.

Kurzweil argues that the significance of this data supports his "law of accelerating returns," a fundamental component of his *Singularity*—the expectation that we are rapidly approaching a point at which overwhelming technological change will completely redefine humanity.

FIGURE 12-6: PARADIGM SHIFTS–COMPARING 15 STUDIES ON CHANGE

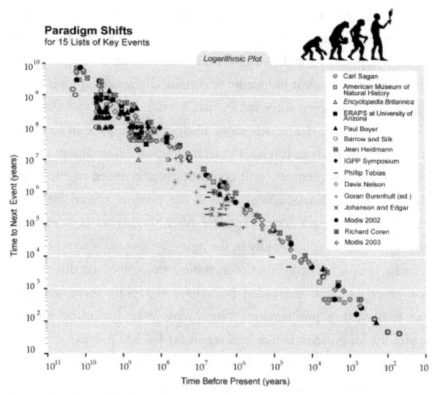

Source: Ray Kurzweil, The Singularity is Near, Viking, 2005.

THE FUTURE AHEAD

What's ahead in the future? We don't really know, but we can make some educated guesses. Because we know that change and development have been with

279

us all along, and that the rate of that change has been accelerating (perhaps exponentially) for much of human history, we can safely predict more (much more) of the same ahead.

With this history, why would anyone predict a slowing in the rate of change? Barring a significant reset (though this could indeed happen through a significant step backward, resulting, for instance, from nuclear holocaust or climate change collapse) it seems highly unlikely, even impossible, that human change and development would stall. It's much more likely that the pace of development—particularly as it relates to technological development and its associated consequences—will continue to gain speed in the years, decades, and centuries ahead. This is the picture offered by many futurists, including Kurzweil and the other Singularitarians, who see change accelerating so rapidly in the next 35-50 years as to render the human species virtually unrecognizable from today. In this world, computer and machine-aided humans will rapidly solve many of the most-vexing problems we face today, even including human mortality. Singularitarianism still seems far-fetched for many, but it's gathering some steam in the futurist community. More importantly, whether or not humans experience this rapid acceleration toward the Singularity—by 2045 as Kurzweil describes, or perhaps 50, 100, or 200 years after that.

It seems almost certain that human change and development will continue, and will accelerate toward a mind-boggling new paradigm, and not so far from now.

280

A FEW MORE THOUGHTS ON CHANGE

On the macro-scale, it's clear that change—developments in language, technology, information, and culture—has resulted in many improvements in human life. Overall, it seems like change and innovation are themselves subject to a sort of evolutionary force—a "survival of the fittest" process that accepts and inculcates useful change, while rejecting new ideas and actions that provide little use, or are on balance negative contributions. It's also true that the usefulness of some change is clearly in the eye of the beholder. Advances in military strategy or weaponry, for example, have benefited some groups at the expense of others. In some sense, all change is like this—with winners and losers depending on the outcomes.

Additionally, each individual has a unique perspective on, and orientation to, change—an important understanding I've come increasingly to appreciate in my own life and work.

I am one who is positively oriented to change—invigorated by new developments, circumstances, and context. I (and others like me) draw energy from the changing environment, and the open of opportunities and possibilities ahead. We are easily bored with stasis—with living in a comfortable and predictable environment.

I'm not arguing that this "changeophilic" orientation is all good. Along with a positive orientation to change, I'm frankly too easily enamored with and distracted by new stuff, which impedes focus, and staying on task with important priorities. Some excel with new and developing areas of business and life, in building and creating out of "white space." However, success in creating order out of chaos leads at times to a predictable decline in passion and productivity. Changeophiles are not usually maintainers, and must find a new opportunity to maintain their interest.

Clearly, this orientation does not fit for everyone. In fact, my own anecdotal evidence suggests that this "change positive" orientation is uncommon—perhaps 20 percent of the population, and certainly not 80 percent. Much more common are those on the other side, at the other end of the spectrum, with a love of order and predictability, and a generally negative orientation toward change. Most appreciate their ability to control (to varying degrees) their environment of life and work. These folks often resist change *per se*; for them, change is essentially negative by definition. Many in this camp desire not only the current reality, but also (sometimes irrationally) the "good old days" of the past.

It's important to note that each of us exhibits a different orientation to change in different parts of our existence. Some are aggressive change agents in their personal life (church, volunteer associations, or local community), while being strong resisters at work. Others show the opposite: movers and shakers at the office, while strongly conservative and status quo-oriented at home. And, of course, people themselves change and develop over time, through the course of their learning and experience. One can certainly develop a greater appreciation for the positive aspects of change. One can also (of course) become more conservative (especially as you capture life success and positions/possessions to protect).

These differences in orientation to change—whether in individuals or teams—are conceptually obvious. That said, it's not uncommon to forget it, especially when dealing one-to-one with other people. In a more personal context, we often work pretty hard to convince others that our ideas, approach, beliefs are right—and the only right way.

But awareness that people, in fact, view change differently is critically important to the change agent, and to successful leadership of the change initiative. First, one must develop a self-awareness and appreciation for both the positive and negative implications of change on our personal situation. Second, one then must build an understanding of how change is viewed by and affects others around us.

Important also is appreciating that these different orientations to change each have value, and that no one perspective is better than another.

This took a good deal of time for me to grasp and, ultimately, to leverage. I thought for years that my desire for the new and different, the uncertain and unknown, was of higher value—the perspective and orientation of visionary leaders who were simply "out ahead" of the others. But this isn't true. Yes, the group does need some with the change positive orientation—to see possibilities where others do not, to pursue opportunities where others see threats, to dream and create new ideas, approaches and solutions. However, it's clear that a group composed solely of these sorts of individuals cannot usually be successful—first because these change agents often work better alone, and second (and more importantly), because developing new ideas is only one part of success; *execution* of ideas is at least as important as is creating them. Change agents need the contributions of others to successfully deliver. In fact, though it's been a difficult learning for me personally, I've come to believe strongly today (as others have long claimed) that *execution* of ideas is the single most important contributor to success. So while I'm still at times impatient with the naysayers, I've come to appreciate a great deal those who force a disciplined, structured, and pragmatic view of the opportunities of change ahead.

SO WHAT?

Here are a few examples of the type of questions concerning change that you and your organization should consider:

▶ What are the major take-home implications of working in a business environment of constant, pervasive, and accelerating change?

▶ What must we change about our business (or our beliefs) in order to be more successful in a constantly shifting environment?

▶ Are there areas of our business or company that are built around *control* of the environment, that can (or should) be reengineered around *adaptability* to the environment?

▶ What are the key attributes of organizations that thrive and succeed in changing environments?

▶ If the pace of change really is accelerating, then what does it mean for us that we will experience "ten years of change in the next five years?"

▶ Perhaps you and or your team see something else ahead—a moderating, or even reversing, of the increase in the pace of development. If so, what is your hypothesis, your forecast, and your evidence for this alternative view?

► How are you personally oriented to change at work? In your life? What are you doing about it?

► How about the team, and its preparedness for the change ahead? Should the team be adjusted or enhanced to increase the odds of success in a constantly changing environment? Are there others who should be added to the team, and if so, who/what?

PART III
CONCLUSIONS
AND THE ACTION
AGENDA

13

Agenda- What to Do with the Fast Future Ahead

"Not failure, but low aim, is the crime."
—Henry David Thoreau

We've looked in depth now at 10 large-scale, transformational uber-trends that together will likely reshape everything about our 21st-century business and world. And indeed, we're fascinated with this future—though our primary goal is to understand its impact on our business and self. So we've kept close at hand our arsenal of "so what?" questions to aid our analysis. Ultimately, we want to take action, to create, to compete—and to win.

It's clear from our brief journey that we know few of the details about the road ahead. We see the macro-trends all right, but debate even these, argue about the overall pace of change, wrestle with the meaning of the transformation, and struggle to determine how best to move. And as we dig deeper, we collect few answers and more questions. Still, we believe that in asking these questions we will uncover the clues for strategy, action, and competitive edge.

Moreover, we are reminded yet again that while we cannot control the uncontrollable future, we can indeed control ourselves, our team, and our enterprise. We have little power over change, but nearly complete power over our reaction to the change. This is extraordinarily good news.

I'm often asked (by clearly exasperated firm leaders) to "cut through the crap and tell me what to do." The future itself seems complex and uncertain, and many leaders expect the answers to be complex, as well. But interestingly (and sometimes disappointingly), my answer is much simpler. With near-constant change in our environment, the list of focal points for business success remains itself largely unchanged. Similar to improving the relationship with a spouse, you probably already know what to do (listen more, invest more, care more). Business answers are similar, simple. By this, I don't mean easy—because the road to success is rarely easy—but it doesn't have to be complex.

If you're looking for a prescription for business health and longevity—growth, profit, and sustainable 21st-century success— I'm going to strongly suggest you follow a simple, straightforward, and back-to-basics approach. As described in Figure 14-1, my *Super-Seven Response Framework* contains these important components, which together form the basis of "what I most need to do." These seven components are *mission, vision, strategy, alignment, marketing, operations,* and *people*. Bolstering the organization in these seven areas offers a (virtual) shoo-in for success, because (1) most everything important happening in the organization is covered here, and (2) very few firms do enough in any of these areas. In other words, working on these seven areas is both valuable and rare. The *Super-Seven Response Framework* is simple, but it's not easy. Execution takes courage and guts—and a good deal of effort.

FIGURE 13-1. THE FAST FUTURE SUPER-SEVEN RESPONSE FRAMEWORK

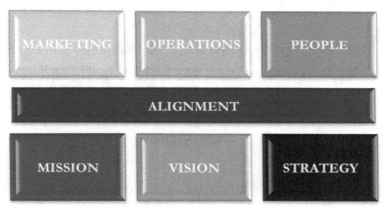

Source: J. Doehring & Co., LLC, 2014.

This approach begins with creating a strong foundation of clarity around three important concepts: mission (why we exist), vision (where we're headed), and strategy (how we'll get there). Done right, the answers to these questions will inevitably attract interest—of people and resources—to the organization. And clarity and consensus on the big things leads to an even more powerful outcome: *organization alignment*, which transforms camaraderie into commitment, and commitment into performance. This is the fundamental purpose of the firm—accomplishing together what individuals cannot accomplish alone. Without this sense of alignment, great performance simply isn't possible.

On top of this foundational alignment, we focus next on the three primary functions of the enterprise: (1) marketing (capturing the business), (2) operations (executing the business), and (3) people (building and growing the one true asset of the firm). Of course, each of these three areas includes a multitude of component parts, issues, and opportunities. The model is simplified on purpose. Focus on just a few of the issues in any of these areas, and the company will likely be better for it. Focus effort in several areas, and success will come much, much faster.

Let's take a brief look at each of the components of the *Super-Seven Response Framework*, and see what's involved in each.

MISSION

"To boldly go where no man has gone before."
—(Star Trek)

All of us want to make a difference, and to do work that has meaning. No one wants to belong to a company without a clear sense of purpose. Mahatma Gandhi once said, "A small body of determined spirits, fired by an unquenchable faith in their mission, can alter the course of history." Yes, this mission stuff is powerful.

An organization's *mission* answers the questions of *why*. It articulates the core purpose, the raison d'être. Sometimes the mission is expressed as a tagline, but it's much more than that. A clear and powerful mission creates true clarity of direction, aligns important stakeholders, and bubbles up the passion necessary for success.

Why does your company exist? What is its primary purpose? What drives your team—owners, principals, managers, and staff? What is the mission?

To be fair, in a general sense, the mission of every business enterprise is essentially the same—it's the mission of the corporation. This generic mission includes providing (1) products and services for customers, (2) gainful employment for staff, and (3) profit for investor-shareholders. This is the bottom line, and it's not too sexy (though it's still important).

But what is most interesting, and ultimately most compelling, about a firm is not generic similarity, but instead what's distinctive about the company. Each organization differs in many ways—in its focus, priority, and aspirations. Some zero-in like a laser on *customers*, and consider their mission primarily in the light of serving these. Others emphasize *staff* as the top priority. Still others focus first on shareholders, and on delivering a profit. And organizations also differ in the size of their dreams—the scale, scope, pace, and intensity of their aspirations. Some firms want to rule the universe, others just a small corner of it.

Great mission statements (which grow from great missions) are interesting and compelling. They articulate meaning and attract attention. Indeed, almost all great mission statements share a set of descriptive attributes: they're short, memorable, meaningful, compelling, and bold. Because of this, these statements (and the missions behind them) break through the clutter of average.

Want an example of a really great mission statement? I suppose my all-time favorite is from Star Trek: "To boldly go where no man has gone before." Or the whole of it: "To explore strange new worlds. To seek out new life and new civilizations. To boldly go where no man has gone before." If you're over the age of 30, this is a familiar mission (though it first appeared on TV in the mid 1960s, and then only for three years).[1] It's a great one because it's short, memorable, meaningful, and bold—and it's really distinctive.

Okay, so not all of us are involved in pursuits as lofty or as different as Star Trek. Still, most of us are all looking for purpose and meaning in our work. In the confusing and uber-noisy future ahead, this meaning will become ever more valuable, and it's worth some effort to get it right today.

VISION

"Nothing happens unless first a dream."
—Carl Sandburg

What is the most important part of the organization's foundation? For my money, it's vision. I'm vision driven. More important to me than virtually anything else is the desired destination, the big objective. My motivation comes from seeing and understanding the dream.

For years, I assumed everyone was like this, but it isn't so. In fact, I've learned that individuals are motivated by many different things. Visionists look for the big objective. Purpose-driven folks are excited more by mission (the why), and still others by strategy (how we're going to do it). Some care less about any of these, and more about momentum, making progress. These are the Executers, and their primary interest is action.

Vision provides the response to the questions of *where?* In simple terms, it clarifies where the company is headed. A great vision is both *aspirational* (desired but not yet achieved), and *motivational* (creating the energy for action). A vision statement helps to paint a picture, a *visual* (same root) of the goal. For organizational clarity—and consensus, alignment, and commitment—clear vision is a must.

A client once remarked that vision was critically important in his firm, so much so that indeed they had several! He was joking, but the point is important. An organization must have one aligning vision, not several. (You can't expect everyone to agree with 100 percent of it, but all can agree that it is *their* objective together.) Any firm with multiple and/or conflicting ideas, or (even worse) a free-for-all of "you have yours and I'll have mine," has in reality no vision at all.

A clear vision is necessary not only for initial alignment, but also along the way, aiding leaders with key decisions through time. This works because strategic choices must make sense in the context of the big objective (does doing this thing help us to achieve the vision). If the organization's vision doesn't function this way, then something is wrong.

Given its importance, it's frankly astounding just how many firms are unsuccessful with visioning. Indeed, most companies have a vision *statement*, but too often it's simply junk. Carefully conceived and word-smithed, watered down, middle of the road, plain vanilla—the vision statement says and stands for nothing, and won't help with strategic choices. Non-threatening generalizations and MBA gobble-dygook is not what we're after.

Unfortunately, these are common, because firm leaders lack the courage to do something different. A compelling vision requires tough choices, taking a stand, and shooting for objectives that are risky and not guaranteed. And courage is today in short supply.

An example of a truly extraordinary vision is the famous, often-cited Cold War US space program initiative, articulated by President John F. Kennedy in May 1961:

"I believe that this nation should commit itself to achieving the goal, before this decade is out, of landing a man on the moon and returning him safely to the Earth."[2]

This was extraordinarily bold, and (especially by today's political standards) brave. There was no lack of clarity in this objective. Landing on the moon, and coming home safe. A clear goal, with little wiggle room for interpretation.

Even more importantly, the moon shot was profoundly compelling and extraordinarily difficult. Yes, some criticized it, but most Americans quickly got behind the program. Rarely does a leader (especially a politician) reach for a goal so big, challenging, and uncertain—and beyond the capabilities of the group at that moment. But in a direct way, this was the point. As Kennedy later explained it, the goal was chosen not because it was easy, but specifically because it was hard—and, therefore, would unite the nation in a single-minded focus (beating the Russians in the Cold War).

Perhaps (you'll say) this is an example too grand, especially when considering the possibilities of a business? I get the point, but I don't agree.

Bold and daring visioning is needed in organizations today, and it's absent in most. Most firms are (frankly) boring, focused on benchmarking the average, on surviving another quarter, on muddling through. How many of these companies (and the individuals within them) have the capacity to accomplish much more, to reach for the truly extraordinary? What is needed today is more bold and courageous vision.

There are other pitfalls in the work of organization visioning, though the lack of ambition to "go big" is probably the most common. A related issue is the short-term focus of most managers and leaders—not looking far enough out on the horizon. Want to do something big? That takes time. A bold, compelling vision isn't about next year's business plan. Or to paraphrase a Steven Covey idea, it's not about how one can slash a trail through the jungle, but about determining (in the first place) what jungle one should be slashing in. In addition to these, misalignment and head-butting of the firm's senior leaders, and a general (and often irrational) aversion to risk are also common pitfalls to success with visioning.

So, creating vision is crucial for business success and, in my view, the most important foundational concept of business. As the poet Carl Sandburg said, "Nothing happens unless first a dream."

STRATEGY

> *"All men can see these tactics whereby*
> *I conquer, but what none can see is the*
> *strategy out of which victory is evolved".*
> —Sun Tzu

Strategy—it's one of the most commonly talked about (but still misused) concepts in business. Today, the idea of strategy is just too much gobbledygook—over generalized and lacking any real meaning. (A potential client once remarked that "strategic" meant I was probably going to charge him more for the work.) Few managers apply the concept of strategy particularly well. So, clarifying what strategy is, and its important role in the organization, is a powerful step in the process of improving the company.

Simply stated, strategy answers the questions of "how?" In the firm, it's how the organization will pursue the mission and achieve the vision. Born originally in a military context, strategy focuses on *how* to win the battle.

Though conceptually straightforward, there is frankly little that is easy about crafting and executing good strategy. *Competitive advantage* and *market differentiation* are understandable ideas, but often extraordinarily hard to achieve. It's not uncommon for firm leaders to start off on the right track but then to lose courage along the challenging path. *Persistence* is a virtue in the strategic enterprise.

Beyond persistence, a couple of other strategy attributes are important. First, strategy is fundamentally about *choice*, selecting a course of action from among the options. The choice required is often difficult, because more than one way looks attractive. This choice suggests that organizations (and individuals) must, well, *choose*. The reason is focus. To excel, one cannot simultaneously pursue multiple goals. You can be average at many things, but truly excellent at perhaps just one.

Second, strategy is—as Harvard Professor Michael Porter said—about being *different*.[3] In the marketplace, this involves assessing the strategic choices of others, and then selecting a road that's different. It's this difference that bolsters the organization's competitive edge—its focus, strengths, and advantages. Consumers don't want a bunch of car companies all making Chevys. What they want is choice—Fords, Toyotas, Hondas, and BMWs. Strategy is about being different.

Strategy is a concept that can be applied at multiple levels in the firm. At the highest level, strategy defines the *how* approach of the entire *enterprise*, the firm as a whole. Some refer to this as the "business model," and I often call it the "Big S" strategy. In contrast, "Little S" strategies are those that focus on more specific parts of the business, like *functions* (marketing, human resources, finance and accounting), *disciplines* (structural engineering, tax law, architecture), or *markets* (commercial real estate, pharmaceuticals, health care). Most companies employ quite a few of the Little S strategies in their operations, and ideally these will be well aligned with the larger Big S enterprise strategy.

Strategy is also appropriately applied at the project or job level. Examples include the marketing team's "pursuit strategy" for an upcoming proposal, a project manager's "staffing strategy" for a new project, or the finance group's "integration strategy" for a completed acquisition. Strategy can be applied in various contexts and levels of company management, though it's always properly used in support of addressing the questions of *how*.

Also, strategy and *leadership* are closely related and commonly intertwined. Jim Collins's now-famous book *Good to Great* helped many of us to understand the crucial importance of leadership.[4] Great ideas without great people simply don't get you very far. Tough medicine at first for those of us enamored with ideas—but good medicine. And after still more years of working with it, I've further concluded that, in fact, strategy and leadership *are almost the same thing*—two sides of the same coin. Choose and develop the right people, and as leaders they can't help but define, articulate, and execute good business strategy. This is what leaders do, thinking and acting differently from others. Being strategic.

Similarly, there is an important relationship between strategy and *structure*. Alfred Chandler wrote of this in 1962,[5] and I first read about it in *In Search of Excellence* (Tom Peters and Robert Waterman).[6] These authors concluded (correctly, I think) that structure comes after strategy, that form follows function. This simple premise made sense to me then, and it still does today. As far as I'm concerned, the issue is settled. However, despite the good sense here, business leaders often act as though the opposite were true. (Have a problem in the organization, and you can bet that someone is busy reorganizing something.) Worse yet, some leaders seem to think that structure *is* strategy, that reorganizing itself is all that's necessary. This is wrong and it never works, though the temptation remains. Maybe it just feels right doing something.

Finally, in my experience, the most common challenge today is not that organizations and their leaders don't understand strategy, but that they've chosen poorly (or not at all), and that their strategies simply aren't working well. Yes, one must choose, but one must chose wisely.

Poor strategy choices show up again and again. Some I've seen include:

1. *Say yes!*—a purely opportunistic approach of going after everything, in an unfocused, haphazard way
2. *The customer is always right*—focusing nearly exclusively on external issues (clients and markets) and insufficiently on optimizing internal operations
3. *Utilization is it!*—an overly introverted focus on internal efficiency and not on markets and customers
4. *Line-item anarchy*—a near free-for-all, in a highly decentralized, autonomous organization lacking overarching alignment

Like other foundational concepts of our framework, strategy is a straightforward idea, not overly complex but certainly not easy to accomplish. The key points of good strategy are choice, difference, focus, and persistence.

ALIGNMENT

"If you're in a round boat (with your colleagues),
paddling and spinning but not getting
anywhere, then paddling faster won't help."
—John Doehring

Organization alignment is another of our simple but important concepts, and it is indeed elusive in organizations. Alignment comes through sustained agreement in the team, and this is difficult to grasp and hold. Still, the effort is worth it, because organization alignment is one of the most powerful inputs of business success.

Alignment is the state in the business in which *all members of the group are on the same page about the big and important stuff.* In this all-too-rare condition, leaders, managers, and staff in the firm agree, and work productively together in the business. Note that I don't mean technical or discipline-based conformity—staff agreeing on how to do engineering, dentistry, or scientific discovery. Most professions and business functions do a pretty good job of self-policing their core expertise. Instead, I mean alignment around the organization's major *business* issues—specifically the why, where, and how questions of (respectively) mission, vision, and strategy. This is challenging because few employees focus on the enterprise itself (working *on* the business rather than *in* it), and fewer still focus on the *entire* enterprise (reaching beyond the natural consensus of their functional, project, or geographic teams).

I've been asked before if organization alignment—as important as it is—is really an *objective* of the firm per se (something that leaders must explicitly achieve), or more accurately an *outcome* of pursuing the mission, vision, and strategy. That's a good question.

My answer is both yes and no. Alignment is for sure a key outcome of consensus in the foundational issues of mission, vision, and strategy. And, as we've said, the objective of these is to clarify the why, where, and how—in order to attract attention, resources, and talent to the business—and to compel action towards success. So organization alignment is a key *outcome* of that effort, as depicted in Figure 13-2.

FIGURE 13-2. THE PATH THROUGH FOUNDATIONAL OBJECTIVES TO ORGANIZATIONAL ALIGNMENT

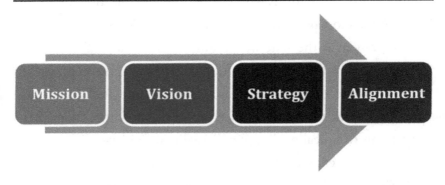

Source: J. Doehring & Co., LLC, 2014

On the other hand, alignment is itself so very important to firm success that I believe it must also be viewed as a key *objective* of the team. I mean that it's not enough to assume that alignment will occur through these other pursuits. Instead, it should be sought after explicitly, aggressively, and proactively. With this view, alignment is also a strategic objective.

If alignment is this central to business success, then why are so many organizations lacking in it? There are multiple reasons. First, firms are inherently complicated and messy, composed of many different people, perspectives, and goals. Many organizations are highly decentralized, autonomous, even disorganized by nature, while others are rigidly controlled, and hardened into impenetrable silos of noncooperation. Second, in quite a few markets and industries, competitive firms haven't really had to align themselves much at the *enterprise* level—a strong "one-company" approach just wasn't necessary in the past, and it's only the new pressures of the Fast Future that demand it today. Third, it's sometimes in our nature as humans to be negative, self-centered, and selfish. Altruism takes work. We view the organization as a zero-sum game—where when others succeed, we fail. This condition makes alignment (and cooperation) difficult, but it also means that those who achieve strong alignment earn a real advantage.

Fourth, alignment also requires considerable trust. Trust is a big deal for all of us: it's developed only over time (but can be squandered in a heartbeat), and it too is in short supply in most organizations. Employees are reluctant to extend their precious trust because it's easy to get burned. The rewards sometimes don't seem worth the risk. What's needed to combat this is strong leadership, a sense of mission, and clear vision. A brave soul or two thinking and acting differently (and with courage) can make a big difference in breaking through the fear and cynicism. Trust is in short supply, but its effect on alignment is magical. As Jean-Paul Sartre once pointed out, "In love, one and one are one."

MARKETING

"Next to doing the right thing, the most important thing is to let people know you are doing the right thing."
—J. D. Rockefeller

Marketing is the magic of *persuasion*, and it's both science and art. Marketing efforts create awareness, visibility, and demand for products and services. It's a simple and straightforward premise, and we all get it. We're all more or less willing (even enthusiastic) participants in the marketing game, especially as consumers. It's a bit more challenging at work, on the selling side of the ledger. There are several reasons for our reluctance to market our offerings to others.

First, and to be honest, many in business (both inside and outside the firm) consider marketing to be at best a necessary requirement, and at worst something considerably more evil. In some business segments (including professional services), descriptors such as inapplicable, inappropriate, unethical—and even illegal—have previously been associated with marketing. The idea of promoting oneself to build business seemed unnecessary, and rather beneath the dignity of the professional.

Second, in the latter half of the last century, many businesses really didn't need to do much marketing. Their success came primarily through simply *being*—following a strategy I call "the diploma and phone." In other words, business owners had some capability (the diploma) and some position/visibility in the local market (the phone). This combination—and a good deal of hard work—was usually enough, without much overt marketing.

Third, many businesses who did invest in marketing initiatives didn't see much in the way of results, or return on their effort. Their lack of success was due itself to several factors, including insufficient expertise and experience; poorly conceived marketing plans; subpar execution of those plans; and an inordinate focus on other aspects of the business (like billable project work) at the expense of marketing.

In practice, many managers get most of their marketing wrong. In firm after firm, what is described as *marketing* is really almost exclusively *sales*. (There's nothing wrong with sales, of course, but it's only a part of the marketing puzzle.) These downstream-oriented, opportunity-focused efforts in sales—without the corresponding upstream and general demand initiatives of marketing—just don't work very well. It's inefficient and ineffective to pursue new business with sales alone.

Worse still, too many organizations operate as though there are only two business development modes in total: sales and off. When project teams are busy, these companies cut back on all business development work (why market now)? When work is needed, they toggle back to sales, but by this time the stomach is growling (hungry for work); it's a poor time to think comprehensively about growth (or to plant a healthy vegetable garden). Poorly conceived approaches lead most often to poorly achieved results.

This overreliance on sales efforts leads also to an over-focus on downstream metrics of success—such as sales, profits, and cash. I'm not suggesting that these objectives aren't important, or aren't the ultimate outcomes we're after—just that measuring these alone will shed very little light on performance across the marketing system. And it's a systematic and systems-focused marketing process that we're after.

A few years back, I developed a new framework for marketing success and called it the *Made to Measure (M2M) Marketing System*. My M2M system envisions a more comprehensive framework for marketing—including defined objectives, goals, and metrics across four operational levels in the firm. These four, cascading levels are outlined in Figure 13-3, and include *strategic business objectives* (for instance, the size, pace, and quality of growth, and the firm's defi-nition of target markets), *strategic marketing objectives* (positioning; strategies in product, price, placement, promotion, process, and people; marketing organization, execution, management, planning, and training), *tactical marketing objectives* (day-to-day execution of the communications, events, and business development plans), and *marketing results objectives* (e.g., dollars won, checks cashed, and profits enjoyed).

FIGURE 13-3: A COMPREHENSIVE CASCADING SYSTEM FOR MARKETING

MANAGEMENT

Source: J. Doehring & Co., LLC, 2014.

Many argue that measuring final results—the endpoint objectives—is all that really matters. I wholeheartedly disagree. Not only must the firm steward these endpoint results like sales, revenues, and profit, but it must also develop interim measures within each of the four operational levels. The idea is to create a connected system of initiatives and outcomes, all tied in to the (eventual) results of growth and profit. Measuring both activity and results across this system improves both the execution of marketing activities and the ultimate performance achieved.

As markets change rapidly today, so too does the need for marketing to change. In fact, the field of marketing is undergoing its own radical transformation, as the traditional approaches of outbound, interruption-based marketing (marketer in control) work less and less effectively. Many new forms of inbound, permission-based marketing (customer in control) are quickly developing and evolving. This is the new paradigm of 21st-century business growth.

Most organizations are (or will be soon) wrestling with the need for more innovative marketing efforts that better match this new order. And most businesses will in the Fast Future need to do much more marketing work than they have done in the past.

OPERATIONS

"Change is not necessary. Survival is not mandatory."
—W. Edwards Deming

At the core, the business of running a company is pretty simple. There are really just a handful of important tasks, like winning the work (new customers), doing the work (executing projects), and getting paid for it (and a few other related administrative matters). But, of course, there's a great deal of effort, struggle, and anguish involved in each of these functions. Business is simple (or should be), but it's rarely easy.

An important step in improving any business is to consider just how *productivity*—the good stuff—is defined by the firm. In many companies, productivity is defined simply by the total hours worked. If employees are on the clock, then they are assumed to be productive, accomplishing the necessary tasks of their job. This is, of course, only an approximation, since (1) employees can be at work but not doing anything, or otherwise wasting time and resources; and (2) staff may be achieving work it believes to be productive, but that is of limited or no value to the client.

In many professional services firms, productivity is equivalent to (and measured primarily by) *utilization*. Utilization is defined by whether or not the employee is currently *billable* to the client project, or is alternatively focused on non-billable (usually) administrative tasks. Utilization is zealously over-emphasized in many of these organizations, and this focus causes myriad issues. An organization full of people, all running around doing things—but with incomplete understanding of whether these are the right things, are done right, or are ultimately of client value—is ridiculous. Moreover, efficiency and effectiveness are not independent variables, but are related and sometimes causal. As efficiency climbs, gains in effectiveness must eventually slow, and possibly even decline. This is "busy work" and subject to diminishing returns—hours-worked increases, but value-per-hour decreases. And it shouldn't matter (though sadly it does) that today's clients are still in the dark, and routinely pay for this low value added. This won't last.

Moreover, despite the truth that professionals often care deeply about the *quality* of their work, the organization's drumbeating on utilization (and very little else) results not in focus on quality, but rather on quantity. This is true in many other types of business as well—manufacturing, distribution, and retail. The siren song of top-line growth, and increasing production throughput for greater revenues, is constantly at work to drown out the focus of quality. Firms must guard against this by watching a suite of success metrics, beyond the singular measure of utilization.

Additionally, it's not enough to think of productivity as an on–off switch (either you have it or you don't). There are different types of productive effort in an organization, beyond that of satisfying customer needs. These involve *investing* in the business (plant, property, equipment) and/or the staff, and both are of value. Improving the business always requires this investment. These initiatives don't always pay off quickly, so short-term "productivity" may suffer in creating sustainable productivity over the longer haul.

Many projects that improve the business are small in scale, and can be handled by local project or functional teams. And the overall return on these investments, added up across the organization, can be extraordinary. However, some improvement efforts are quite large— enterprise-scale initiatives that require both coordination in interdisciplinary teams, and also a wider, systems-thinking perspective. For example, working only on sales and marketing strategies without considering their effect on financial services, or on operations, may have limited value. Systems thinking in these situations is necessary, though this is particularly challenging in decentralized firms where local, project, or functional teams don't commonly work outside of their own fence posts.

The extraordinary changes of the Fast Future will pressure today's organizations to change much about how they collaborate internally for operations improvement, and indeed for basic company operations. As the business environment becomes more competitive and complex, firm leaders must improve their organizational capabilities—either through centralization, standardization, and simplification of operating practices and procedures, or through increasing the capabilities of individual contributors on the team. It's likely that the most progressive firms will pursue improvement along both of these avenues.

The list of potential business improvement initiatives in the firm is virtually endless. Even the best of organizations have a myriad of opportunities to better both productivity and business results. Figure 13-4 catalogs some of these.

FIGURE 13-4. SOME IDEAS FOR BUSINESS OPERATIONS IMPROVEMENT

Planning	Organizations must plan explicitly for business improvement, not simply expect it to happen. Clear objectives, action agenda, an execution plan.
Communications	There's no such thing as *too much communication*. Effective communication is in short supply everywhere, and it's a powerful competitive advantage.
Project Management	In the future, much more of work will become "projectized," and effective project management skill and experience will increase in value. Even today's project-oriented organizations can still improve a great deal.
Pricing/Contracting	Pricing and contracting work based on hourly rates is a shortcoming, and properly incentivizes neither the firm nor the client. A shift toward *value-based pricing* represents a huge operational and profit improvement opportunity.
People Development	People are the key in every business. The best of firms will continue to strengthen their advantage through significant investment in training, development, mentoring, and experiential learning.
Incentives	Compensation and other rewards is a complex, lightning-rod issue. One-size solutions rarely fit. In an increasingly meritocratic business environment, incentive-based compensation will reward those who produce real results.
Measuring Success	Metrics is a hot topic, but for most businesses it's really not that complicated. The real trick to measurement is not in choosing the perfect metrics, but in paying attention to those that are chosen. What's needed most are our simple management systems, and then significant focus on using them.
Client Feedback	Understanding the customer's perspective is crucial. Today, too few firms don't invest enough in feedback. Improved technology, information, and communication tools will help in this regard, and the best firms will continue to engage clients in more robust, collaborative, and mutually beneficial relationships.

Source: J. Doehring & Co., LLC, 2014.

Finally, no plan to improve business is fully complete until it is understood as a *process*, rather than a one-time event. Business solutions are never perfect, and environmental conditions are constantly changing. The leader's role is to stay focused and keep at it, to lead the organization and team forward through both success and challenge, and with a view towards sustained commitment. The continuous improvement paradigm suggests *activity*—and a collaborative and inclusive approach to change. In the Fast Future ahead (where complexity grows, change is unrelenting, and the road ahead uncertain), this everyone-in approach makes perfect sense. Opportunities and challenges are big, fast moving, quickly missed. The whole team must be involved.

PEOPLE

"The firm that builds the best team—wins."
—John Doehring

People are central to business, and few leaders would disagree with their importance. Still, our experience breeds a certain skepticism with this, doesn't it? We've long heard it said that "people are our greatest asset," but then the organization's actions suggest something altogether different. In many companies, it seems the real priority is almost exclusively customers—and not employees. Why is that? Of course, customers are important. They're the reason the firm is in business. But for my money, getting the staff (people) part right is what holds the enterprise together.

Building an employee team involves several important processes: recruiting, selection, on-boarding, training and development, mentoring and coaching, job experiences, performance assessment, career-pathing, professional development, compensation, and benefits. The first step in an integrated people system is *recruiting*.

Many firms approach recruiting in an ineffective approach that is remarkably similar to the mistakes they make with marketing. In fact, the analogy between human resources and marketing is strong. If the firm invests very little work in the finding and attracting of talent until it has actual job openings, this organization is acting very much in "sales" mode. Recruiting is transactional (filling the open slot) and not the more robust, ongoing, and sustained work of talent management, which is akin to an ongoing marketing effort. And just as with the shortcomings in marketing, in recruiting the transactional focus results in a suboptimal, start-and-stop, herky-jerky process to fill jobs only when the organization is hungry to get them filled. Instead, progressive, people-oriented companies work on recruiting all the time, and as a result they attract and select from a better talent pool overall.

Some organizations hire only one type of recruit, with a certain background, education, or experience level. Others view their team-building opportunities more broadly, and add new talent when and where they find it. This contrast of approaches is a bit like the difference between sports teams who only draft to fill a specific position, versus those who always draft the best player available (irrespective of need). In businesses, there are potential opportunities at three general levels of the organization: junior, mid-career, and principal. Junior professionals are usually taken right from college or university, while mid-career professionals are most often discovered in similar (and even competitive) organizations. Senior-level professionals often appear haphazardly, and they can (admittedly) be challenging to fit into existing firm structure. Nevertheless, almost all organizations should be looking for opportunities not in one, but in *all three* of these areas—as if their very survival depended on it. That's because, ultimately, it does. The best of companies spend much more time in recruiting and selection (up to one-third of their senior team's time and effort), and they involve many more of their staff (up and down the organization) in the work. HR folks help to facilitate the process, but recruiting in these firms is the responsibility of managers and staff in line operations.

There's much more to say about people and the people processes in the organization, largely beyond the scope of this book. Figure 13-5 captures a few additional thoughts about the people process for our consideration.

FIGURE 13-5. SOME KEY AREAS OF FOCUS IN THE PEOPLE PROCESS OF THE FIRM

Diversity	Today, *diversity* is focused on the obvious things–gender, race, and ethnicity. Soon the concept of diversity will expand to describe much more important dimensions–like the diversity of *ideas*.
Engagement	In the complexity of the Fast Future, it's less likely that any one person will have all the answers. Collaboration and engagement in the broader team will become essential.
Democracy	Collaborative organizations will become more democratic, with shared management, leadership, and ownership–and flat organization structures. In the future we'll see more powerful *meritocracies*–with rewards for the doers.
Learning	Learning opportunities and requirements will be more dispersed through a career, and we won't finish all of our formal learning up front before we begin our careers.
Know How	At some point, knowledge itself will become the last sustaining asset. The ability to use and to *acquire* knowledge, and to use it for good, will matter more and more.
Process	Building, nurturing, and developing the team takes time, commitment, and ongoing effort. It's a *process*, not an event.
Continuous improvement	Continuous, short cycle improvement (Japanese *kaisen)* will become a normative approach, the focus of an agile and adaptive society, and will define how successful work is done almost everywhere.
Culture	All organizations have culture, but not all have a culture they really want. Good culture starts with mission, vision, and enterprise strategy–and is bolstered and developed through a great team.
Leadership	In the end, perhaps nothing matters as much as leadership. Today, much of the effort of professional development is focused on discipline expertise (engineering, science, medicine, law). In the future, *leadership* itself will become the primary discipline.

Source: J. Doehring & Co., LLC, 2014.

A FINAL THOUGHT

The Fast Future isn't just coming—it's already here. The details aren't clear (and may never be), but what's ahead in the next 25 years will transform our globe in profound, astounding, and astonishing dimensions. Everything will change in our businesses, societies, and world. At times, the disruption will be extraordinarily positive (for instance, enjoying longer and healthier lives), but at other times the changes will be extraordinarily challenging (loss of jobs and careers, dissolving markets and industries, evolution and revolution of governments and nations).

As quality management guru Ed Deming once said, "Change is not necessary, [because] survival is not mandatory." Of course, you don't have to agree with the Fast Future thesis I've sketched out here, or even see the future as changing in any way. You and I don't have to understand the future unfolding, ponder its implications, or think about change and adaptation in our business.

We don't have to do anything at all—except to accept the consequences of our action or inaction.

We're free to choose any path, but we must live with the fallout of that choice.

Nevertheless, we should, I think, keep in mind that—especially in our topsy-turvy, highly volatile, and unpredictably mutating universe—that the "do nothing" strategy (maintaining today's status quo) is not itself without risk. In fact, this seemingly safe and secure choice might be the riskiest strategy of all. (By now, you can guess how I view this approach.)

My own bias is for action—make that *bold* action—moving forward with mission, vision, enterprise strategy, and full alignment of the team. These components—and a long-term commitment to continuously adapting and improving the business—provide the path for moving out into an uncertain future, but one with bright prospects.

None of us will control the Fast Future that lies ahead, but neither must we be victims, completely out of control in an unrelenting, unabated, malevolent storm. If we are smart, diligent, and committed—tireless in our efforts and vigilance—and if we have a little good fortune along the way, then we might (as business owners, leaders, professionals, and entrepreneurs) catch one of these really big, uber-waves of the Fast Future storm—and take it on the ride of a lifetime.

I'll leave you with that thought, and a wish that you too will catch your own wave, and enjoy the ride to transformational success in the Fast Future ahead.

Here it comes.

Notes

PART 1 - INTRODUCTION

CHAPTER 1. THE CHALLENGE OF THE FUTURE - TODAY

CHAPTER 2. THE ECONOMY, FORECASTING, AND THE ROAD AHEAD

1. CIA World Fact Book, at https://www.cia.gov/library/publications/the-world-factbook/rankorder/2001rank.html.
2. U.S. Bureau of Economic Analysis, at http://www.bea.gov/newsreleases/national/gdp/gdp_glance.htm.
3. U.S. Bureau of Economic Analysis, at http://www.bea.gov/newsreleases/national/gdp/gdp_glance.htm.
4. US Bureau of Labor Statistics, at http://www.bls.gov/news.release/empsit.nr0.htm.
5. US Bureau of Labor Statistics, at http://www.bls.gov/web/laus/mstrtcr1.gif.
6. USA Today and IHS-Global Insight, at http://www.usatoday.com/money/economy/story/Economic-Outlook/35290148/1.
7. U.S. Census Bureau, at http://www.census.gov/compendia/statab/cats/population.html.
8. U.S. Census Bureau, Population Division, "Interim State Population Projections," 2005; at http://www.census.gov/population/projections/files/stateproj/PressTab1.xls.
9. *Megaregions, at www.america2050.org.*

PART II - UBER-TRENDS

CHAPTER 3. THE ASTOUNDING ACCELERATION OF TECHNOLOGY

1. TOP 500 Supercomputer Sites, at http://www.top500.org.
2. *Source: Ray Kurzweil and KurzweilAI.net.*
3. "Pushing the Limits of Computer Chip Miniaturization," and "New '3-D' Transistors Promising Future Chips, Lighter laptops," in Science Daily, at http://www.sciencedaily.com/releases/2008/01/0801112083626.htm, and /2011/12/111206151536.htm, retrieved 3/5/2012.
4. "Grid Computing," from Wikipedia, retrieved 11/17/2014.

5. "The Convention on Biological Diversity at(http://www.biodiv.org/convention/convention. shtml)," United Nations, 1992, as referenced in *Biotechnology*, from Wikipedia, retrieved 12/8/2011.

6. "Diamond v. Chakrabarty, 447 U.S. 303 (1980), No.79-139 (http://caselaw.lp.findlaw.com/ scripts/getcase.pl?court-us&vol=447&invol=303), United States Supreme Court, June 16, 1980," as referenced in *Biotechnology*, from Wikipedia, retrieved 12/8/2011.

7. "Nanotechnology," from Wikipedia, retrieved 12/8/2011.

8. "Nanotechnology," from Wikipedia, retrieved 12/8/2011.

9. "Analysis: This is the first publicly available on-line inventory of nanotechnology-based consumer products," at (http://www.nanotechproject.org/inventories/consumer/ analysis_draft), The Project on Emerging *Nanotechnologies*, 2008, in Nanotechnology, from Wikipedia, retrieved 12/8/2011.

10. Kurzweil, Ray, *The Singularity is Near, When Humans Transcend Biology*, Viking, 2005.

11. Grossman, Lev, "2045, The Year Man Becomes Immortal," in *Time Magazine*, February 21, 2011.

CHAPTER 4. INFORMATION UBIQUITY AND THE RISING VALUE OF KNOWLEDGE

1. Horn, Sam, live presentation, at the 2012 National Speaker's Association Annual Conference, Indianapolis, IN.

2. Friedman, Thomas L., *The World is Flat, A Brief History of the Twenty-First Century*, Picador, 2007.

3. McLeod, Scott and Karl Fisch, *Did You Know*, at http://shifthappens.wikispaces.com/, 2008, 2009, 2011.

4. Internet World Stats, Usage and Population Statistics, at http://www.internetworldstats. com/stats.htm, retrieved 6/30/2011.

5. Internet World Stats, Usage and Population Statistics, at http://www.internetworldstats. com/stats.htm, retrieved 6/30/2011.

6. Rosen, Jay, "The People Formerly Known as the Audience," *Huff Post Media*, at http:// huffingtonpost.com/jay-rosen/the-people-formerly-known_1_b_24113.html., 5/25/2011.

7. *Facebook*, at http://facebook.com/press/info.php?timeline, updated 4/11/2014.

8. Dugan, Laura, "Twitter is Growing Faster than Facebook in the US [Stats]," *AllTwitter Blog at MediaBistro*, http://www.mediabistro.com/alltwitter, March 6, 2012.

9. *Twitter*, at http://twitter.com/company, retrieved 4/11/2014.

10. *LinkedIn*, at http://linkedin.com/about, retrieved 4/11/2014.

11. *YouTube*, at https://www.youtube.com/yt/press/statistics.html, retrieved 4/11/2014.

12. *MySpace*, at https://myspace.com/pressroom, 2011, and updated 4/11/2014.

13. Zeleny, Jeff and Katherine Q. Seelye, "More Money is Pouring In for Clinton and Obama," in *The New York Times*, Politics, March 7, 2008 at http://www.nytimes.com/2008/03/07/us/ politics/07campaign.html.

14. Lewis, M. Paul, Gary F. Simons, and Charles D. Fennig (eds.), *2014 Ethnologue: Languages of the World, Seventeenth Edition*, SIL International, at http://www.ethnologue.com.

15. Grimes, Barbara F. (ed.), *2000 Ethnologue: Languages of the World, Fourteenth Edition*, SIL International, at http://www.ethnologue.com/14.

16. Shirky, Clay, *Cognitive Surplus*, Penguin Press, 2010.

17. Jarvis, Jeff, "Disruption," a live presentation at the 2012 National Speakers Association Annual Conference, Indianapolis, IN.

18. Reed, James, "Fans Kickstart Amanda Palmer's Album, Tour," The Boston Globe, July 26, 2012, at http://www.bostonglobe.com/arts/2012/07/25/amanda-palmer-connection-with-fans-fans-view-kickstarter-success-summer-tour/shT4Gpt6ETTOAlrxmuwXJO/story.html.

19. Chorost, Michael, "A World Wide Mind: The Coming Collective Telempathy," in *The Futurist Magazine*, March/April 2012.

20. Lehrer, Jonah, "Groupthink, The Brainstorming Myth," in *The New Yorker, Annals of Ideas*, January 30, 2012, at http://www.newyorker.com/magazine/2012/01/30/groupthink.

CHAPTER 5. THE GREAT GLOBALIZING GLOBE

1. "Globalization," Dictionary.com. *Dictionary.com Unabridged.* Random House, Inc. at http://dictionary.reference.com/browse/globalization, retrieved 3/9/2012.

2. "Globalization," Dictionary.com. *Collins English Dictionary - Complete & Unabridged 10th Edition.* HarperCollins Publishers. At http://dictionary.reference.com/browse/globalization, retrieved 3/9/2012.

3. "Globalization," at Wikipedia, http://en.wikipedia.org/wiki/globalization, retrieved 3/9/2012.

4. "Summary of the Annual Review of Developments in Globalization and Regional Integration in the Countries of the ESCWA Region," United Nations Economic and Social Commission for Western Asia, in "globalization," at Wikipedia, http://en.wikipedia.org/wiki/globalization, retrieved 3/9/2012.

5. IMF Team, 2000, "Globalization: Threats or Opportunity," 12th April 2000, IMF Publications, in "globalization," at Wikipedia, http://en.wikipedia.org/wiki/globalization, retrieved 3/9/2012.

6. "Globalization," at Wikipedia, http://en.wikipedia.org/wiki/globalization, retrieved 3/9/2012.

7. Friedman, Thomas L., *The World is Flat, A Brief History of the Twenty-First Century*, Picador, 2007.

8. "Globalisation Shakes the World," BBC News 1/21/2007, at http://news.bbc.co.uk/2hi/business/6279679.stm, in "globalization," at Wikipedia, http://en.wikipedia.org/wiki/globalization, retrieved 3/9/2012.

9. Politzer, Malia, "China and Africa" Stronger Economic Ties Mean More Migration," *Migration Information Source*, August 2008, and "Africa, China's New Frontier," Times Online, 2/10/2008, both in "globalization," at Wikipedia, http://en.wikipedia.org/wiki/globalization, retrieved 3/9/2012.

10. United Nations Development Program, 1992, "1992 Human Development Report," Oxford University Press, in "globalization," at Wikipedia, http://en.wikipedia.org/wiki/globalization, retrieved 3/9/2012.

11. Hanksworth, John and Gordon Cookson, "The World in 2050, Beyond the BRICS: A Broader Look at Emerging Market Growth Prospects," PriceWaterhouseCoopers LLP, http://www.pwc.com/gx/en/world-2050/pdf/world_2050_brics.pdf, in "globalization," at Wikipedia, http://en.wikipedia.org/wiki/globalization, retrieved 3/9/2012.

12. "EM Equity in Two Decades, A Changing Landscape," Global Economics Paper No. 204, Goldman Sachs Global Economics, Commodities and Strategies Research, 9/8/2010, http://disinvestment.com/fileadmin/images/pictures/0809_Global_Econ_Paper_No_204_Final.pdf, in "globalization," at Wikipedia, http://en.wikipedia.org/wiki/globalization, retrieved 3/9/2012.

13. Lewis, M. Paul, Gary F. Simons, and Charles D. Fennig (eds.), *2014 Ethnologue: Languages of the World, Seventeenth Edition*, SIL International, at http://www.ethnologue.com.

CHAPTER 6. THE MORPHING, MUTATING, SHAPE-SHIFTING MARKETPLACE

1. "Sex and Suffering in the Afternoon". *Time*. January 12, 1976, as listed in "soap opera" at Wikipedia, http://en.wikipedia.org/wiki/soap_opera.

2. Gitomer, Jeffrey, *The Little Red Book of Selling*, 2005, Bard Press, and at http://www.gitomer.com/.

3. Godin, Seth, *Permission Marketing*, 1999, Simon & Schuster.

4. Halligan, Brian, "Inbound Marketing," at http://www.hubspot.com/.

5. Scott, David Meerman, at http://www.davidmeermanscott.com/.

6. ZweigWhite, "AEC Outsourcing Study," unpublished, personal engagement.

7. Friedman, Thomas L., *The World is Flat, A Brief History of the Twenty-First Century*, Picador, 2007.

8. "Amazon Mechanical Turk," at Wikipedia, http://en.wikipedia.org/wiki/Amazon_Mechanical_Turk.

9. Shirky, Clay, *Here Comes Everybody*, Penguin Group, 2008.

10. U.S. Census Bureau, Business Database, 2007, at http://www.census.gov/econ/.

CHAPTER 7. URBANIZATION, MOBILITY, AND THE POWER OF INFRASTRUCTURE

1. "Neolithic," in Wikipedia at http://em.wikipedia.org/wiki/Neolithic, retrieved 3/23/2012.

2. Jacobs, Jane, The Economy of Cities, 1969, Random House, referenced in "city" in Wikipedia, at http://en.wikipedia.org/wiki/city, retrieved 8/8/2011.

3. Jacobs, Jane, The Economy of Cities, 1969, Random House, referenced in "city" in Wikipedia, at http://en.wikipedia.org/wiki/city, retrieved 8/8/2011.

4. "City" in Wikipedia, at http://en.wikipedia.org/wiki/city, retrieved 8/8/2011.

5. "City" in Wikipedia, at http://en.wikipedia.org/wiki/city, retrieved 8/8/2011.

6. "City" in Wikipedia, at http://en.wikipedia.org/wiki/city, retrieved 8/8/2011.

7. *Four Thousand Years of Urban Growth: An Historical Census*, 1987, St. David's University Press, retrieved at http://geography.about.com/library/weekly/aa011201a.htm.

8. "City" in Wikipedia, at http://en.wikipedia.org/wiki/city, retrieved 8/8/2011.

9. "City" in Wikipedia, at http://en.wikipedia.org/wiki/city, retrieved 8/8/2011.

10. O'Flaherty, Brenden, City Economics, 2005, Harvard University Press, as referenced in "city" in Wikipedia, at http://en.wikipedia.org/wiki/city, retrieved 8/8/2011.

11. Ambrose Stephen E., *Nothing Like It in the World*, 2000, Simon & Schuster.

12. "Levittown, New York," in Wikipedia, at http://en.wikipedia.org/wiki/Levittown_New_York, retrieved 8/15/2011.

13. United Nations, Department of Economic and Social Affairs, Population Division: *World Urbanization Prospects, the 2011 Revision.* New York, 2012.

14. Cohen, Barney, National Research Council, "Urban Growth in Developing Countries: A Review of Current Trends and a Caution Regarding Existing Forecasts," 2004.

15. United Nations, Department of Economic and Social Affairs, Population Division: *World Urbanization Prospects*, the 2011 Revision. New York, 2012.

16. United Nations, Department of Economic and Social Affairs, Population Division: *World Urbanization Prospects*, the 2011 Revision. New York, 2012.

17. United Nations, Department of Economic and Social Affairs, Population Division: *World Urbanization Prospects*, the 2011 Revision. New York, 2012.

18. United Nations, Department of Economic and Social Affairs, Population Division: *World Urbanization Prospects*, the 2011 Revision. New York, 2012.

19. IHS Global Insight, "Global Construction Outlook: Executive Overview," Second Quarter 2010, at http://www.ihs.com.

20. Hofstra University, The Geography of Transport Systems, "Rail Track Mileage and Number of Class I Rail Carriers, United States, 1830-2008," at https://people.hofstra.edu/geotrans/eng/ch3en/conc3en/usrail18402003.html, retrieved 11/7/2012.

21. U.S. Department of Transportation, Federal Highway Administration, "Eisenhower Interstate Highway System," at http://fhwa.dot.gove/interstate/faq/htm., retrieved 11/7/2012.

22. Council on Tall Buildings and Urban Habitat, (http://ctbuh.org/), list at http://buildingdb.ctbuh.org/create.php?search=yes&status_COM=on&type_building=on.

23. American Society of Civil Engineers (ASCE), "2009 Report Card on America's Infrastructure," at http://www.infrastructurereportcard.org/.

24. Patar, Oliver, Live Presentation at the IMC-USA Confab, Reno, NV 2011.

CHAPTER 8. EMBRACING DIVERSITY, AND THE ASCENDING GLOBAL MERITOCRACY

1. Lewis, M. Paul, Gary F. Simons, and Charles D. Fennig (eds.), *2014 Ethnologue: Languages of the World, Seventeenth Edition*, SIL International, at http://www.ethnologue.com.

2. EUROPA, "Population Projections," at http://europa.eu/rapid/pressreleasesaction.do?reference=STAT/08/119, 2008, in "Demographics of the European Union," in Wikipedia, at http://en.wikipedia.org/wiki/Demographics_of_the_European_Union," retrieved 6/5/2012.

3. "Demographics of the European Union," in Wikipedia, at http://en.wikipedia.org/wiki/Demographics_of_the_European_Union," retrieved 6/5/2012.

4. "The Future of the Global Muslim Population," Pew Center Publications, 2011, at http://www.pewforum.org/2011/01/27/the-future-of-the-global-muslim-population/, retrieved 6/25/2012.

5. "The Future of the Global Muslim Population," Pew Center Publications, 2011, at http://www.pewforum.org/2011/01/27/the-future-of-the-global-muslim-population/, retrieved 6/25/2012.

6. European Commission, Eurostat, Statistics Explained, at http://epp.eurostat.ec.europa.eu/statistics_explained/index.php/Fertility_statistics - retrieved 10/03/2014.

7. U.S. Census Bureau, Decennial Censuses 1970, 1980, 1990, and 2000; 7/1/2011 Population Estimates, 2008 National Population Projections.

8. U.S. Census Bureau, Population Estimates, 2000-2010, July 1, 2011.

9. U.S. Census Bureau, Population Estimates, July 1, 2011.

10. U.S. Census Bureau, Population Estimates, July 1, 2011.

11. U.S. Census Bureau, 2010 Census.

12. "List of Cities in China by Population," in Wikipedia, at http://en.wikipedia.org/wiki/List_of_cities_in_the_People%27s_Republic_of_China_by_population.

13. Friedman, Thomas L., *The World is Flat, A Brief History of the Twenty-First Century*, Picador, 2007.

14. "Soviet Union," in Wikipedia at http://en.wikipedia.org/wiki/Soviet_Union.

15. "Arab Spring," in Wikipedia at http://en.wikipedia.org/wiki/Arab_Spring.

16. "Iran Elections: A Twitter Revolution?" The Washington Post, 6/17/2009, at http://www.washingtonpost.com/wp-dyn/content/discussion/2009/06/17/DI2009061702232.html.

17. "Secretary of State Hillary Clinton to Make Landmark Visit to Burma," Fox News Insider, 11/18/2011, at http://insider.foxnews.com/2011/11/18/secretary-of-state-hillary-clinton-to-make-landmark-visit-to-burma.

18. "World in 2050, The BRICs and beyond: prospects, challenges and opportunities," PwC Economics, January 2013, at http://www.pwc.com/en_GX/gx/world-2050/assets/pwc-world-in-2050-report-january-2013.pdf.

19. *World Health Statistics 2012*, World Health Organization, at http://www.who.int/gho/publications/world_health_statistics/2012/en/.

20. *World Health Statistics 2012*, World Health Organization, at http://www.who.int/gho/publications/world_health_statistics/2012/en/.

21. Mishel, Lawrence, "CEO to Worker Pay Imbalance Grows," 6/21/2006, Economic Policy Institute, at http://www.epi.org/publication/webfeatures_snapshots_20060621/.

22. WorldBlu, at http://www.worldblu.com/.

CHAPTER 9. LONGEVITY, HEALTHY LIVING, AND THE BIO-CENTURY

1. "Life Expectancy at Birth," Central Intelligence Agency World FactBook, at https://www.cia.gov/library/publications/the-world-factbook/rankorder/2012rank.html, retrieved 03.27.13.

2. "Life Expectancy at Birth," United Nations, *World Population Prospects*, Department of Economic and Social Affairs, Population Division, File Mort/7.1.

3. "Water and Sanitation," World Health Organization Global Health Observatory (GHO), at http://www.who.int/gho/mdg/environmental_sustainability/en/index/html, retrieved 06.26.12.

4. "Child Health," World Health Organization Global Health Observatory (GHO), at http://www.who.int/gho/child_health/en/index/html, retrieved 06.26.12.

5. World Health Organization Global Health Observatory (GHO), at http://www.who.int/gho/hiv/en/index/html, retrieved 06.26.12.

6. "Life Expectancy at Birth," United Nations, *World Population Prospects*, Department of Economic and Social Affairs, Population Division, File Mort/7.1.

7. "Underweight Children" and "Obesity Rates," Central Intelligence Agency World Factbook, at https://www.cia.gov/library/publications/the-world-factbook/rankorder/rawdata_2224.txt, and https://www.cia.gov/library/publications/the-world-factbook/rankorder/rawdata_2228.txt, retrieved 06.26.12.

8. "Youth Unemployment," Central Intelligence Agency World Factbook, at https://www.cia.gov/library/publications/the-world-factbook/rankorder/2229rank.html, retrieved 03.27.13.

9. Mayes, Randall, "Where Will the Century of Biology Lead Us?" in The Futurist Magazine, May-June 2014.

10. Mesko, Bertalan, "Rx Disruption: Technology Trends in Medicine and Health Care," in The Futurist Magazine, May-June 2014.

CHAPTER 10. CLIMATE CHANGE, ENVIRONMENTALISM, AND ENERGY

1. Moore, Thomas A., "Comparing Climate Change to Your Sick Child," Arizona State University Center for Bioenergy & photosynthesis, at http://bioenergy.asu.edu/faculty/tmoore/discussion2.html, retrieved 4/23/2014.

2. U.S. Energy Information Administration, Monthly Energy Review, March 2012.

3. U.S. Energy Information Administration, Monthly Energy Review, April 2012.

4. U.S. Energy Information Administration, "Primary Energy Consumption Estimates by Source," at http://www.eia.gov/totalenergy/data/annual/pdf/sec1_8.pdf

5. U.S. Energy Information Administration, "Energy Perspectives," 2012.

6. Wood, John H., Gary R. Long, David F. Morehouse, "Long-Term World Oil Supply Scenarios, The Future Is Neither as Bleak or Rosy as Some Assert," 2004, at U.S. Energy Information Administration, at http://www.eia.gov/pub/oil_gas/petroleum/feature_articles/2004/worldoilsupply/oilsupply04.html

CHAPTER 11. THE NEW LOOK OF COMMUNITY

1. Facebook, at http://newsroom.fb.com/Key-Facts, retrieved 04.08.13.

2. Facebook, at http://newsroom.fb.com/Key-Facts, retrieved 04.08.13.

3. Shirky, Clay, Cognitive Surplus, Penguin Press, 2010.

4. Pappano, Laura, "The Year of the MOOC," The New York Times, Education Life, 11/2/2012, at http://www.nytimes.com/2012/11/04/education/edlife/massive-open-online-courses-are-multiplying-at-a-rapid-pace.html?_r=0.

5. Shirky, Clay, Cognitive Surplus, Penguin Press, 2010.

CHAPTER 12. A FUTURE OF CHANGE

1. Viegas, Jennifer, "Get Ready for More Proto-Humans," Discovery News, 5/21/2010, at http://news.discovery.com/get-ready-for-more-proto-humans.html.

2. "Homo," in Wikipedia, at http://en.wkipedia.org/wiki/homo., retrieved 3/23/2012.

3. "Paleolithic," in Wikipedia, at http://en.wkipedia.org/wiki/paleolithic., retrieved 3/23/2012.

4. "Neolithic," in Wikipedia, at http://en.wkipedia.org/wiki/neolithic., retrieved 3/23/2012.

5. "Bronze Age," in Wikipedia, at http://en.wkipedia.org/wiki/bronze_age, retrieved 3/23/2012.

6. United Nations, at http://www.un.org/cyberschoolbus/briefing/technology/tech.pdf., in the presentation "Did You Know," by McLeod, Scott and Karl Fisch, at http://shifthappens. wikispaces.com/, 2008, 2009, 2011.

7. Apple, Inc., Press Release, "First Weekend iPhone Sales Top 10 Million, Set New Record," 9/22/2014, at http://www.apple.com/pr/library/2014/09/22First-Weekend-iPhone-Sales-Top-10-Million-Set-New-Record.html.

PART III - CONCLUSIONS, AND THE ACTION AGENDA

CHAPTER 13. ACTION- ON WHAT TO DO WITH THE FAST FUTURE AHEAD

1. Star Trek, The Original Series, at http://www.startrek.com/page/star-trek-the-original-series.

2. Kennedy, John F., President's Speech before a Joint Session of Congress, (The Decision to go to the Moon), May 25, 1961, http://history.nasa.gov/moondec.html.

3. Porter, Michael, On Competition, Harvard Business School Press, 1998.

4. Collins, Jim *Good to Great: Why Some Companies Make the Leap... and Others Don't*, HarperCollins, 2001.

5. Chandler, Alfred Dupont, *Strategy and Structure: Chapters in the History of the Industrial Enterprise*, 1962.

6. Peters, Thomas J. and Robert H. Waterman, Jr., *In Search of Excellence, Lessons from America's Best Run Companies*, Warner Books, 1982.

LIST OF FIGURES